Praise for *What to Expect When N...*

"A powerful argument that the only thing worse than having children is not having them. I'm reading *What To Expect When No One's Expecting* aloud to the three little arguments for birth control at my house in hope they'll quit squabbling and making messes and start acting so cute that all my neighbors decide to conceive."
— P.J. O'Rourke, author of *Holidays in Heck*

"Jonathan Last has measured the full and unhappy consequences of decades' worth of anti-natalism and asks the rest of us to do the same—before the West goes into a demographic death-spiral. His book is a welcome refutation of 'population bomb' nonsense and a clarion call to build the kind of culture and society that can cherish children once again. For no matter how messy, annoying, and expensive the little people may be, they are the future. Without them, there is no future. If you don't believe that, look at Greece and Italy."
— George Weigel, Distinguished Senior Fellow,
Ethics and Public Policy Center, and author of
Witness to Hope: The Biography of Pope John Paul II

"Jonathan Last masterfully describes the key facts and concepts any literate person should know about the sea change in global demography and speculates wisely and soberly about the implications for the future of humanity. Avoiding the alarmism, sexism, and racial chauvinism that mars so much other writing on this subject, Last is an insightful and trustworthy guide."
— Phillip Longman, Senior Fellow, New America Foundation,
and author of *The Empty Cradle: How Falling Birthrates
Threaten World Prosperity and What to Do About It*

"Jonathan Last's writing matches his reasoning: as clear as a shot of gin, and just as bracing. America is changing more quickly than ever before, and this book explains why. A terrific, important read."
— Tucker Carlson, Editor, *The Daily Caller*

"Jonathan Last has pulled off an amazing feat. He's written a book that's at once lively and profound, that deals with weighty matters with a light touch, and that explains a complex subject clearly. It might make you laugh, it could make you cry—but above all it will make you think."
— William Kristol, Editor, *The Weekly Standard*

"This book explodes old ways of thinking. Not moralizing, not blaming, Jonathan Last peers methodically ahead at the cold consequences of plunging global birth rates."

—Michael Novak, recipient of the Templeton Prize (1994),
and author of *The Spirit of Democratic Capitalism*

"The Malthusian paranoia of a coming population boom has nothing on the reality of a coming population implosion. Frankly it kinda makes a girl want to procreate."

—S. E. Cupp, host of CNN's *Crossfire*

"Imagine a merger of Mark Steyn and David Brooks, with a Supreme Court-imposed page limit."

—Hugh Hewitt, host of *The Hugh Hewitt Show*

Jonathan V. Last is "an extremely sharp writer with a great eye for telling details and revealing anecdotes. . . . *What To Expect When No One's Expecting* is a rich and detailed read, well worth the price of admission just for Last's cogent summarizing of long-term demographic trends."

—Nick Gillespie, *Bookforum*

"Among the many virtues of this slim, sprightly volume is that the author offers no easy solutions."

—William McGurn, *Wall Street Journal*

"Provocative and engaging."

—W. Bradford Wilcox, *National Review*

"Controversial."

—Lauren Sandler, *Time*

"Jonathan Last's new *What To Expect When No One's Expecting* is the best-written, most engaging, and funniest book on the social cost of low birth rates and population decline. . . . Highly recommended."

—Bryan Caplan, author of *Selfish Reasons to Have More Kids*

"Last takes a vigorous look at the policy and political issues resulting from this still-underappreciated seismic shift in the human condition. Even those who do not share his basically conservative outlook on many fertility and family-policy issues will find this a stimulating and enlightening read."

—Walter Russell Mead, *Foreign Affairs*

One of *World* magazine's "Top Ten Books of the Year"

"Well-written and enjoyable."
—David P. Goldman, *Claremont Review of Books*

"Riveting."
—Mary Eberstadt, author of *How the West Really Lost God*

"Last's tightly argued and deftly navigated tour through perhaps the most important social transition in modern history is a valuable contribution to our understanding of the need for innovation in social policy."
—Ari N. Schulman, *Commentary*

"It's a pity *What to Expect When No One's Expecting* . . . was not available prior to the latest election. In fewer than 200 pages, Last surveys America's challenging demographic future and delivers an uncomfortable truth: the vibrant, dynamic and optimistic social model of twentieth-century America is fundamentally incompatible with modernity. . . . Last demonstrates impressive restraint in presenting a small-'c' conservative outlook on what can be done to combat the ever-collapsing birth rates in the United States."
—The Daily Beast

The book "documents a remarkable demographic shift: the global baby un-boom."
—Heather Wilhelm, RealClearBooks

"Jonathan Last's thoughtful and important new book, *What to Expect When No One's Expecting* is a fun read. Policy questions aside, Last provides a fascinating and crystal-clear account of America's demographic decline. There's plenty to learn on related issues as well. . . . Do yourself a favor and have a look."
—Stanley Kurtz, *National Review Online*
"Last synthesizes scholarly research with an engaging blend of statistics, anecdotes, and judicious observations. His is very much a book for contemporary readers."
—Scott Yenor, *Public Discourse*

"Because the seeds of our demographic destruction are not American-made, but rather a design flaw of the modern age, *What to Expect* has a thesis with global implications. Mr. Last artfully teases these out."
—David DesRosiers, *Washington Times*

"A much needed wakeup call for the nation: we need more children, and we need them now."

—William Donohue, President, The Catholic League

"Last vigorously applies his analytical shears to the thorny problem of plummeting birth rates in the United States, the Western world, and beyond, and clears the path for an incisive look at the key economic ramifications of the fertility drop."

—Michael Rosen, *The American*

"A reader-friendly but thorough analysis of the demographic crisis afflicting the West. . . . Clearly argued and entertainingly written."

—*Defining Ideas*

"*What to Expect When No One's Expecting* is a surprisingly entertaining tour of demographics. A talented writer, Last takes a dry, academic subject and makes it come alive."

—Julia Shaw, *The Family in America*

"Last delivers his warning with humor."

—*The Independent Review*

"Jonathan Last provides a reader-friendly, but thorough analysis of the demographic crisis afflicting the West and the very bad things that will follow population decline."

—*Capital*

"In his very good new book on population and demography . . . Last explains how difficult modern society makes it to have children."

—Austin Ruse, *Crisis*

Jonathan V. Last "catalogues the current fertility crisis [and] puts parochial worries . . . in a larger context. . . . Last explains that the current below replacement-level birth rate is a national, even global, affliction for which there are multiple explanations . . . and which we ignore at our peril."

—Abby W. Schachter, *Jewish Review of Books*

What to Expect When No One's Expecting

America's Coming Demographic Disaster

Jonathan V. Last

ENCOUNTER BOOKS NEW YORK • LONDON

First American edition published in 2013 by Encounter Books,
an activity of Encounter for Culture and Education, Inc.,
a nonprofit, tax exempt corporation.
Encounter Books website address: www.encounterbooks.com

Manufactured in the United States and printed on
acid-free paper. The paper used in this publication meets
the minimum requirements of ANSI/NISO Z39.48 1992
(R 1997) (*Permanence of Paper*).

First paperback edition published in 2014.
Paperback edition ISBN: 978-1-59403-731-3

THE LIBRARY OF CONGRESS HAS CATALOGED
THE HARDCOVER EDITION AS FOLLOWS:

Last, Jonathan V., 1974–
What to expect when no one's expecting: America's coming
demographic disaster/Jonathan V. Last.
p. cm.
Includes bibliographical references and index.
ISBN 978-1-59403-641-5 (hbk.: alk. paper)
ISBN 978-1-59403-654-5 (ebook)
1. United States—Population. 2. Population forecasting—United States.
3. Age distribution (Demography)—United States. I. Title.
HB3505.L37 2013
304.60973'01—dc23
2012010870

For Shannon Leigh Mary Last

Demography is the key factor. If you are not able to maintain yourself biologically, how do you expect to maintain yourself economically, politically, and militarily? It's impossible. The answer of letting people from other countries come in . . . that could be an economic solution, but it's not a solution of your real sickness, that you are not able to maintain your own civilization.

— VIKTOR ORBÁN, PRIME MINISTER OF HUNGARY, 2012

Contents

Preface

What was true then is true now. Only more so.

When this book first appeared in 2013, I began by describing some of the lunatic ways people treat their dogs these days. I don't want to ruin the surprise—it's just five pages down the road—but if anything, the crazy has gotten worse. For instance, a friend of mine reported recently that during a stay at the Rome Cavalieri Hotel she noticed a room-service menu for dogs. Thirty-five euros for a three-course meal. For pets with a less discriminating palate, the "Yaffbar" was released. Its makers describe it as "the world's first energy bar created for you . . . to share with your dog!" Then there's the yoga studio in Philadelphia offering classes for people and their dogs. Because, as the "doga" instructor explained to a local reporter, "your dog helps you to find yourself." But at least the Yaffbar and the doga keep the pooches active. The past year also saw the debut of DogTV, a premium-cable channel for dogs. No, not a channel *about* dogs. It's *for* dogs. You leave it on while you're at work and the dogs zone out to TV shows designed just for them. Really.

Meanwhile, demographic trends have gone on pretty much as expected, too, with continuing declines across the globe. In America, the birth rate dropped (again), hitting a new historic low (again). In Germany, demographers discovered that the country has 1.5 million fewer people than they had previously thought. The wave of geriatrics created by low fertility rates over there continues to cause all sorts of social dislocations. For instance, there's now a cottage industry of "emigrant nursing homes"—meaning that Germans ship their parents to old-folks homes in Poland because they're so much cheaper. (It could be worse, I suppose—surely this is the least alarming German invasion in Polish history.)

Japan suffered the largest one-year drop in population since the end of World War II. And in China, the demographic math became daunting enough that the ruling Communist Party has kind-of, sort-of revoked the One Child policy. Lots of coercive measures are still in place for people who have unauthorized children. But the government will now allow parents to have a second child, provided that either the father or the mother was an only child. The upshot is that the Chinese have now embarked on a grand experiment to see if One Child functioned as an upward limit on their fertility, or if it lastingly changed their culture's ideas about ideal family size.

But like I said, I don't want to spoil the book. Instead, I'd like to plant a seed with you concerning a question which I've never been able to fully resolve.

When *What to Expect When No One's Expecting* was released, one of the big surprises for me was a dog (so to speak) that didn't bark: I expected a feminist-socialist critique. But it never materialized. I find that puzzling, disappointing and—truth be told—a little worrisome. Let me explain for just a minute and then I promise you can move on to the good stuff.

* * *

At its heart, *What to Expect* is about the changes in our world which have led people to have fewer children. Some of these changes have been, objectively speaking, wonderful. For one example, infant mortality levels have dropped, which pushes fertility down. Great! For another, higher levels of educational attainment for men and women—but particularly women—have also pushed fertility down. As you'll see, I think we can get carried away with education-mania—do you really need a master's degree if you're going to work for the Post Office? But viewed through the long lens of human history, high levels of education are, again, a great good.

On the other hand, some of the drivers of fertility decline are—remember, we're talking objectively—not good. Divorce and out-of-wedlock births (both of which result in sub-optimal outcomes in education, health, income, and other measures for the adults and children involved) have also contributed to fertility decline. We ought not celebrate such developments.

There are many, many other causes, but the net result is that, first, society isn't making enough babies to sustain itself, and second, men and women are having fewer babies than they say they would like to have.

All of which is why I expected someone from the feminist-socialist school to make something like the following argument:

> Our free-market system drastically undervalues human capital to the point of its own dysfunction. Families are the building blocks of society, yet capitalism views the family as, at best, an externality and, at worst, an inefficiency which needs to be wrung out of the equation. Instead, our society urges us to work and consume to the exclusion of all other human activities.
>
> This consumptive, capitalist orgy has created a culture in which women are continually unable to achieve their fertility ideals. After generations of women were forced to have *more* children than they wanted, women finally mastered their fertil-

ity only to have the American system force them into having *fewer* children than they want.

The failure of women to achieve their fertility ideals is made even more grotesque by the fact that women underachieve them by larger margins as they move up the economic and educational ladders. There is no better proof that our red-in-tooth-and-claw capitalist system simply doesn't work. After 30 years of venerating the free market and dismissing alternative forms of economic organization, our demographic problems suggest that the free market is failing us all—and especially women—in the most fundamental way.

Now, you might argue that the capitalist system misunderstands the worth of children, and of women, and has set up an adversarial dynamic where the economy doesn't function well without the dynamism of women in the workplace. But the truth is even worse. Yes, the free market presents women with an impossible choice: Be a producer (in economic terms) or be a mother. But the most insidious part of the bargain is the unmistakable message to women that, either way, you're on your own. As Elizabeth Warren reported in her 2003 book *The Two-Income Trap*, "*Having a child is now the single best predictor that a woman will end up in financial collapse.*" Any society in which this is the case is neither fair, nor wise, nor sustainable.

You get the picture. Now to be honest, I wouldn't entirely disagree with such a critique—and not just because Elizabeth Warren is my progressive pin-up. (Seriously. For me, Warren is the *belle idéale* of progressive intellectuals.) But after *What to Expect* was released, this line of argument was nowhere to be found.

Instead, the feminist response seemed to be more of what we might call anti-natalism. That is, many parts of the feminist left merely insisted that whatever problems low fertility might present for society, the economy, or the welfare state, the highest priority is to protect a woman's right not to have children. "Back off the baby talk," they seemed to say, "so that women can work hard, make money, and buy cool stuff."

I'm paraphrasing, of course. But the message was pretty unmistakable: We're all free-marketeers now, for better or worse.

* * *

I'm not a Marxist myself. I understand the immense good that market economies have achieved in lifting hundreds of millions of people out of abject poverty and providing the space for liberalism and freedom to flower. But I'm pink enough to appreciate the need for counterbalancing forces in society—to have progressives pointing to the inherent shallowness of consumerism and the intense, values-warping, gravitational pull of the free market. And so it saddens me that progressive feminists seem to have abdicated that role. Because if even the radical feminists have decided that shopping at Restoration Hardware is the apex of the human condition, then what hope do the rest of us have?

The question I kept asking myself was, *Why?* Why did the feminists decide to circle the wagons around a woman's right to be child-free? (Which, so far as I can tell, exactly no one is suggesting should be impinged on.) Why didn't they instead attack the heartless free market for failing women who *want* children? (Which, the data clearly indicate, is most of them.) A few possible explanations occurred to me, which might be worth keeping in the back of your head while you read *What to Expect*.

It could simply be that, with the close of the Cold War and the End of History, feminism—like all the other -isms of the left—has made its peace with capitalism and consumerism. The feminist war with the free market is over and the University of Chicago's econ department won.

Or it could be the result of more pedestrian political calculations. The progressive coalition these days includes both feminists and radical environmentalists, who have some conflicting goals. The radical environmentalists want to reduce the number of people on the planet, which is in direct tension with any notion about empowering women to have whatever size families they want. For the good of the coalition, then, it's better to fixate on the right to be child-free.

Or perhaps it comes from tensions within the feminist project itself. Talking about demographics and babies requires, at the most general and abstract level, making value judgments about sex. *If* you accept that society needs a certain number of babies to prosper *then* you have to believe that it is both good and necessary for people to have babies sometimes. Which is a value judgment.

Now, I don't see this proposition as an express elevator to full-on, fundamentalist theocracy, myself. But you must never underestimate the extent to which our culture in general, and today's left in particular, views non-judgmentalism about *any* aspect of sexuality as the prime directive.

Or maybe it was none of these and the silence of the feminists meant something else altogether. But I suspect it means something.

We're getting ahead of ourselves, though, aren't we? Let's put all of this intellectual intrigue aside so I can tell you a story.

It's the story of a boy and a girl who fell very much in love. They were married and built for themselves a beautiful, wonder-filled life. They traveled and read great books. They had stimulating conversations and went running together. And then they had a baby.

It's a story about cribs and car seats and college tuition.

And coffee.

—JVL
January 14, 2014

One Child for All!

Once upon a time, my wife and I lived in Old Town Alexandria, one of the most historic and desirable suburbs of our nation's capital. Old Town is like a wildlife preserve for yuppies. There are cobblestone streets and high-end kitchen-and-bath stores and designer dress boutiques and hipster eateries and coffee shops. Lots and lots of coffee shops. On Royal Street in Old Town there's a place called Grape + Bean, which sells wine and coffee. They have a Clover machine, which uses a brew-process so scientifically advanced that the coffee—not a latté or a cappuccino, just normal coffee—costs $4 a cup. A few blocks away is a shop called Misha's. They brew coffee the old-fashioned way. But they also roast their own beans on premises. Above Misha's, in the same early nineteenth-century white-brick building, is a yoga studio.

In 2008, a new shopping hub opened just down the street from our lovely little riverfront condo in Old Town. Naturally, the development was anchored by a coffee shop. It was also home to an upscale gastro-pub, a smoothie café, a salon, a Russian gourmet market, a dry cleaner, and a children's clothing store. After 18 months of sluggish sales, the children's boutique, preciously named "Tutto Bambini," went out of business. It was replaced by a doggie spa. Which would be unremarkable except that the turnover left Old Town with six luxury pet stores and only two shops dedicated to clothing children.

The pet market has been steadily increasing in America since the 1980s, with people not only acquiring more furry little dependents, but spending more on them, too.[1] In 1994 Americans spent $17 billion on pets; by 2008 that number had risen to $43 billion.[2] By 2010, even in the face of a massive recession, it had climbed over $48 billion.[3] The evidence suggests that pets are increasingly treated like actual family members: In 1998, the average dog-owning American household spent $383 on medical care for their dogs; by 2006, that figure had risen to $672.[4] Expenditures on doggie grooming aids more than doubled from $59 to $127.[5] In surveys from 1947 to 1985, fewer than half of Americans reported that they owned a pet.[6] Today American pets outnumber American children by more than four to one.[7]

Those numbers, of course, don't reveal the full scope of America's pet mania: Auto insurance companies now offer policies for pets traveling in cars. Wealthy dog owners have successfully lobbied for changes in estate law allowing pets to legally receive inheritances and trust funds.[8] A bill put forward in Congress recently called for a $3,500 tax break for pet-care expenses—which is more than families get for a child.[9] The HAPPY Act (Humanity and Pets Partnered through the Years) happily failed to reach a vote on the floor of the House.[10]

At the micro level, the pet boom is even more unsettling. When people in Old Town go on holiday, they might drop their pooch off at a local kennel called Dog Town, where each precious pup stays in a private, miniature house, complete with beds, a covered deck, framed pictures on the walls, and air conditioning.[11] Or perhaps they might choose the nearby Happy Tracks, where dogs are given report cards at the end of their boarding, telling dog-parents how well little Mr. Darcy ate, slept, and played with others.

This obsession with pets is not unique to America. In Japan, for instance, it is common to see canines paraded around in strollers by childless adult women. The "dog mommy" has become a common Japanese stereotype, with dogs now outnumbering children under age 10.[12] Italy is also experiencing a pet boom, with ownership and expenditures, mostly on dogs, increasing by more than 70 percent since 1994.[13] There is a common thread. In all three countries, educated, middle-class people have all but stopped having babies. Pets have become fuzzy, low-maintenance replacements for children.

In order for a country to maintain a steady population, it needs a fertility rate of 2.1—remember this as the Golden Number. If the rate is higher, the country's population grows; lower, and it shrinks. Which means that the Japanese and Italians (with fertility rates of about 1.4[14]) are on the verge of downsizing their countries. Their cities are dwindling; some small towns are on the cusp of simply closing. With only-children the rule, the average person in Japan and Italy will soon have no brothers, sisters, aunts, or uncles. But they'll have plenty of places to pamper their dogs. As for the American fertility rate, we'll talk about that in a second.

America's Falling Fertility

But first, let's jump back to Old Town. Behind its façade of cafés and doggie spas are roughly the demographics you'd expect. The city's education rate is remarkably high: 68 percent of adults over the age of 25 have at least a bachelor's degree. If you strip out the part of town that contains large amounts of public housing, that figure jumps to 80 percent. In 2000, one out of every five households in Old Town made over $150,000. The average income is more than twice the national average. Seventy percent of working people in Old Town have jobs in management or the professional classes—lots of lawyers, doctors, lobbyists, and engineers.[15]

Old Towners are an impressive bunch. There's just one category in which they're below average. In the country at large, 33 percent of households contain children under the age of 18. In Old Town, only 12 percent of households have children. And even those intrepid enough to start families don't have very many kids: The average family in Old Town consists of a mother, a father, and 0.57 children.[16] That's right: The average married couple has a wee bit more than half a child.

When you look at the numbers, it was inevitable that Tutto Bambini would fold. The spa that replaced it only accepts dogs by appointment and is exclusive enough that it does not publish its prices. Yet even three years later, in the midst of an economic downturn, Hairy Situations—all of these pet-fancy places have insipid names—has even expanded its space. That's because people in Old Town have dogs, not children.

In that sense, they're not much different from the rest of the country: Middle-class Americans don't have very many babies these days. In case you're wondering, the American fertility rate currently sits at 1.93.[17] That sounds pretty good, but the number is deceptive. To understand why, we'll have to talk a little math—but I promise, it won't hurt.

Fertility Math for Dummies

Demographers measure fertility in different ways. They start with the simplest observation: the number of births each year plotted against the numbers and ages of the rest of the population. From there they calculate the "crude birth rate," which is the number of children born per 1,000 people in that particular year. The crude birth rate isn't particularly useful, but for sake of context, the U.S. population was about 312 million in 2011 and about 4 million babies were born, so the U.S. crude birth rate was around 13. By combining the crude birth rate with other census data, you can determine "completed fertility," which is the number of babies actually born to each woman in America by the time she's 50 and hanging up her spurs. And finally, there's the "total fertility rate." The TFR is closely related to completed fertility: It's the number of babies the average woman would bear over the course of her life *if* she were to survive until the end of her reproductive years *and* the age-specific birth rate were to remain constant. In other words, it's a snapshot. The TFR is usually higher than completed fertility because it assumes children born to women who have not had the chance (and assumes no change in the birth rate). Both completed fertility and the total fertility rate are useful numbers. However, in this book, when I say "fertility rate," I'm referring to the TFR, unless I say otherwise. There are other metrics but we needn't burden ourselves with them.[18]*

With all of that in mind, let's unpack America's total fertility rate. For starters, it's important to understand that these numbers are not inviolable. Because calculating TFR is a statistical exercise, and not pure math, you'll often see reliable sources reporting slightly different numbers. For one thing, new data sets are often incomplete, and must rely on projections. So while the CDC put the 2008 TFR at 2.084, the Census Bureau had the 2008 number pegged at 2.182.[19] What's important here aren't the tiny variances, but the bigger pictures and trends.

As it stands, even a TFR of 1.93 is a pretty fair mark. It's close to our Golden Number of 2.1 and would probably be higher if not for the Great Recession, which, beginning in 2007, tamped down the

---

* An aside for those undeterred by math: There are a number of subtle distinctions to be made when it comes to demographic numbers, the most important of which is the difference between period and cohort fertility. The period fertility rate is the TFR derived by taking into account all women, right now. But when you break down this rate by cohorts—that is, groups of women about the same age—the numbers sometimes change. The demographer John Bongaarts proposes that as women's childbearing patterns have changed (they get married and begin having children much later than they once did), this delayed action skews the overall (period) fertility rate, making it look artificially low. Bongaarts argues that cohort fertility is a more accurate measure and that once women have completed their fertility, the overall TFR will rebound. This phenomenon is called the "tempo effect" and it undoubtedly explains some—though not all, or even a large part—of the West's fertility decline. Some demographers use it to calculate an "adjusted total fertility rate," which is probably a better measure than the plain TFR. (However, the lack of availability of calculated adjusted-TFRs makes it harder to compare data across time and space.) Other nuances exist the deeper you get into the data. That said, it is possible to both acknowledge these mathematical distinctions and not lose sight of the larger, thematic trends. For an exhaustive list of measures, see the Population Reference Bureau's Glossary: http://www.prb.org/Educators/Resources/Glossary.aspx.

number of births after several years of small, but steady, growth.[20] What's more, for a First World country, 1.93 is exceptionally high. Few industrialized nations are even in that ballpark.[21] But the closer you look, the less reassuring our number is. When you break it out by demographic group, you see that black women have a healthy TFR of 1.96. White women, on the other hand, have a TFR of 1.79. Our national average is only boosted because Hispanic women are doing most of the heavy lifting, having an average of 2.35 babies. Take out Hispanics, and America's fertility picture begins to look quite different.

It gets even worse when you look at socioeconomic markers. The Census Bureau puts the number for an average woman's "completed fertility" at 1.90 (remember, we expect this number to be lower than the TFR). For women who graduated from college, the number drops to 1.78. For women with a graduate degree, it slumps to 1.61.[22] Now, we're not comparing apples to apples with these numbers; it's the shape of the curve that's important. And the message is unmistakable: America's fertility rate may be holding up, but America's middle-class women are reproducing at rates far below the Golden Number.

Why is this? That's the subject of this book and I'll give you the full tour in a minute. But if you're looking to get ahead of the class, reasons include: the ubiquity of college, the delay of marriage, the birth-control pill, car seat laws, religious participation, the rise of the thousand-dollar stroller, and Social Security. This is a partial list. But what's really fascinating is that this phenomenon is not new. The fertility rate in America has been falling since the country's founding, with only one major moment of increase.

The Incredible Shrinking Country

The more pressing question you probably have is: Why should we care? After all, America seems pretty crowded as it is. Why should it matter if, in a few decades, we don't have as many people clogging up the freeways and malls? The short answer is that sub-replacement fertility rates eventually lead to a shrinking of population—and throughout recorded human history, declining populations have *always* followed or been followed by Very Bad Things. Disease. War. Economic stagnation or collapse. And these grim tidings from history may be in our future, since population contraction is where most of the world is headed.

Let's jump back for a moment to the two other pet-crazy countries, Japan and Italy. Their fertility rates (now around 1.4) are within a range demographers call "lowest-low." This is a mathematical tipping point at which a country's population could decline by 50 percent within 45 years. It is a death spiral from which, demographers believe, it might be impossible to escape. Then again, that's just theory. Modern history has never seen fertility rates so low. Next to them, America's 1.93 looks pretty great. The large-scale, continual influx of immigrants we receive is enough to keep the American population at a steady state, or even growing slowly. The question is whether our 1.93 is sustainable, or if it's headed further south.

Contrary to rumor, demography is not destiny. In 1968 Paul Ehrlich wrote one of the most spectacularly foolish books ever published—*The Population Bomb*. Ehrlich claimed that overpopulation was, within a few years, going to ravage the planet Earth. Just so you don't think I'm exaggerating, here's how Ehrlich begins:

> The battle to feed all of humanity is over. In the 1970s the world will undergo famines—hundreds of millions of people are going to starve to death in spite of any crash programs embarked upon now. At this late date nothing can prevent a substantial increase in the world death rate.[23]

And on and on he went. What makes Ehrlich's rant so fascinating isn't just that he was totally and completely wrong—hundreds of millions have not starved to death and nowadays most famines are caused by corrupt political establishments, not overpopulation. No, what's so wonderful about Ehrlich's silly book is that he was wrong at the exact moment when the *very opposite* of his prediction was unfolding:

Fertility rates in America and across the world had been declining gradually for decades, but beginning in 1968 they sank like a stone.

Ehrlich became a huge celebrity. Johnny Carson had him on *The Tonight Show* several times—once devoting the entire program to him.[24] His book sold some 2 million copies and became a bible for politicians, government planners, and academics in the 1970s.[25] The Dutch government was so alarmed that it issued a report in 1979, which concluded, "We recommend the government to aim for an end to natural population growth as fast as possible."[26] Even today, thanks to Ehrlich, many people still believe that "overpopulation" is a looming problem. But in reality, from Africa to Asia, from South America to Eastern Europe, and from Third World jungles to the wealthy desert petro-kingdoms, nearly every country in every region is experiencing declines in fertility. In 1979, the world's fertility rate was 6.0; today it's 2.52.[27] From a current population of 6.9 billion, the United Nations and others predict that world population will peak somewhere between 10 billion and 12 billion in the next 85 years and then begin the long, inexorable process of shrinking back down.[28] The reason for these predictions is that all but a handful of countries are experiencing long-term declines in their fertility rates. All First World countries are already below the 2.1 line. And while the fertility rates in many parts of the developing world are still above the 2.1 mark, their *rates of decline* are, in most cases, even steeper than in the First World.

Unlike Ehrlich, I'm not selling doom. (Unless that's good for book-buying. In which case, we're doomed.) The numbers tell us with a great deal of accuracy where we are now, and how we got here. And they tell us with pretty fair confidence where we'll be in the near future, because all of the next generation's parents have already been born. But the numbers can't tell us for certain where we'll end up in the long run, because the current trajectories may not remain constant.

Consider Poland. What we do know is that the Polish fertility rate is 1.32 and that for the last few years Poland's population has been hovering around 38 million.[29] We know that right now in Poland the current cohort of children aged 0 to 14 years is 40 percent smaller than the cohort currently in its prime reproductive years.[30] And we know that because of this math, the United Nations projects that by 2100, Poland's population will decline by 25 percent, to 29 million people.[31]

That's the rosy scenario, by the way. For Poland to "only" lose a quarter of its population, the United Nations simply assumes that the country's TFR will reverse 60 years of constant decline and begin 80 years of constant increase starting, well, tomorrow. This best-case scenario has Poland's fertility rate rising all the way back to 2.0 by 2080. If things don't work out so well—if, say, Poland's fertility rate were to remain right where it is now? Well, in that case, the country's population would plummet from 38 million today to 16.4 million in 2100.[32]

Could Poland escape the future that demography predicts? Absolutely. In order to hold the country's population stable, all that would have to happen is that, once they become adults, the little girls in Poland today (and the women who follow them) would need to have an average of about four babies each.[33] Is it possible that a country working on three generations of steadily declining, sub-replacement fertility will spontaneously decide to increase its output of children by 300 percent? Possible? Yes. Likely? I wouldn't bet the milk money on it.

A few caveats before we begin. First, the study of demographics has sometimes carried an unpleasant undertone of racism. Americans have been worried about fertility issues for a long time. Margaret Sanger, the mother of Planned Parenthood and a saint to America's progressives, pioneered the birth-control movement in large part because she wanted to stop "ignorant people" and "dysgenic types" from "breeding."[34] But the proper concern from America's point of view is actually quite the opposite: As we mentioned before, white Americans are far below replacement fertility and the national average is buoyed only by the Hispanic population. But our concern isn't that Hispanic Americans are having too many babies. No, what should worry us is that while recent Hispanic immigrants have large families, their own children are likely to quickly decline toward the national average. The problem with the elevated fertility level of Hispanic Americans is that it isn't likely to last.

Second, please understand I am not arguing that correlation equals causation. In the coming pages, I will often point to a societal development that coincides with a data trend. Unless I say otherwise, I am not insisting that the former is the cause of the latter. What I am hoping to do is layer enough of these trends upon enough of these data points to convince you that each trend is probably contributing in some part to the outcomes you'll see.

I'd also like to offer a preemptive defense against readers who may take this book to be a criticism of the modern American woman. Nothing could be further from my intent. The constellation of factors that drive the baby-making decisions of couples is so vast that it's often impossible to pinpoint exactly why some women have four children and other women have none. But that should not prevent us from noticing important trends. For example, as we just noted, one of the great predictors of fertility is a woman's level of education. The more educated a woman is, on average, the fewer children she will have. To observe this is not to argue that women should be barefoot, pregnant, and waiting at home for their husbands every night with a cocktail and a smile.

Finally, this book is not an attempt to convince you to have babies. Children are wonderful, in their way. But you'll find no sentimentalizing about them here. To raise a child is to submit to a staggering amount of work, much of which is deeply unpleasant. It would be crazy to have children if they weren't so damned important.

So with this housekeeping behind us, let's put America's fertility problem into the starkest relief possible. China is famous for its One-Child Policy. Instituted in 1979, One-Child decimated the country's fertility, driving the TFR downward and preventing, over the course of 30 years, somewhere between 100 million and 400 million births.[35] The One-Child Policy employs an array of coercive measures to prevent couples from having babies—violators are often taxed or fired from their jobs; there are forced sterilizations and forced abortions; sometimes their homes are razed as punishment. As a result of One-Child, the fertility rate in China is roughly 1.54.[36] In America, the fertility rate for white, college-educated women—we'll use them because they serve as a fair proxy for our middle class—is 1.6. In other words, America has created its very own One-Child Policy. It's soft and unintentional, the result of accidents of history and thousands of little choices. But it has been just as effective.

CHAPTER ONE

America's Falling Fertility

Right-thinking Westerners have lauded China's One-Child Policy for over three decades. So much so that you might think that having Americans hew to a rough equivalent isn't such a bad thing after all. China sure looks like the future. If you tuned in to any of the 2008 Beijing Olympics you saw a country full of shiny, modernist buildings. The nation's industrial sector makes everything from spools of thread to iPhones. Futuristic maglev trains crisscross the landscape. China's public works projects are so massive that they're difficult to comprehend in the abstract. (The Three Gorges Dam, for instance, is *six times* as long as the Hoover Dam. The Hoover Dam has a spillway capacity of 400,000 cubic feet per second. The Three Gorges Dam's spillway capacity is 4.1 *million* cubic feet per second.) Our wise men frequently lecture us about how we will eventually submit to our new Chinese overlords and the One-Child Policy is often given credit for their coming supremacy. In his 2008 book *Hot, Flat, and Crowded*, for instance, Tom Friedman lauded One-Child for saving China from "a population calamity."[1]

But Friedman and other Sinophiles misunderstand China's One-Child Policy. Rather than saving China from calamity, it has created a slow-rolling demographic catastrophe that should scare the living bejesus out of anyone paying attention to more than the buildings, factories, trains, and dams.

The Original One-Child Policy

Between 1950 and 1970, the average Chinese woman had roughly six children during her lifetime. Beginning in 1970, the Chinese government began urging a course of "late, long, few"—instructing women to wait until later in life to have babies, put longer periods of time between births, and have fewer children overall. In a decade, the country's fertility rate dropped from 5.5 to 2.7.[2] That wasn't enough for the government, so in 1979 it formulated the One-Child Policy.

The policy is more complicated than its name suggests. Under One-Child, couples wanting a baby were originally required to obtain permission from local officials first. (In 2002, the government relaxed this provision; couples can now have one child without government clearance.) After having one child, urban residents and government employees were forbidden from having another, with very few exceptions. In rural areas, couples were often allowed to have a second baby five years after the first. Any more than two, however, and the government instituted penalties. Sanctions ranged from heavy fines to confiscation of belongings to dismissal from work. In addition, that is, to the occasional forced abortion and sterilization.[3] The overall result is a Chinese fertility rate that now sits somewhere between 1.9 and 1.3, depending on who's doing the tabulating. Demographer Nicholas Eberstadt notes that, "In some major population centers—Beijing, Shanghai, and Tianjin among them—it appears that the average number of births per woman is amazingly low: below one baby per lifetime."[4]

By 2050 the age structure in China will be such that there are only two workers to support each retiree.[5] Because the extended family has been dismantled and there is no pension system, the government will be forced to either: (1) substantially cut spending in such areas as defense and public works in order to shift resources to care for the elderly; or (2) impose radically higher tax burdens on younger workers. The first option risks China's international and military ambitions; the second risks revolution.

Of course, there is a third option: The Chinese government could simply send its old people to the countryside to die. It seems unthinkable, but remember that this is a regime that, within living memory, intentionally starved to death between 20 million and 40 million of its own people.[6] A proposal that sounds monstrous to our ears may be a legitimate policy option for the Chinese Communist Party. To avoid these unpleasant scenarios, all China has to do is convince its citizens to have more babies, starting now. This, it turns out, is harder—much harder—than it sounds.

American (Fertility) History 101

American fertility has been headed south almost since the Founding. When the Constitution was first ratified it called for a national census, which our newly formed government first conducted in 1790.[7] A few years ago, economist Michael Haines combined data from that first census with other data sets to determine that in 1800, the fertility rate for white Americans was 7.04.[8] The earliest reliable estimate of the fertility rate for black Americans, from the 1850s, puts it at 7.90.[9] By 1890, the fertility rate for whites had fallen to 3.87, while staying relatively high for blacks, at 6.56. (All early population numbers were kept separately by race.)

Over the next half-century, however, the black fertility rate went into free-fall, reaching 2.87 in 1940—a drop of 56 percent in less than three generations. Meanwhile, the white fertility rate exhibited a more gradual decline, settling at 2.22 in 1940.[10] At the end of the Second

World War, America experienced the Baby Boom, about which you probably know quite a lot. For 20 years, the fertility rate spiked, reaching a height in 1960 of 3.53 for whites and 4.52 for blacks.[11] What made the Baby Boom so exceptional wasn't just its magnitude, but its longevity—it lasted an entire generation, creating a population bulge that still bloats our demographic profile.

Yet despite its size, the Baby Boom proved temporary. In the cultural moment that followed during the 1960s and 1970s, the fertility rate in America—and the rest of the world—went bust. In Canada, the United States, Japan, and Western Europe—in every single industrialized nation—the fertility rate plummeted. In the Netherlands, for instance, the fertility rate went from 3.1 in 1960 to 1.6 in 1980; in Canada it slipped from 3.8 to 1.8; in West Germany it fell from 2.3 to 1.5.[12]

America followed suit. From a combined TFR of 3.7 in 1960 (the end of the Baby Boom), the fertility rate in the United States dropped to 1.8 in 1980, a 50 percent decline in a single generation. Since that low point, we've rebounded slightly. Our TFR went as high as 2.12 in 2007 before slumping back to 2.01 in 2009.[13] But again, that rebound was largely driven by the high fertility of immigrants, whose numbers surged from the 1980s through the early part of the 2000s. Let's have a look.

In 1990, America's fertility rate was 2.08, which seemed ideal. But that number belied two very different realities. Non-Hispanic whites had a TFR of 2.00 that year, while the Hispanic fertility rate was 2.96.[14] By 2000 the overall fertility rate had dipped to 2.06, even though fertility for non-Hispanic whites actually ticked upward to 2.05.[15] The reason: The Hispanic rate dropped, to 2.73—where it stayed through 2009.[16] (This 9 percent drop between 2007 and 2009 was the largest decline among the racial cohorts.[17]) In 2010, it plummeted to 2.35. Which suggests, as I mentioned earlier, that the trouble with Hispanic fertility in America is that it's sliding toward the national average. We'll talk about this in more detail later.

To get a sense of what these differing fertility rates mean in the real world, here are some numbers from the 2010 census: In 1990, there were 22.35 million people of Hispanic origin in America, making up 9 percent of our total population.[18] By 2000, that number rose to 35.3 million, or 12.5 percent.[19] In 2010, 50.5 million Americans—16.3 percent of the population—were Hispanic. That's more than a doubling of the Hispanic population in just 20 years. To put it even more starkly: Between 2000 and 2010, the *total* population of the United States increased by 27.3 million, yet more than half of *the entire increase* came just from Hispanics.

Most of that increase was due to fertility. Between 2000 and 2010, a net of 7.02 million people immigrated to the United States from south of the border.[20] Which means that, over the last decade, 30 percent of America's total population growth was the result of the labors of a group that makes up only 16 percent of the country.

This should scare you quite a lot, though not for the reasons you might think. The problem isn't that America is about to be overrun with Hispanic immigrants and their children. The problem is that our population profile is so dependent on Hispanic fertility that if this group continues falling toward the national average—and everything about American history suggests that it will—then our 1.93 fertility rate will take a nosedive.

One Child for All

So the decline in American fertility is a real and longstanding trend. The question is: Why? I would argue that it's the result of a complex constellation of factors, operating independently, with both foreseeable and unintended consequences. From big things—like the decline in church attendance and the increase of women in the workforce—to little things—like a law mandating car seats in Tennessee or the reform of divorce statutes in California—our modern world has evolved in such a way as to subtly discourage childbearing. It's not a conspiracy. None of these changes was intended to drive down fertility. But the fact that there's no conspiracy makes it even more worrisome, because every country across the globe is witnessing the same phenomenon—even though their individual circumstances could not be more different. Which means that there is something about modernity itself that tends toward fewer children.

But that kind of talk is gauzy, so let's start with something concrete. Stripped down to its most basic cause, our declining fertility is first and foremost about the decline of infant mortality. In 1850, 2 out of every 10 white babies and 3.4 out of every 10 black babies died during infancy.[21] Steady improvements in medicine, sanitation, and nutrition vastly reduced infant mortality—to just 5.98 deaths for every 1,000 live births today.[22] This very happy development is such an enormous driver of current fertility that its contribution is—again, happily—beyond measure.

Another quantitative factor has been the decline of "desired fertility." The Gallup organization has been asking Americans about their "ideal family size" since 1936. When Gallup first asked the question, 64 percent of Americans said that three or more children were ideal; 34 percent said that zero, one, or two children were ideal. Those percentages remained reasonably stable until the late 1960s. In 1967, a sudden decline in desired family size began. By 1973, 48 percent of Americans wanted zero, one, or two children and only 43 percent wanted three or more. The percentage wanting smaller families grew until the 1990s, when roughly 60 percent of Americans thought a smaller family (or no family at all) was ideal. Today only 33 percent of Americans think that a family with three or more children is ideal.[23]

It is important to remember that with easy access to birth control and abortion, increased educational demands, and the rising cost of raising children, the "desired fertility" metric is an upward limit on "actual fertility." In practice, actual fertility is often much lower than desired. In 2011, 58 percent of women said that an ideal family would have zero, one, or two children. But in reality, 20.4 percent of women completed their childbearing years with no children; 16.9 percent had only one child; and 34.4 percent had two children.[24] All told, 71.7 percent of women wound up with small, or no, families. So when Gallup reports that 2.5 children is the ideal family size for Americans, it

Figure 1. Ideal Family Size Trend.
(*Source: Lydia Saad, Gallup News Service, June 30, 2011.*)

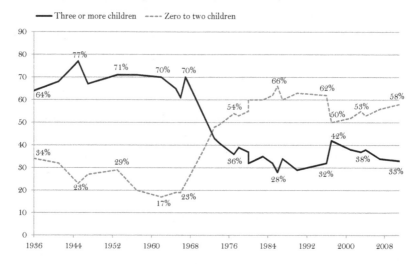

means that even in a perfect world, 2.5 is the upper limit on America's fertility rate.

There are other large-scale contributors to our fertility decline. During the Industrial Revolution, Americans began migrating from rural areas to cities (which have always had lower fertility), as they transitioned from farm work to factories.[25] These changes made children both less useful and more expensive. Social changes affected fertility, too. The routinization of divorce allowed married couples to split before they finished having children. The widespread practice of abortion culled an entire generation's worth of babies that otherwise might have been born. The growing acceptance of homosexuality liberated gay men and women who, in the past, often unhappily made do with heterosexual life. Women began going to college in greater numbers and then fanning out in the workforce. And the birth-control pill changed the consequences of sex. (The Pill first became available in America—and much of the West—in 1960, just before fertility rates dropped through the floor.)

These observations are not meant as indictments. Many of these cultural changes have proven to be genuine benefits for both individuals and society at large. And in any case, there's no going back now, even if society collectively decided that it wanted to. Genies, bottles, etc. But cultural changes also carry costs. Some of these costs—like the influence on fertility—are hidden.

In general, that's how fertility works. Both the world's influence on it, and its influence on the world, can be hard to see. Fertility is, as the brilliant demographer Phillip Longman puts it, like the tectonic plates moving beneath the Earth's crust. Again, demography is not destiny, and we should be careful never to confuse the two. But we would do well to understand how it influences the world we face today and will be forced to confront tomorrow.

Demography and Destiny

Before we begin delving into causes and effects, let's take a little tour of American fertility so you can get a glimpse of those plates shifting beneath our feet. Once you start looking for it, fertility helps explain all sorts of mundane things. Like politics.

Fertility varies widely within the 50 states. In 2008, Utah sported the highest TFR in the land, at 2.60, while Vermont had the lowest, 1.67.[26] That's a difference of 55 percent. Or, to give you a sense of scale, the fertility gap between Utah and Vermont is proportionally larger than the gap between the highest-fertility country in Europe (Ireland, 2.01) and the lowest (Lithuania, 1.27).[27] As you might expect, this differential tends to matter a great deal in American political life.[28] Today the states with the highest fertility are found mostly in the West: Utah (2.60), Arizona (2.31), Idaho (2.47), South Dakota (2.35), Texas (2.36), Nevada (2.31), and Wyoming (2.28) are all in the top ten. (In case you're curious, the other three are Alaska, Hawaii, and Nebraska.) The states with the lowest fertility are found mostly in the industrialized Northeast: Vermont (1.67), Rhode Island (1.73), New Hampshire (1.71), Maine (1.74), Massachusetts (1.77), New York (1.89), Connecticut (1.88), and Pennsylvania (1.94) account for eight of the ten lowest fertility rates. (The other two in the bottom ten are West Virginia and Michigan.)

Obviously, the higher-fertility states tend to be more rural; lower-fertility states more urban. This has always been true. As far back as 1700—when New York was still a colony—there was a wide gap between the fertility rates of those living in the southern tip of Manhattan Island and those living in the more bucolic rest of the county.[29] This gap between urban and rural residents has been persistent, spanning centuries, with the two populations moving in near parallel through periods of decline and boom.

What other trends can we see in these two groups of states? Well, our higher-fertility states tend to have lower land costs, and hence, costs of living. And then there's one other unifying feature: When it comes to politics, the highest-fertility states are (with the exceptions of Nevada and Hawaii) Republican strongholds, while the lowest-fertility states are heavily Democratic.

The cultural demographer Steve Sailer makes a persuasive case that the cost of real estate is an important driver in political alignment.[30] Sailer reports that in 2004, George W. Bush won the 26 states with the least inflation in housing prices between 1980 and 2004. What Sailer was one of the first to notice is that land costs, fertility, and political choice are inseparable, with the cost of real estate driving fertility and fertility driving political choice. Sailer calls this the "dirt gap." Married people with children vote disproportionately Republican. For example, in 2004, President Bush won the 25 states where non-Hispanic white women were married the most years on average—as well as the 19 states with the highest fertility among non-Hispanic whites.[31] In 2008, one of the few groups John McCain actually won was married voters with children, taking them 51 percent to 48 percent over Barack Obama (even though Obama won the general popular vote by 53 to 46 percent).[32]

Once you use the fertility rate as a lens, all kinds of contradictions begin to resolve. For instance, California has a relatively high fertility rate—2.15, ranking it 17th among the states. Yet California has some of the highest land costs in the country and is one of the bluest, most Democratic states. If Sailer's dirt gap theory and the linkage of fertility rates and voting behavior are real, then how can that be? The explanation is that 27 percent of Californians are foreign-born immigrants.[33] This is, by far, the highest percentage in the country. (The next highest is New York, with 21 percent.) These immigrants drive up the state's fertility rate: In California, non-Hispanic whites have a TFR of 1.83; Hispanics have a TFR of 2.33.[34] California's 2.15 really means that the state has an abundance of Hispanics, who are a core Democratic demographic group.

To more fully comprehend immigration's impact on fertility in California, let's pull back and examine the state's past. In 1970, California had a TFR of 2.3 (already slightly below the national average, which was then 2.5).[35] It was about to career over the cliff. By 1972, California's TFR had fallen to 1.9. It would remain below replacement level until 1987, by which time it was steadily climbing, going as high as 2.5 in 1990. What happened? An explosion of immigrant births—the raw totals of which increased by 50 percent between 1982 and 1997. How fecund is California's foreign-born, Hispanic population? In 2000, Hispanics were 30 percent of the state's population, but contributed 50 percent of the state's births.[36]

The Case of the Disappearing Demographic Momentum

Again, none of this is meant as fear-mongering about America's growing Hispanic population. Certainly, mass immigration on the scale we've experienced for the last 30 years presents very real problems. To pick only the most obvious from the list: Illegal immigration creates downward pressure at the low end of the wage scale. It puts stress on social services for those most in need and makes it hard for natives who aren't college graduates to earn a living. And as Robert Putnam found—much to his dismay—mass-scale "diversity" tends to make everyone more insular and less engaged in civil society.[37] But in the broader view, these are all high-class problems to have. Because for all the challenges presented by our recent immigration experience, lots of countries would kill to have a steady supply of Mexicans and South Americans shuffling across their borders.

Let's jump back again, for a minute, to Japan and Italy. With their lowest-low fertility rates, both of those countries are already seeing their populations shrink. As we will see later, nothing good is going to come of this. America's fertility rate has been sub-replacement for most of the last 40 years. Yet our overall population isn't shrinking. In fact, it's still growing. Even stripping out increases due to immigration, America's population grew by 21 million between 2000 and 2010. How can population increase even when the fertility rate is below the Golden Number of 2.1? The answer is demographic momentum.

The principle of demographic momentum is simple, but requires a tiny bit more math. Consider a town composed of 10 young couples (population: 20). Each couple then has three children, giving our town a total population of 50. If those children all marry and each couple has two children of their own, the population swells to 80. On the surface, it looks as though our town is growing, even as fertility is slowing. Now suppose the next generation has (on average) 1.5 children per couple. Even as our original inhabitants die off, the town's population increases again, to 83.

Our little town's fertility rate has fallen by 50 percent! Yet its population kept growing because of demographic momentum—the built-up supply of people from earlier generations. The rule of demographic momentum is this: *You don't see the effects of fertility decreases until the last above-replacement generation dies.* Now, let's say the fourth generation in our town now holds the fertility line at 1.5. The town's second generation is elderly and as they set off for the undiscovered country, population finally contracts, falling to 70.

This is the cycle of sub-replacement fertility. Populations grow as fertility rates drop. But the rate of growth slows until an inflection point is reached when the last above-replacement generation dies. After that, the population begins contracting, relentlessly. We have yet to witness the effects of our low fertility rate in America because the first generation of sub-replacement-level parents, those who came of age in the 1960s, is (blessedly) still with us. So until they begin to peg out, America's population will continue to increase.

What could our future look like if we continue to have too few babies? Again, Italy and Japan are instructive. Explaining the seriousness of the situation for Italy, demographer Letizia Mencarini told the *New York Times*, "In the 1960s, the overall fertility rate in Italy was around two children per couple. Now it is about 1.3, and for some towns in Italy it is less than 1. This is considered pathological."[38] In 1995, Italy had 58.3 million people.[39] That was the inflection point. By 2008, the slow decline had begun and Italy's population slipped backward to 58.1 million. In 2010, there were 25,500 more deaths than births in Italy.[40]

Yet the Italians had *some* luck. Their overall population actually ticked upward because they've recently averaged 300,000 new immigrants per year. With their demographic momentum spent, these new immigrants—mostly from Albania—are all that's standing between Italy and serious shrinkage. And soon even they won't be enough. Back in 2001, the United Nations Population Division projected that even with heavy immigration, Italy's population would fall to 51 million by 2025 and 41 million by 2050.[41] Then, in 2010, the Population Division revised its projections, suggesting that Italy's population decline wouldn't be so bad after all. The UN simply assumed that Italy's fertility rate would march right back up to replacement level over the next few decades.[42] (More on this assumption in a moment.) If the current revision is wrong and Italy's fertility holds constant, its population will fall to 37 million by the end of the century, even with high levels of immigration.[43]

Japan is facing the same situation, only without the benefit of immigration. In 1995, Japan had 125.51 million people and a fertility rate of 1.56, but thanks to momentum its population was still growing.[44] By 2000, Japan had grown, slightly, to 126.55 million.[45] That tiny rate of increase disappeared as Japan's population teetered at the tipping point (127.46 million) from 2006 to 2007.[46] In 2008 the decline began; by 2011 Japan had already lost a million people.[47] These losses will accelerate. Between now and 2025, the country's population will drop by another 6 million.[48] If Japanese fertility were to somehow rebound (the United Nations assumes that *all* industrial nations will rise to

2.0), Japan will "only" lose 30 percent of its population by 2100.[49] If Japan's fertility stays where it is, the country will contract by more than half—to 56.8 million—by the end of the century.[50]

Let me offer a brief aside about the recent fertility assumptions of the United Nations: It's guesswork, pure and simple. The UN assumes that nearly every industrialized nation in the world, no matter its current TFR, rates of immigration, or culture, will begin a steady climb in fertility over the next 70 years, and will settle at 2.0, permanently. The UN assumes this for countries where fertility has been in uninterrupted decline for more than half a century. It assumes this for countries with high rates of immigration—and countries with no immigration at all. The same projection can't logically be made for both.

Not to put too fine a point on it: This entire exercise was little more than wishful thinking. Now, if Walt Disney taught us anything, it's that sometimes wishes come true—so maybe we really are about to see a rebound in fertility rates across the industrialized world. That would be good news for everyone! (Except, possibly, for those of us writing books about fertility decline.) But it would also be utterly unheard-of. And the nice stat-geeks at the United Nations know this. Because in 1997, back before things got really, *really* bad, they wrote in their population projection that "There exists no compelling and quantifiable theory of reproductive behavior in low-fertility societies."[51] Just a few years later, the UN admitted that "The recent experience of low-fertility countries suggests that there is no reason to assume that their fertility will return anytime soon to the above-replacement level."[52] Nothing has changed since then. As researchers Philip Morgan and Miles Taylor noted in a 2006 survey of low fertility in the twenty-first century, "No country has transitioned back to replacement-level fertility (for any five-year period) once falling below it."[53] In other words, the UN has suddenly changed its mind and invented a model which it previously claimed was impossible.

But enough about survey methodology—back to Italy and Japan. I'm not just cherry-picking countries where the news is dire. Fertility decline is a global problem. The United Nations projects that by 2050, only three members of the European Union will *not* be experiencing population decline. (The lucky three are France, Ireland, and Luxembourg.)[54] By that time, Greece may have lost 20 percent of its people, Portugal 17 percent, Belgium 11 percent—the dismal list goes on and on.

In other parts of Europe, the future is now. Since 1989, Latvia has lost 13 percent of its population.[55] Germany is shedding 100,000 people a year. (When I spoke with the country's family minister in 2006 she muttered darkly, "We will have to turn the lights out.") In Russia, matters are considerably worse. In 1995, Russia had 149.6 million people.[56] Today, Russia is home to 138 million.[57] By 2050, its population will be nearly a third smaller than it is today. This impending catastrophe is not lost on the Russian government, which released a study in 2001 concluding that the country's contracting population was a threat to national security.[58] The report caused Vladimir Putin, in his first annual state of the nation address, to warn his countrymen that they were "facing the serious threat of turning into a decaying nation."

Old Guys Rule

There can be a dissonance between what we see with our eyes every day and what the demographic math tells us. Vladimir Putin worries that low fertility leads to decay, but Russia's fertility rate isn't much lower than what we had in Old Town Alexandria, that glorious preserve of eco-conscious yoga and free-range coffee. My neighbors had wonderfully comfortable lives in part because they didn't take on the expense of raising children. If we treated Old Town as a closed system—a little nation-state of its own—you might wonder why population decline is such a bad thing. After all, fewer people just means less crowding at the good restaurants on Saturday night, right?

Well, not exactly. Population decline is the most obvious effect of sub-replacement fertility. The more subtle effect is that low fertility reshapes a society's age structure. In a steady-state country with a fertility rate of 2.1, the age structure looks something like the nib of a fountain pen, with its tip pointed toward the sky. The younger age cohorts are close in size to the cohorts that are in their prime reproductive years, and the cohorts above reproductive age get steadily smaller. Figure 2 shows a snapshot of America's age distribution, circa 2000.

As fertility rates drop, the structure begins to invert, with more adults, and eventually more retirees, than children. For example, Figure 3 shows the age structure Russia will face in 2050, as its population continues contracting. Note how the youngest cohort, from ages 0 to 5 years, is smaller than every cohort except for the ones composed of the very elderly (75 and older).

America's age structure is already shifting. Between 2005 and 2025, the number of U.S. citizens over 65 will increase by 72 percent. One out of every five Americans will reach retirement age by 2050. The population of 65-and-overs will outnumber the population of 14-and-unders by 13 million.[59] Roughly speaking, America as a whole will have an age structure similar to Florida's age structure today.

Figure 2. Age-Sex Structure of the United States, 2000.
(*Source: United Nations Population Division, Replacement Migration, 2000.*
http://www.un.org/esa/population/publications/migration/usa.pdf)

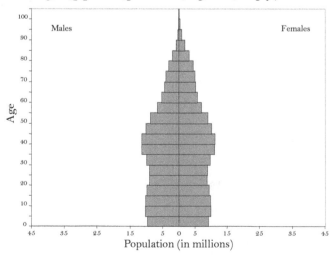

The consequences of this change are enormous. At the most mundane level, entitlement programs such as Social Security and Medicare will consume ever-larger portions of the federal budget. Fewer working-age people supporting more retirees means that something will have to give: Either benefits will be scaled back, non-entitlement spending cut, or taxes raised.

Yet there are hidden consequences, too. Demographer Phillip Longman notes that the pace of human progress has slowed considerably since 1972—just after Western fertility began to collapse. Longman observes that between 1913 and 1972, America's "total-factor productivity" (a measure of economic dynamism) increased annually by 1.08 percent. Between 1972 and 1995, that rate of increase declined by more than 80 percent.[60] There is vigorous debate as to the cause of this decline, but it is not unreasonable to suspect that America's older, grayer population structure may have something to do with it. As Longman puts it, "After the proportion of elders increases in

Figure 3. Age-Sex Structure of Russia, 2050.
(*Source: United Nations Population Division, Replacement Migration, 2000.* *http://www.un.org/esa/population/publications/ReplMigED/RusFed.pdf*)

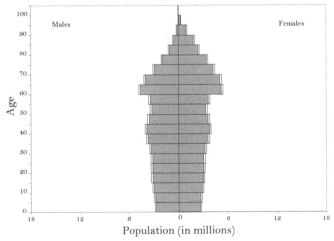

a society beyond a certain point, the level of entrepreneurship and inventiveness decreases."[61]

Older citizens necessarily seek less risky employment and investments. Their consumption becomes focused in sectors that do not necessarily spur innovation in the wider economy. Again, here is Longman: "As growth in population dwindles, so does the need to increase the supply of just about everything, except healthcare."[62]

Finally, an older society with fewer children will find it difficult to project power in the wider world. America's military spending is already loaded down by retirement benefits. The Pentagon now spends 84 cents on pensions for every dollar it spends on basic pay.[63] And whatever form our future military does take, families with just one child will be less willing to accept military casualties. The loss of a child will represent not just a tragedy, but in most cases, the end of the family line. As David Goldman ruefully notes, "A people without progeny will not accept a single military casualty."[64]

There is reason to believe that low fertility has had a pacifying effect on Europe, and although it is a complicated question, the general pattern holds when one glances across the globe. Countries frequently at war tend to have high fertility rates. Perpetually war-torn Rwanda, for instance, has a fertility rate of 5.43, one of the highest in Africa. Afghanistan, home to three generations of near-continuous conflict, has a fertility rate of 6.8, the highest in Asia. The Palestinian territories, a hotbed of violence, have a fertility rate of 4.7, one of the highest in the Middle East.[65]

By contrast, even in unstable regions, the countries with relatively low fertility rates tend to be more peaceable. Mauritius, South Africa, and Gabon have the lowest fertility rates in Africa, and are among the continent's most stable nations. Israel and Qatar have the lowest fertility rates in the Middle East and are two of the least belligerent states in the neighborhood. In volatile South Central Asia, the lowest fertility rate is claimed by Kazakhstan, a stable, modernizing country.

No More Babies

If countries with lower fertility make less trouble, then why should we be worried about falling fertility rates and population contraction? As it happens, some people aren't worried at all. They celebrate childlessness and are looking forward to the coming population crunch.

Back in 1968, Paul Ehrlich's *Population Bomb* claimed that hundreds of millions would die as overpopulation ravaged the world. As previously noted, Ehrlich couldn't have been more wrong. Yet the '60s and '70s were full of population hysteria. Groups such as the Ford Foundation and the International Planned Parenthood Federation pushed to introduce birth control and abortion in developing countries. When Lyndon Johnson signed the Food for Peace Act he required USAID officers to "exert the maximum leverage and influence" on the countries we were helping so that they'd cut down on their baby-making.[66] In 1972, the Club of Rome published a tract, *The Limits to Growth*, echoing Ehrlich's forecast. (Among other things, the Club of Rome predicted that the planet's oil reserves would be exhausted by 1992.) The movement was in such a lather that in 1967, Disney produced a movie for the Population Council, titled *Family Planning*. The movie, translated into 24 different languages and featuring Donald Duck, lectured viewers that if families didn't drastically cut back the number of kids they had, "the children will be sickly and unhappy, with little hope for the future."[67]

The hysteria might be funny in hindsight, except that lots of people are still under its spell. Including Ehrlich. Undeterred by having his life's work completely discredited, the octogenarian professor is mad about the perils of overpopulation, even to this day. In 1990, long after his initial thesis was disproved, he doubled down and published *The Population Explosion*, in which he claimed that overpopulation was more. Dangerous. THAN. EVER! "It's insane to consider low birthrate as a crisis," he said recently. "Basically every person I know in my section of the National Academy of Sciences thinks it's wonderful that rich countries are starting to shrink their populations to sustainable levels. We have to do that because we're wrecking our life-support system."[68] (Ehrlich now explains the lack of mass starvation in the 1970s by admitting that "repeatedly in my career it has turned out things I never would have imagined were huge factors."[69] No kidding.)

Ehrlich isn't alone in thinking that population growth is still an unsustainable danger. The group Californians for Population Stabilization claims that "population growth [is] wildly out of control" and is causing "further degradation of America's natural treasures."[70] The Dalai Lama warns that overpopulation is "very serious—very, very serious."[71] The United Nations, which has done a great deal of study on the downward spiral of falling fertility rates through its Population Division, nonetheless sponsors a "World Population Day" to raise awareness about overpopulation.[72]

In 2008, a government report in Australia proclaimed that babies were a drag on the economy.[73] A recent study at Oregon State University warned that children were terrible contributors to global warming and advised that responsible couples should have (at least!) one fewer child than they might otherwise wish.[74] In the London *Independent*, columnist Johann Hari worried that, "It will be easier for 6 billion people to cope on a heaving, boiling planet than for 9 or 10 billion."[75] In *Hot, Flat, and Crowded*, Tom Friedman argued that overpopulation is one of the drivers of a coming global catastrophe and talked about the "steady population growth" the world will experience in the future as if he'd never seen a fertility chart.[76] The group Earth First! went so far as to publish articles saying that "The AIDS epidemic, rather than being a scourge, is a welcome development in the inevitable reduction of human population" and if AIDS "didn't exist, radical environmentalists would have to invent [it]."[77]

The lamentations continue. In 2009, Canada's *Financial Post* called fertility "the real inconvenient truth" and called for a "planetary law" limiting women to one child in order to "reverse the disastrous global birthrate" which is, the authors claimed, responsible for climate change.[78] China agrees. "Dealing with climate change is not simply an issue of CO_2 emission reduction but a comprehensive challenge involving political, economic, social, cultural and ecological issues, and the population concern fits right into the picture," said Zhao Baige, one of China's representatives to the 2009 Copenhagen conference on climate change.[79]*

The environmentalist group Population Matters has called for a world with "fewer emitters, lower emissions."[80] ("Emitter" may be the most charming euphemism ever conceived for an infant.) Population Matters runs a program whereby environmentally conscious Westerners purchase carbon-offsetting family-planning credits. In other words, concerned citizens give the group money to fund birth control in developing countries to make up for their own carbon-gobbling lifestyle. In case you're curious, Population Matters estimates that it only takes $144.20 per year to keep enough of the great unwashed from reproducing to offset a typical American's existence.[81]

---

* The environmentalist case against children doesn't stand up to scrutiny. The three main environmental population worries are (1) overcrowding; (2) scarcity of resources; and (3) climate change due to carbon dioxide emissions. Let's take these in order. (1) Sure, America's city centers and major highways are more crowded than ever. But on the other hand, it's a big country. (Have you been to Montana—or even rural Maryland?) And it's important not to let provincialism distort your understanding of the world. For instance, if you live in Manhattan, you might think that America is becoming overcrowded, because New York City is overcrowded. But there is more to America than our city cores. For instance, there are fewer people living in the Rust Belt today than there were in the 1930s. There's still plenty of room out there. (2) As economist Bryan Caplan points out, population growth has historically led to conservation through innovation. And as the work of economist Ester Boserup made clear, innovation is a byproduct of increasing population. That's why commodities prices—a good measure of scarcity—have dropped about 1 percent a year since the Civil War. It's why air and water quality are markedly better today—in both America and the rest of the West—than they were in the 1970s, when there were fewer people. (3) The only environmentalist concern that population might legitimately affect is climate change, a subject so fraught with theological division that I'll leave it be. I'll only say that even if you take climate change to be real, and serious, and man-made, you still have to reckon that the environmental impact of "overpopulation" is, at worst, a mixed bag.

Child-Free and Loving It!

Even if you don't buy into radical environmental politics, there's a movement that pushes childlessness as a superior lifestyle choice. The term of art here is "child-free" and the raft of books on the subject is both hysterical and clarifying: from Madelyn Cain's *The Childless Revolution* to Terri Casey's *Pride and Joy: The Lives and Passion of Women without Children* to Nicki Defago's *Childfree and Loving It!* to Laura Carroll's *Families of Two: Interviews with Happily Married Couples without Children by Choice.* My favorite is Laura Scott's *Two Is Enough: A Couple's Guide to Living Childless by Choice.*

The child-free life is championed with the vigor and conviction of the early Marxists. Corinne Maier's *No Kids: 40 Good Reasons NOT to Have Children,* became a sensation across Europe with its frank and unabashed assault on the odiousness of babies. Bill McKibben issued a more serious call to the child-free life in 1998 with *Maybe One: A Case for Smaller Families.* Philosophy professor David Benatar published a book titled *Better Never to Have Been: The Harm of Coming into Existence*—which is either a work of performance art, comedy, or astonishing foolishness. He dedicates it "To my parents, even though they brought me into existence; and to my brothers, each of whose existence, although a harm to him, is a great benefit to the rest of us."

The child-free movement is so strident that its adherents often charge that society is giving *them* the short end of the stick. They want America to become even *more* anti-child. In *The Baby Boon: How Family-Friendly America Cheats the Childless*, Elinor Burkett argues that the child-free are forced to put in overtime so that colleagues with kids can take "leave from work to watch Susi dance *Swan Lake.*" The entire family-benefits system, she cries, is "affirmative action for mothers." (One suspects that Burkett, a down-the-line liberal, rather likes affirmative action—so long as it's tied to race.) Other liberals, such as *Mother Jones* reporter Stephanie Mencimer, argue that it is precisely America's "right-wing" system of making life hard on working mothers that has led women to "boycott" having children.[82]

When the child-free encounter families in the wild, the results can be unpleasant. In 2010, the *Washington Post* reported on a conflict between parents and the child-free in the District of Columbia's fancy Lincoln Park neighborhood. A sudden outpouring of babies sparked altercations between parents, who brought their children, and childless adults, who brought their dogs, to play in the neighborhood's idyllic park.[83]

Lincoln Park is gentrified and expensive—even post-bubble, the median price for a row house is near $1 million. The dog owners, who laid claim to the neighborhood first, were annoyed at being asked to share space with the new human dependents. In an attempt to bring peace, a local pet coach calling herself the Doggy Lama held "dog citizen" workshops to help pet owners learn to deal peaceably with the interlopers.

It was tough sledding. One dog owner interviewed by the *Post* said that she wished the *kids* could be confined to a fenced-in area of the park. "I find people with children to be tyrants," she explained. "As someone who doesn't have children, I think children are fine. I don't think they own everything." The *Post* detailed similar scuffles in other neighborhoods. The article generated nearly 500 comments on the paper's website, with sentiment running about 60-to-40 against parents and children.[84] Some sample entries:

> **CAC2**: keep your nasty little snotty kid away from me, PLEASE!!!! Do not let your stickly offspring rush up to me in Whole Foods and grab my $250 Ralph Lauren silk skirt with it's grubby, crusty hands. One of the benefits of not having children is not having to wear the Mommy Wardrobe. Do not make those of us who are not forced into wash and wear to pay extra for the dry cleaner to remove child goo. Do not allow your offspring to lean over the seat of a restaurant and try to initiate "conversation" with me when I am enjoying a meal with friends
>
> **graylandgal**: I won't make any apologies: I hate kids, especially babies. If parents can't afford or locate a sitter, then

stay home. I am bloody sick of having my feet and Achilles tendon rammed by knobby-tired strollers the size of Smart Cars; I am bitter about extortion for baby showers, christening gift, etc., for droolers who won't thank me now any more than they will when graduation extortions start; I am nauseated by the stench of dirty diapers changed in public areas because a lazy-ass parent won't adjourn to a restroom I am tired of "friends" dragging their hyper-active germ-spreaders to my antiques- and breakable-filled home for events clearly meant for grown-ups because, gee, everybody thinks they're SO cute; and I weary of replying "hi" 467 times to a toddler who hangs over the back of an adjoining restaurant booth because the parents won't make it sit down and shut up. Bitter? You bet. . . . My parents did not inflict me on society until I developed continence, self-ambulation, and social skills.[85]

All the outrage, bile, misspellings, and unintelligibility are in the originals, I'm afraid. Yet as unattractive as these comments might be, they're not (completely) insane. It is a hard truth that living child-free in a place like Lincoln Park or Old Town Alexandria can be a glorious, wonder-filled existence. Having children is often a one-way ticket out of Eden into some soulless suburb lined with big box stores, chain restaurants, and strip-malls. It is nearly impossible to have both. And so, as Nikolai Botev of the United Nations Population Fund put it to the *New York Times*, in the modern pleasure carnival, "childlessness emerges as an ideal lifestyle."[86]

"All of this has happened before..."

Pope Benedict XVI had it right when he observed that children are now "perceived as a threat to the present" in the West. But while low-fertility population contraction is something new in modern times, it's not unheard-of in human history. The Greek historian Polybius observed the consequences of falling fertility among his countrymen in the second century B.C. in words that sound eerily familiar. He wrote:

> In our time all Greece was visited by a dearth of children and generally a decay of population, owing to which the cities were denuded of inhabitants, and a failure of productiveness resulted, though there were no long-continued wars or serious pestilences among us. If, then, anyone had advised our sending to ask the gods in regard to this, what we were to do or say in order to become more numerous and better fill our cities — would he not have seemed a futile person, when the case was manifest and the cure in our own hands?
>
> For this evil grew upon us rapidly, and without attracting attention, by our men becoming perverted to a passion for show and money and the pleasures of an idle life, and accordingly either not marrying at all, or, if they did marry, refusing to rear the children that were born, or, at most one or two out of a great number, for the sake of leaving them well off or bringing them up in extravagant luxury.
>
> For when there are only one or two sons, it is evident that, if war or pestilence carries one off, the houses must be left heirless: and, like swarms of bees, little by little the cities become sparsely inhabited and weak.[87]

The Roman Empire also eroded because of declining fertility. In his seminal *Concise History of World Population*, the brilliant Italian demographer Massimo Livi-Bacci explains that between 400 B.C. and the birth of Christ, the world's population increased from about 153 million to 252 million.[88] For the next 200 years, growth slowed to a halt. Then, between A.D. 200 and 600, population shrank from 257 million to 208 million, because of falling fertility. We commonly refer to that period as the descent into the Dark Ages. Early on, Caesar Augustus attempted to combat the dearth of children with a bachelor tax on single men; it had little effect.[89] World population also declined steeply between 1340 and 1400, shrinking from 443 million to 374 million. This was not a period of environmental and social harmony; it was the reign of the Black Death.[90]

As Livi-Bacci observes, "Historically, areas depopulated or in the process of losing population have almost always been characterized by backward economies." Or, as Adam Smith noted in *The Wealth of Nations*, "the most decisive mark of prosperity of any country is the increase of the number of its inhabitants." Or perhaps the great Mark Steyn puts it best—if most starkly—when he cautions that "there is no precedent in human history for economic growth on declining human capital."[91]

These are gloomy thoughts. However, before you get too depressed, there is good news. Remember that fertility rates are not constant across all populations. There may be tumult, but in the long run, the groups that breed will (literally) inherit the future. What will that future look like? How will differing fertility rates affect America, both at home and abroad? And, finally, is it possible to change the trend line we're on now?

Those are all very big questions, so let's start with a task that's somewhat smaller: Where did America's one-child policy come from? And to begin an answer, let's try an even more discrete question. Let's pretend that you and your spouse wake up one Saturday morning in your charming little loft in Old Town. You're sitting at the bistro table in your kitchen, surrounded by stainless steel appliances and exposed-brick walls, munching on croissants and sipping espresso. You trade sections of the *Wall Street Journal* back and forth as you finish your breakfast until one of you absently mentions that, well, maybe it's time to think about having a baby together. The other one—the sensible one—nods noncommittally while a single thought shoves its way to the front of the brainpan: *What's this going to cost me?*

CHAPTER TWO

The Roots of One-Child

The company Posh Tots offers an amazing array of products for children and their parents. They have mini-rosaries made of pearls and diaper bags featuring antique brass hardware. They have vintage Barbie prints and heirloom changing tables constructed from hardwoods that have been hand-rubbed to a distressed, yet perfect, finish. The star of the catalog is the Red Beard's Revenge Pirate Playhouse. It looks as if it has washed ashore from a movie. Made from poplar and mahogany, it's 18 feet along the keel and 11 feet across the beam. It features 17 working windows and ornate detailing—wide moldings, an elaborate captain's wheel, and the carved figurehead of a wolf mounted on the bow. There's room enough for four adults in the captain's quarters, where you can sit on padded benches. (Which double as sleeping berths.) Red Beard's Revenge costs $52,000.

Red Beard's Revenge is, of course, a sensational example of parental insanity. No one—not even the really rich—needs a backyard play set that costs more than a base Mercedes. And it's not as if these glittering pirate ships are flying off the shelves. Posh Tots won't disclose how many it sells and will say only that the ships are made to order. But even when you back away from the outliers, "normal" can be pretty insane these days. If you're a middle-class parent who wants to put a swing set in your back yard—nothing fancy, just a slide, a ladder, and a couple swings, the kind of thing you buy at Home Depot and assemble yourself—you can expect to drop at least $1,200. And it's easy to spend a lot more. Even at Wal-Mart, the nicer sets run over $3,000.

The Most Expensive Decision You'll Ever Make

It's clichéd to complain about $800 baby strollers and designer children's clothing. But even the clichés no longer capture the lunacy of it all. One popular baby stroller, the Bugaboo Cameleon, now retails for $880. That's a bargain compared with Avila's innovative "round" crib. Crafted from cherry wood, it goes for $1,285. Back in Old Town we had a store called Pink & Brown, which billed itself as "An Organic & Trendy Children's Boutique." Over by Pink & Brown I came across a flyer one afternoon for "Seichou Karate," which teaches martial arts, "dojo etiquette," and Japanese calligraphy to children. The company's description of itself is beyond parody:

> There's no better training for the mind, body and spirit of a Child than the combination of Seichou Karate and Yoga. Let us bring out your Child's peaceful power with our hybrid curriculum!
> We're unique because our Ivy League educated director is a full-contact karate champion and an expert on Japanese culture. Also, all of our instructors possess masters degrees [sic throughout].

Seichou summer camp sessions cost $295 a week. You can, perhaps, imagine the type of parent to whom the graduate-school credentials of a karate teacher are important. It's the same kind of parent who insists on both organic food *and* organic clothing. And odds are, it's not a parent with more than two children.

But even for sensible parents—who buy $30 umbrella strollers, get clothes secondhand, and don't send their kids to Peaceful Power karate camp—the cost of raising a child is staggering. And the extent to which these expenses have grown is easy to measure because the U.S. Department of Agriculture has kept track of them for 50 years. Its findings are remarkable.

In 1960 the USDA estimated that the total amount of money needed to cover medical care for a child from birth until age 18 was $1,062. Education spending until 18 was $372. Clothing—a big-ticket item—was costed out at $2,718. All told, the USDA figured that a child born in 1960 would cost his parents $25,229 (about $193,000 in 2011 dollars).[2]

Over the next 25 years, the cost of raising a child remained reasonably constant, rising and falling by minor degrees. By 1985 it stood at $90,100, which, adjusted for inflation, was actually slightly cheaper than it had been in 1960.[3] But after 1985 children became steadily more expensive. By 2007 the cost of raising a child had risen 15 percent (in real dollars) over the 1960 level.[4] And that figure belies the speed with which children's expenses rose—the cost had actually increased 17.5 percent in just 22 years.

Yet even these numbers don't give the whole story. The USDA estimates leave out many of the little costs of parenthood—maternity clothes, baby furniture, toys, vitamins.[5] (In her book on the baby market, Pamela Paul reports that the global market for this bric-a-brac is $1.7 trillion a year.[6]) But those items are just nickels and dimes. The real money is in three big-ticket items that the USDA does not take fully into account: child care, college tuition, and mothers' forgone salaries.

Let's start with child care. The 2007 USDA survey reported that the average family spent a total of $4,000 on child care during the first two years of a child's life. True, only half of the survey's respondents spent any money on child care at all. Yet in the real world, that $4,000 is little more than a mathematical construct. The National Association of Child Care Resource and Referral Agencies reports that in 2008, the average cost of full-time care (40 hours a week) for an infant from a babysitter or nanny was $9,630 per year.[7] The average cost of full-time care for an infant in a day-care center was even more jaw-dropping: $14,591 per year.

The Terror of the Thick Envelope

The USDA also ignores the expense of college. Today, the majority of children—and an even greater majority of middle-class children—attend college. In 2006, 66 percent of high school graduates enrolled in either a two- or four-year degree program within a year of completing high school.[8]

The costs beggar belief. The College Board reports that for the 2010–2011 school year, the average tuition to a state college was $7,613.[9] Private colleges averaged $27,265. Neither of those figures includes room and board, which was roughly $9,000 for full-time students not living at home. So a child starting college today will cost her parents somewhere from $66,452 (for an average state-school degree) to $145,060 (for an average private degree). Remember, please, that we're talking averages here. If your bundle of joy is lucky enough to gain entrance to an elite university, the four-year tab will easily top $200,000.

Yet even *that* isn't the end of the bad news. During the last 35 years, the period during which college became a necessary expense for middle-class life, the price of college increased—in real dollars—by *1,000 percent.* Fortunately, over the last decade, the real price increase has slowed to an average of "only" 2.4 percent per year (remember, that's the real growth, not counting inflation).[10] If this slow-growth trend continues, a baby born in 2011 will need north of $260,000 (in today's dollars) to pay for a private college diploma by 2030.

The Cost of Parenting

Yet before Mom and Dad arrive at the bittersweet moment when they watch their little princess walk toward her freshmen orientation, ready to soak up the great books of Western civilization (that is, when she's not binge-drinking and hooking up with lacrosse players), there are other hidden costs of parenting. One of them is the time cost. And like everything else we've looked at, it, too, has exploded since the Baby Boom years.

In 1965—"the '60s," as we popularly conceive of them, didn't actually start until 1968—middle-class families were very close in structure to the popular stereotype: Sixty percent of all children lived in a family with a working father and a stay-at-home mom. The Baby Boom had just ended, but the fertility rate was still quite high at 2.93.[11] How much time did parents spend taking care of their kids? You might be surprised. The average married mother spent 10.6 hours per week on the kids. The average married father spent 2.6 hours per week.[12]

These numbers may sound fishy, but they're actually fairly reliable because they're not theoretical, socio-economic constructs. No, they were composed by actual parents recording their activities contemporaneously in time diaries. You might be thinking, *That's crazy, even a mother with a nanny spends more than 10.6 hours per week on the kids.* But remember that these numbers are the averages for all families—so mothers and fathers with toddlers who were putting in lots of hours were balanced out by parents with kids in high school.[13]

Here's where it gets interesting: From 1965 to 1985, mothers actually spent *less* time taking care of the kids (just 8.8 hours per week in 1975 and 9.3 hours per week in 1985) while fathers inched their numbers up a tiny bit, to 3 hours per week. After 1985, both moms and dads started doing more—lots more. By 2000, married fathers more than doubled their time with the kids, clocking 6.5 hours a week.[14]

Overall, American fathers have become more involved in raising their children. So much so that, as economist Bryan Caplan jokes, they could almost pass for '6os-era mothers.[15] But what's really astounding is what mothers have done. By 2000, more than 60 percent of married mothers worked outside the home. In doing so, they increased their number of paid work hours per week from 6.0 in 1965 to 23.8.[16] Yet even as they moved out of the house to pursue careers, they also increased the amount of time they spent with their children, cranking it up to a bracing 12.6 hours per week.[17]

Now, on the one hand, this is a happy development. It's a good thing to have parents taking a more active role in their kids' lives. But on the other hand, these numbers explain why parents are so frayed and stressed these days: Because however nice it is to be spending more time with your children, it's also a rising cost. There are only 24 hours in a day and if people are spending more time on kids, those hours have to come from somewhere.

If you want to be really blown away by mothers, consider this: A working mom today spends almost as much time with her kids as a stay-at-home mom did in prelapsarian 1965.[18] And if we were to construct a new statistic—something like "parental hours per week per child"—it would really go off the charts. Because of the big drop in fertility, parents are spending more time looking after fewer children.

What about mothers who still stay at home? They're now spending an average of 17.2 hours per week with the kids—more than a working mother and father *combined*. Which brings with it yet another cost. Recall that in its cost estimate for kids, the USDA assumes virtually no expenditures for child care. This implies that one parent (for sexism's sake, we'll assume the mother) stays home at least until the child reaches school age. In *The Empty Cradle*, Phillip Longman explores the cost of lost income by mothers:

> Consider Sherri and Mike, a hypothetical middle-class, dual-income/no children ("DINK") family. Two years into their marriage, both were 30 years old and working full-time, each making $45,000 a year. But then came baby. Sherri immediately quit her job to stay home with Mike Jr., causing their

family income to fall by half. After Mike Jr. reaches kinder-
garten, she hopes to begin working half-time. . . . She does
not plan to return to full-time work until Junior goes off to
college.[19]

Under this perfectly plausible scenario—and assuming Sherri is
able to find work whenever she wants it—Longman's couple is forgo-
ing $823,736 in lost wages between the birth of the baby and the time
the child turns 18.

Look at that number again: $823,736. Now add it to the other
numbers we've seen: $207,800 for USDA-accounted expenses and
between $66,452 and $145,060 for college. Even if you eschew the
insanities of the baby market, that's over $1.1 million—*$1.1 million*—to
raise a single child. That's a lot of money for a middle-class couple. In
2007, the median income for a person with a bachelor's degree was
$47,240.[20] The median income for Americans in their prime childbear-
ing years (ages 25 to 34) was much lower: $30,846 for all individuals and
$40,739 for people with a college degree.[21] To give some perspective,
the median price of a home in 2008 was $180,100.[22] It is commonly
said that buying a house is the biggest purchase most Americans will
ever make. Well, having a baby is like buying six houses, all at once.
Except you can't sell your children, they never appreciate in value,
and there's a good chance that, somewhere around age 16, they'll
announce: "I hate you."

Children as a Marker of Poverty

Fertility correlates with income—just not as you might expect. The
poorest families, those with annual incomes under $20,000, have the
second-highest fertility rate, 2.038. The highest fertility is found among
lower-middle-class families, those with incomes between $35,000 and
$49,999. They have a TFR of 2.052. But as you slide up the scale
to more solidly middle-class and upper-class families, fertility drops
(before ticking up slightly for families making over $100,000 a year).

Household Income Level	Total Fertility Rate
Under $20,000	2.038
$20,000 to $29,999	1.988
$35,000 to $49,999	2.052
$50,000 to $74,999	1.734
$75,000 to $99,999	1.752
$100,000 and over	1.832
Source: Jane Lawler Dye, U.S. Census Bureau, "Fertility of American Women: 2006," August 2008.	

What we have, then, is a picture of an American middle class that is surprisingly barren: 37 percent of women have no children or one child; only 6 percent of women have four or more children. Women who go to college or graduate school are unlikely to have even two children. It's the same for families making more than $50,000 a year. It's a kind of reverse Darwinism where the traditional markers of success make one *less* likely to reproduce.

Take this in conjunction with the costs of raising kids and you reach an alarming possibility: In part, the poorer families may be poor because they have chosen to invest their money in children and richer families may be rich because they have not. In other words, the soaring cost of childbearing has created a gargantuan societal maladaptation: Children have gone from being a *marker of* economic success to a *barrier to* economic success. It was not always thus.

The Worst Investment You'll Ever Make

There was a time, not long ago, when children served a very practical economic purpose: They cared for their parents in old age. Oftentimes physically; always financially. The arrangement dates to before Biblical times and, in America, to before the Founding. Having children made good financial sense. You invested your resources in raising them so that they would be able to provide for you when you could no longer work. Beginning with the New Deal, the logistics of this social compact began to change.

In 1935, President Franklin Roosevelt signed the Social Security Act which, for the first time in American history, provided government payouts to retirees. These benefits were to be drawn from a new payroll tax levied on the working. Over time, Social Security payments expanded, the Social Security tax increased, and new benefits were added. In 1965, President Lyndon Johnson created Medicare, which placed the government in charge of paying for the medical care of retirees, too.

It's difficult to overstate the effects of these two initiatives. For starters, they created an enormous new tax burden on workers. The Social Security tax rate was only 1.5 percent in 1950 and wages over $3,000 were tax-free.[23] By 2013, the rate was 6.2 percent and wages didn't become tax-free until they went over $113,700. When you add in Medicare, the payroll tax rate is 7.65 percent.[24] And the total tax burden—combining all federal, state, and local taxes—has risen dramatically. In 1955, the median one-income family paid 17.3 percent in taxes. By 1998, the median one-earner family paid 37.6 percent in income taxes; two-earner families paid 39.0 percent.[25]

One of the results of this increasing tax burden was a serious decline in the relative earning power of reproductive-aged men.[26] Since the 1970s, young white men have seen a 40 percent decline in income relative to their fathers (young black men have seen a relative decline of 60 percent), largely because of taxes.[27] So Social Security and Medicare have placed a serious and increasing burden on families, making it more difficult to afford the—also increasing—cost of children.

There were two larger consequences of establishing government-funded programs for care of the elderly. The first was that children were no longer needed to look after their retired parents. Where people's offspring had for centuries seen to the financial needs of their parents, retired people with no offspring now had access to a set of comparable benefits. They could free-ride on the system.

This new system undermined the ancient rationale for childbearing. In a world in which childbearing has no practical benefit—the government will care for you if you don't have children to do so—parenthood becomes a simple act of consumption. People have babies because they want to, seeing it as either an act of self-fulfillment or as some kind of moral imperative.

Such compunctions aren't free, though. Because in addition to reducing the income of young couples and severing the bonds of intergenerational familial dependency, the most insidious effect of the Social Security and Medicare regimes is that they actually *shift* economic incentives *away* from having children. Remember, you and I don't pay for our Social Security benefits. We pay for the generation ahead of us and our benefits come from the taxes paid by the generation of workers behind us.

But where will those workers come from? From the people who have children, of course. Traditionally, parents invested resources in their children not just because they wanted the kids to succeed but in the hopes that, the more successful the children became, the better provided for the parents would be in their dotage. Well today, you can spend your $1.1 million raising a child to become a productive worker, but an increasing share of his labor will go to the government. And the government hands out equal shares of retirement benefits from his labor both to those who spent the money raising children and those who didn't.

Just as welfare at some point ceased to be a safety net and became a disincentive to work, Social Security and Medicare are no longer stopgaps to protect elderly pensioners on the verge of poverty. Those programs are now incentivizing couples to have fewer—or no—children. Recent studies trying to isolate their effects suggest that Social Security and Medicare actually suppress the fertility rate by a staggering 0.5 children per woman.[28] Put simply, these programs are sowing the seeds of their own destruction.

None of this was the intent of the men who built these pillars of the welfare state, of course. But such is the peril of social engineering: The systems of politics and economics and culture which shape

American society are so complicated that you never quite know what's going to happen if you try to change a small piece of one of them.

More School, Fewer Babies

The law of unintended consequences has wreaked havoc on America's fertility in many ways. As I said at the beginning, one of the best predictors of fertility is a woman's education level. Simply put, the more educated a woman is, the fewer children she will have in the course of her lifetime. The total fertility rate for American women without a high school diploma is a healthy 2.45. With each subsequent level of educational attainment, fertility drops.

Education Level	Total Fertility Rate
Not a high school graduate	2.447
High school, 4 years	1.947
College, 1 or more year	1.719
Associate's degree	1.820
Bachelor's degree	1.632
Graduate degree	1.596
Source: Jane Lawler Dye, U.S. Census Bureau, "Fertility of American Women: 2006," August 2008.	

It's worth examining *how* this correlation came to be. From 1879 to 1930, American men and women graduated from college at roughly the same rate. This was as much a function of college being the exclusive preserve of the privileged as it was of gender equality.[29] It wasn't until 1930 that the rates of college graduation between the sexes began diverging, with men becoming markedly better educated. By 1947, 2.3 men graduated from college for every woman.

That divergence was not, as the feminist-industrial complex would have you believe, the result of sexism. The explanation was relatively simple: Before the two World Wars, college was open only to a small pool of wealthy elites and was partaken of by these men and women in roughly equal measure. Even though slightly more men than women were going to college, very few people were enrolled at all—only 9.5 percent of college-aged men and 8.9 percent of college-aged women actually attended a university.[30] The G.I. Bill broadened the accessibility of college to former soldiers who were, naturally, men. As these middle- and lower-middle-class men flooded the classrooms, a gender gap arose.

With the class restriction lifted, however, it was only a matter of time before middle- and lower-middle-class women caught up with their male counterparts. From 1947 on, women began closing the college gender gap. By 1980, the balance was about even again. By 2003, women significantly outnumbered men, with 1.35 women graduating for every man.

As you might expect, as more women graduated from college, more women went into the workforce. From 1956 until 1965, the percentage of women working outside the home was fairly constant, ranging from 41 percent to 44 percent.[31] Beginning in the late 1960s, however, it skyrocketed: In 1967, 48.2 percent of women were in the workforce; by 1980, the number was 61.5; by 1990, it was 69.7 percent. Which is about where it stopped: Since 1990, at any given time, about 70 percent of women have been in the labor force. This may be the natural limit in America. Again, look at the coincidence: After being relatively stable for a generation, women's participation in the workforce jumped by 50 percent in two decades; and these two decades also saw the steepest fertility decline in American history.

I say these two developments are "coincidental" because the raw labor force participation actually might not be all that influential on fertility. In a 2000 study, sociologists Karin Brewster and Ronald Rindfuss noted that when you examine the change in both labor participation rates of women and fertility rates in industrialized countries from 1965 to 1996, you see that many countries with high percentages of women in the workforce also have relatively high fertility rates.[32] So while we might look at the American experience and conclude that the fact of women joining the workforce drove down fertility, that may not be the case. In Italy, for example, women's labor force participation only moved from 34.6 percent in 1965 to 43.2 percent in 1996; yet the nation's fertility rate during that period sank from 2.5 to 1.2. The same correlation exists in Ireland, Spain, Greece, and other low-female workforce, low-fertility countries.

But surely *something* about the massive change in women's work life has influenced their childbearing decisions. So let's wind the clock back to the period stretching from the 1950s to the early 1970s when women started enrolling in college in increasing numbers. What's interesting about this interregnum is what women graduating from college did with their degrees. Nearly half of female graduates were involved in a single field—education. And, as it turns out, being a teacher is very conducive to having babies.

In 1960, for instance, only 39 percent of female college graduates in their twenties and thirties were in the workforce and 73 percent of female college graduates had children at home. As more and more women began attending college, they entered a broader array of fields, many of which were less conducive to family life. For instance, only 36 percent of female graduates from the class of 1980 became teachers. That number has continued to drop.[33]

The Chain Reaction and Marriage

As more women entered other fields, having babies was necessarily postponed. A teacher can reasonably graduate from college at 22, begin working immediately, and if she so chooses, marry and have children in short order without losing ground in her career. By comparison, consider the life of a young woman who becomes a doctor: Graduate with a bachelor's degree at 22; graduate from medical school at 26; finish residency at 29. If our doctor does not pursue any specialization, she can begin her career as she turns 30. Only then is childbearing even theoretically possible, and it will come at some expense to her nascent career.

As you might expect, the first effect of the broadening of women's career paths was to push the average age of marriage upward. In 1950, the average age of first marriage for an American woman was 20.3 years.[34] Between 1950 and 1970—when a large percentage of women were still entering the teaching profession—that number ticked upward only slightly, to 20.8 years. By 1980 it had risen to 22.0 years; by 1990 it was 23.9 years and from there, it was Katy bar the door.

Year	Average Age of First Marriage (Women)
1950	20.3
1970	20.8
1980	22.0
1990	23.9
1995	24.5
1996	24.8
1997	25.0
1998	25.0
1999	25.1
2000	25.1
2001	25.1
2002	25.3
2003	25.3
2004	25.5
2005	25.5
2006	25.9
2007	26.0

Source: U.S. Census Bureau.

The drop in fertility among women with college and advanced degrees, then, is in large part a function of delayed family formation. The longer a woman waits to get married, the longer she will wait to have children. For example, in 1970, the average age of a woman in the United States giving birth to her first child was 21.4 years. In 2000, it was 24.9 years.[35]

Like other aspects of modern life, the American drive for education has both obvious and subtle effects on fertility. For instance, it's not just the length of education that diminishes fertility, or the careers the education makes possible, but the debt load the education incurs. Since 1987, when the Nellie Mae Corporation began keeping statistical track of student loans, the average student-loan burden on college graduates has almost quadrupled, from $7,500 to $27,600 (in constant dollars).[36]

Respondents to Nellie Mae's survey indicated that their debt was increasingly pushing them to delay both marriage and children. In 1987, 9 percent said they were delaying marriage because of their student loans and 12 percent said they were delaying children. By 2002, those numbers had risen; 14 percent said they were delaying marriage and 21 percent said they were postponing having children.

Delaying children is not as simple as it sounds, because while our social institutions are often malleable, biology is not. Between the ages of 24 and 34, a woman's chance of becoming infertile increases from 3 percent to 8 percent.[37] By 35, half of women trying to get pregnant over the course of 8 months will not succeed.[38] After 35 it gets even dicier. By age 39, a woman has a 15 percent chance of being unable to conceive at all. And by a woman's 43rd birthday, her chances of getting pregnant are nearly zero.[39] All of which is why today, 1 out of every 100 babies born in the United States is created via in vitro fertilization.[40] You can only push off pregnancy for so long.

The funny thing is that when they're younger, millions of women go to great lengths to make sure that zero is *precisely* their chance of getting pregnant.

CHAPTER THREE
SEX!
(and maybe marriage)

Margaret Sanger was a weird old bat. You'd never know it today, of course. In feminism's rush to create an apostolic line, Sanger was sainted and mounted on a high shelf, far enough away that future generations couldn't get too good a look at her. Which is a shame, because she deserves as much credit as any one person for shaping the curve of modern fertility.

Sanger was the sixth of eleven children. Her mother died young and Sanger blamed the death on her siblings, believing that the act of bearing this litter of rascals did in her poor mum. (This was an odd claim; her mother died from tuberculosis, not a pregnancy-related illness.[1]) Nevertheless, Sanger made it her life's goal to help women stop having babies, by hook or by crook. In 1912, she told people that she dreamed of a "magic pill" that would keep women from getting pregnant.[2] In 1915 she coined the phrase "birth control" and within a year would be sent to jail for opening the first birth-control clinic in America.[3]

Over time her interest in preventing pregnancy became less about her own personal history and more about her public policy concerns. She was—how to put this nicely?—alarmed by the prospect of "poor" people having babies. "Poor" being a euphemism for certain races of "dysgenic" peoples. She deplored the "racial chaos into which the world has today drifted."[4] In her autobiography, she wrote that this unfortunate problem had been created because "The eugenists wanted to shift the birth control emphasis from less children for the poor to more children for the rich. We went back of that and sought first to stop the multiplication of the unfit. This appeared the most important and greatest step towards race betterment."[5]

In 1923, she defended the idea of birth control in a piece for the *New York Times*, writing that its legalization would usher in "a new era of . . . racial hygiene":

> Birth control is not contraception indiscriminately and
> thoughtlessly practiced. It means the release and cultivation
> of the better racial elements in our society, and the gradual
> suppression, elimination and eventual extirpation of defective
> stocks—those human weeds which threaten the blooming of
> the finest flowers of American civilization.[6]

And in 1935 she attacked President Roosevelt, who was not on board with the birth-control movement, claiming that the entire New Deal was in danger "as long as the procreative instinct is allowed to run reckless riot through our social structure" because the welfare state would "turn into subsidies for the perpetuation of the irresponsible classes of society."[7]

Fifteen years after *that* she wrote to a friend that the fate of civilization hinged on finding "a simple, cheap, safe, contraceptive to be used in poverty stricken slums, jungles, and among the most ignorant people. I believe that now, immediately there should be national sterilization for certain dysgenic types of our population who are being encouraged to breed and would die out were the government not feeding them."[8] Her credo was simple: "More children from the fit, less from the unfit—that is the chief issue of birth control."[9]

I don't mean to pile on here. I'm just trying to make clear that, by any reasonable definition, Margaret Sanger was a crank. And but for an accident of happenstance, she would have remained a crank. What elevated her from the fringe to the center of history is that in September of 1906, Stanley McCormick was diagnosed with schizophrenia.[10]

Poor Stanley was the son of Cyrus McCormick, who, in 1834, had invented the mechanical reaper and later went on to found the International Harvester Company. As a result, Cyrus, and by extension Stanley, became fabulously wealthy. In 1904, Stanley married the second woman to ever graduate from MIT, an impressive lady in her late twenties named Katharine Dexter. Two years later, Stanley was diagnosed with schizophrenia and three years after *that*, was declared legally incompetent. Control over his vast fortune passed to his young wife.

Shortly after she was given rule of the McCormick money, Katharine became a suffragette. Voting rights was the first in what would be a long line of pet causes as she flitted from this issue to that, looking to fill the hole in her life that was created by having her beloved husband locked away. (This isn't to make light of her situation: Stanley became so violent that it was dangerous for him to be in the same room with his wife. It must have been horrible and heartbreaking.) In the 1920s Mrs. McCormick crossed paths with Sanger and agreed to help her smuggle contraceptive diaphragms from Europe. After her institutionalized husband died in 1947, McCormick asked Sanger if she had a wish list that the McCormick fortune might be able to help move along. And so it was that the International Harvester Company gave birth to the Pill.

At the time, no doctors or researchers wanted anything to do with Sanger's crackpot "magic pill" idea. But with a giant bag of cash, Sanger and McCormick knew they'd be able to buy research from someone desperate enough for the work. They bought Gregory Pincus, a Harvard professor who helped pioneer in vitro fertilization in rabbits and found himself widely denounced (and disgraced) for his work. Over the course of the Pill's development, McCormick would pony up more than $2 million of her own money. The result—a drug called "Enovid"—was released in both England and the United States in 1957. Enovid was ostensibly a treatment for "gynecological disorders," but this was a barely-concealed excuse for its true purpose: contraception.

Once Enovid hit the market, pressure quickly mounted to dispose of the prescription pretext. On May 9, 1960, the FDA approved Enovid for daily use as a contraceptive. Nothing would ever be the same. Within two years, 1.2 million women were taking it.[11] By 1964, the number was over 6.5 million, and still growing. The Pill is one of those inventions—like the atomic bomb or the television—which so alter modern life that it's a little crazy to try and quantify the change. But we'll give it a go just the same.

Take the Pill, and Maybe He'll Call You in the Morning

To understand the Pill, you must first have a sense of the topography of baby-making. There are 62 million women in America between the ages of 15 and 44, the rough span demographers consider to be the reproductive window.[12] In any given year, about 10 percent of these women, 6.2 million of them, become pregnant. Half of these pregnancies are planned; half—surprise!—are not. At any given moment, 62 percent of the women in the reproductive window are using contraception of some kind. The most popular method of birth control is the Pill: Seventeen percent of women aged 15 to 44—that's a total of 10.54 million women—use it.[13]

At first blush, you might think, *That's all? Doesn't sound like a "revolutionary" number to me.* But factor out the women who aren't "at risk" for pregnancy—that is, women who aren't sexually active or are already pregnant—and the use of contraception jumps from 62 percent to 89 percent. And usage of the Pill jumps to 28 percent. And among women who have *ever* had sex, 82 percent have at some point used it.[14]

Pill usage is not uniform. It turns out that the Pill is used primarily by well-educated, middle-class, white women who are in their prime reproductive years. In the universe of women who are "at risk" for getting pregnant, 35 percent of women with a college degree use it; 34 percent of middle-class women and 21 percent of white women use it. Among women in their prime childbearing years (ages 20 to 34) 35 percent use the Pill.[15] To put these numbers into some relief, consider this: Fifty-five percent of childless women use the Pill. Only 8 percent of women with 3 or more children use it.

Like the G.I. Bill, the Pill is an example of unintended consequences. Margaret Sanger willed the Pill into existence so that the educated classes would not be "shouldering the burden of the unthinking fecundity of others."[16] Instead, it has been the educated middle class—Sanger's people—who have used the Pill to tamp down their fertility.

There's no way to hang a definitive number on how many births the Pill has prevented. All we can do is note, with the requisite caveats about correlation and causation, that in America usage of the Pill is highest among the demographic groups that have the lowest fertility. And when you look abroad, the correlation is even more striking. In many European countries, usage rates for the Pill are even higher than they are in America. In Belgium and Portugal, for instance, 45 percent of women are on the Pill. Those countries' fertility rates are dismal: 1.7 and 1.3, respectively.

Collateral Damage

The Pill's effect on fertility, however, is not just on the literal act of contraception. It has also helped shape the behaviors that lead to making babies: sex, dating, marriage, and, finally, stork arrival.

In 2002, the average American woman had sex for the first time at 17.4 years of age.[17] From there, the average age of first marriage for women was 25.1 years, followed shortly by the average age of first birth at 26 years. And by the age of 30.9 years, the average woman intended not to have any more children. (The comparable data for men are not particularly important for our purposes.[18]) These numbers are quite different from what they were 50 years ago, before the Pill.

To get at the effects of the Pill on sexual behavior, let's first look at the timing of first sexual intercourse. Just about half of women who were married between 1960 and 1964 had sex for the first time on their wedding night.[19] (Remember, the Pill was approved by the FDA in 1960.) Just 15 years later, the percentage of women having sex for the first time on their wedding night dropped by more than half, to just 21.4 percent. That's an amazing change, but again, the demographics are even more startling. Let's break out the first-sexual-intercourse numbers by race, since the Pill was used disproportionately by white women.

For white women married between 1960 and 1964, 52.6 percent waited until marriage to have sex. For the next cohort—women married between 1965 and 1969—the number declined only a little, to 45.1 percent. The Pill was reaching market saturation by the end of the 1960s. For the next cohort—women married between 1970 and 1974—the percentage that waited until marriage to have sex plummeted to 29.5 percent.

At the same time, the numbers of women who began having sex not just before tying the knot, but long before marriage, began increasing. For the group of white women married from 1960 to 1964, only 1.6 percent of them had sex for the first time five years or more before they walked down the aisle. For the white women married between 1975 and 1979, 21.9 percent first had sex at least five years before saying "I do."

What was happening here? Well, between 1960 and 1975, the average age of first marriage for women moved barely at all, going from 20.3 years to 21.1 years.[20] Which means that after the Pill was released, women started having sex earlier. And then they began to push marriage further back on the horizon.

We've already talked about how far back marriage eventually got pushed—recall that from immediately after World War II until 1975, it remained relatively constant, between 20.1 and 21.1 years old. After 1975, the average age of first marriage increased at a brisk clip: in 2010 it hit 26.1 years old.[21] And while the average age of marriage was creeping up, a relatively new development appeared: cohabitation. Whereas cohabitating couples were rare in 1960, by 2002, it was common for men and women to live together. (We'll talk a lot more about shacking up in a few minutes.)

All of which contributed to putting off having children. In 1968 the average age of a mother at the birth of her first child was 21.4 years old.[22] By 2002 that number had jumped to 25.1 years old. As women began postponing childbirth, they changed the practice of it in two important ways. First, they began having children out of wedlock. In 1960, only 5 percent of births were to single mothers.[23] By 1980, 18 percent of births were.[24] By 2008, 40.6 percent—that's not a typo—of all births were to unmarried women.[25] The illegitimacy rate has always been higher among minorities than among whites. But that big jump from 1980 onward is almost entirely due to an explosion of unmarried white women who were cohabitating with a partner—either as a prelude to, or in place of, marriage.[26]

Second, women began having children much later in life. Not only did the average age of first birth increase, but the rates at which women had children in their thirties and forties began climbing in the late 1970s and have increased steadily ever since.[27] In 2009, fully 37 percent of all births were to women over the age of 30.[28] And funnily enough, you can see evidence of these two changes overlapping. Once upon a time illegitimacy was assumed to be the domain of careless teenagers. In 1970, 50 percent of all illegitimate births were to teens, but by 2007, teens accounted for only 23 percent.[29] The big growth sector for out-of-wedlock births: women over the age of 30, whose percentage of the pie more than doubled during that period.

It's not hard to see why both of these phenomena would work against having larger families. Cohabitating relationships are much less stable than marriages—78 percent of marriages last more than five years; less than 30 percent of cohabitations last even that long.[30] Women with children out of wedlock have relatively little relational—and hence financial—security, and so often can't afford larger families. And women who are having babies in their thirties only have so much time before they run up against the wall of biology.

Sex without "Consequences"

That four-car pileup—younger sexual initiation, more cohabitation, later marriage, and decreased total fertility—are all just the unintended consequences stemming (in part) from Margaret Sanger's Pill. The *intended* consequence was to remove the entire idea of *consequences* from sex. This separation of the act from the messy result nine months later became a cultural imperative in the West with the advent of the Pill. And prophylactic birth control was just the start. The next step was controlling pregnancy after the fact, via abortion.

Before you start flipping ahead, let me make a promise. Yes, I'm one of those anti-abortion nut jobs who thinks that every embryo is sacred life and abortion is killing an innocent and blah-blah-blah. But when it comes to abortion, most Americans aren't crazies like me—they think abortion should be, in essence, legal, but somewhat restricted, and rare. So without my pushing judgments of any kind, let me just give you the brief demographic tour as to how abortion has affected American fertility.

The Supreme Court handed down *Roe v. Wade* in 1973. Before that moment, the political tide in America was turning against abortion. In the late 1960s, a number of states tried to pass reforms that would have turned their restrictive abortion laws into, essentially, abortion-on-demand. Yet these attempts to make abortion more widely available failed across the country, in states as different as Arizona, Georgia, New York, Indiana, North Dakota, New Mexico, Nebraska, Iowa, Minnesota, Nevada, Illinois, Vermont, and Massachusetts.[31] In fact, as Ramesh Ponnuru observes, before *Roe* it was "not at all clear that a majority of the public favored legal abortion even in the first months of pregnancy."[32]

While there had always been abortions in America (the practice dates back to the ancient Greeks, at least), there were relatively few abortions before *Roe*—even though most states allowed for early-term abortions. In 1970, for example, there were 193,491 reported legal abortions performed in America.[33] Certainly, this figure significantly undercounts the total number of abortions because it does not include unreported, illegal abortions. But for the sake of argument, let's take that 200,000 as a baseline. By 1973, the year the Court ruled on *Roe*, creating a universal, non-restricted right to abortion, the number of reported abortions had risen to 744,600.[34] The next year, that number rose by 20 percent, to 898,600 abortions. By this time nearly all abortions were legal, and so we can be confident that this number is fairly accurate. Over the course of the next 15 years, the number of abortions rose quite a bit. By about 100 percent, actually.

Let's leave aside the legal and moral arguments about *Roe* and focus on what the decision meant for the number of children born. In 1973 there were 3.1 million babies born in America. Over the next 10 years that number rose only slightly, despite the fact that America's total population was increasing quickly. Why weren't there more babies born in the decade following *Roe*? Well, because during that time, 34.19 million children were born. And 13.62 million were aborted. Which means that roughly a quarter of all pregnancies ended in abortion.

Live Births vs. Abortions in the First Decade After *Roe*		
Year	*Live Births (in millions)*	*Abortions (in millions)*
1974	3.160	0.899
1975	3.144	1.034
1976	3.168	1.179
1977	3.327	1.317
1978	3.333	1.410
1979	3.494	1.498
1980	3.612	1.554
1981	3.629	1.577
1982	3.681	1.574
1983	3.639	1.575

Sources: *Centers for Disease Control, Vital Statistics of the United States, 1997, Volume 1—Natality (http://www.cdc.gov/nchs/data/statab/t991x01.pdf) and Lawrence B. Finer and Stanley K. Henshaw, "Estimates of U.S. Abortion Incidence, 2001–2003," Guttmacher Institute (http://www.guttmacher.org/pubs/2006/08/03/ ab_incidence.pdf).*

It would be foolish to assume that every one of those abortions would have resulted in a birth had *Roe* not created a universal abortion right. But several facts remain: (1) Post-*Roe*, the number of abortions significantly increased; (2) About half (49 percent in 2008) of abortions are performed on women who are 25 and older, the prime childbearing years; (3) Over 40 percent of women having abortions already have one or more children; (4) 20 percent of women having abortions are married; (5) Since *Roe* more than 49.5 million babies have been aborted in America; and (6) Post-*Roe*, the fertility rate in America has been roughly inverse to the abortion rate, generally declining when abortion is on the rise, and rising when abortion is on the decline.[35] These factors certainly suggest that, absent unfettered access to abortion, at least some of those pregnancies would have resulted in births. Again, we don't want to confuse causation and correlation, but between 2005 and 2010, the abortion rate rose for the first time since 1990—just as the fertility rate, which had been ticking upward, declined.[36]

If you want more data, you can compare the abortion rate to the birth rate across states and what you find is about what you'd expect. States with very high birth rates—Utah, Mississippi, South Dakota, Kentucky—have very low abortion rates. And vice versa.[37] In 2000 the RAND corporation tried to estimate the numerical effect of abortion on the TFR.[38] It concluded that for white America, abortion on demand lowered the fertility rate by about 0.08—or 4 percent. Among black Americans the effect was much stronger: the *Roe* regime pushed fertility down by 0.34—or 13 percent.

Margaret Sanger and her fellow travelers—the ones who were so worried about stopping certain parts of society from having children—would probably count this as a win.

Love and Marriage

While everything relating to sex was changing, so was the institution of marriage itself. As an economic matter, we value marriage for two chief reasons. First, it provides financial stability, which encourages family formation—which then creates new pools of workers, producers, consumers, and taxpayers. As William Galston puckishly notes, you only have to do three things to avoid poverty in America: (1) finish high school; (2) marry before you have a kid; and (3) don't have the kid until after you turn 20. Check off those boxes, and the rest of life generally takes care of itself.[39]

The other big economic benefit of marriage is that the merging of two households provides the economies of scale and incentives to save and invest, which make upward mobility more likely. But the perks of marriage go beyond economics. Look at the surveys of married adults versus single adults and the numbers are fairly unmistakable: Getting married not only improves your chances of being financially successful, but also makes you happier and healthier to boot.[40]

Americans love marriage. We always have. In 1910, 94 percent of both women and men married at some point in their lives.[41] In the early twentieth century, this percentage—it's called the "ever married" number—bounced up and down a bit, going as high as 97.5 percent (for women, in 1920) and as low as 92.8 percent (also for women, in 1930). But World War II triggered a big rush to the altar. From 1945 until 1970, the percentage of ever-married women stayed above 97.2 percent, even going so high as 98.3 percent. This surge in marriage coincided, not surprisingly, with the Baby Boom.

After 1970, the ever-married rate began dropping. It didn't collapse but floated softly down, to 91.6 percent in 1980, 89 percent in 1990, then 88.6 percent in 2000. More and more Americans were opting out of the marriage game altogether. What actually happened was more complicated than it looks. Because it turns out that not *all* Americans were getting out of the marriage business.

Beginning in the 1960s, the lower classes started being disenchanted with the institution of marriage. During the 1970s, 69 percent of married adults with at least a high school education—this is the vast middle-middle class—reported that they were "very happy" with their marriage.[42] Among the lower classes—those who did not complete high school—only 59 percent said they were "very happy."

But over the years, a schism emerged within the middle class. People who graduated from college and got married maintained the same sunny view about having gotten hitched. But the lower half of the middle class—people with a high school degree and perhaps some college—began to sour on it to the point where their views of marriage became almost indistinguishable from the lower class.

(This middle-middle class—demographers refer to them as the "moderately educated"—makes up the majority of America: 58 percent of the adult population is "moderately educated" while only 30 percent is "highly educated"—meaning that these individuals have at least a bachelor's degree.)

As these moderately educated Americans became less happy in marriage, their patterns of marriage also came to resemble the lower classes. They became more likely to cohabitate instead of marry—and to get divorced within 10 years if they did commit to marriage. What's really worrisome is that this downward trend among the moderately educated has taken place at the same time that the *opposite* has happened among the better educated. Believe it or not, today people with at least a college education are *even more likely* to have lasting marriages than they were 30 years ago.[43]

The data on the decline of marriage are fairly unambiguous. In 1960, 69 percent of men and 66 percent of women over the age of 15 were married.[44] By 1998, those percentages dropped to just 58 percent of men and 55 percent of women. Part of the explanation for this change is the marriage disaster that occurred in the black community: In 1960, 59.8 percent of black women were married. By 1998, the percentage had fallen to 36.3 percent. Marriage is yet one more area in which social tragedy besets America's black population. It's impolitic to note these disparities, but it does no one any favors to pretend that they do not exist.

Shacking Up

Another explanation for the decline of marriage is the rise of cohabitation. "Cohabitation"—couples living together in a rough approximation of marital union, but without the marriage contract—isn't a new phenomenon.[45] Before 1970, the percentage of people who lived with a boyfriend (or girlfriend or fiancé) before getting married sat at around 11 percent.[46] But after 1970, people started shacking up more and more, until living in sin (can you even say that anymore?) became almost a matter of course. By the late 1980s, half of all couples getting married lived together first. By 2002, half of *everyone* had cohabitated at some point.[47] And even that number doesn't tell the whole story, because it includes teenagers as young as 15 still under their parents' roof. Among people in the prime marrying years—those aged 25 to 44—over 60 percent had, at some point, shacked up with a girlfriend or boyfriend.

Without passing judgment (you heathen, fornicatin' sinners!) the rise of cohabitation was objectively bad for the institution of marriage. Studies show that in the 1970s and 1980s, when marriage rates were falling and the average age of first marriage was shooting up, the average age of first *union* stayed about the same. Which is to say that people were starting to move in together at about the age that, in preceding decades, they would have gotten married. During this period, cohabitation alone counted for something like 60 percent of the decline in the marriage rate.[48]

Today, cohabitation is so ingrained in society that it's measured like an alternative—if highly inferior—mode of family formation. I say inferior descriptively, not pejoratively, because cohabitations are much less stable unions than marriage. There's a 64 percent chance that a first marriage will last at least 10 years. Fifty percent of cohabitations break down after just the first year. What about people who think that they're just living together as a prelude to marriage? Bad news. White women shacking up with their first live-in boyfriend have a 27 percent chance of getting married after year one and a 59 percent chance of getting married if they make it to year three. If they stick out the relationship for five years, they've got a 73 percent chance that the guy will make an honest woman out of them. Which sounds pretty good, until you realize that this means a woman who lives with a guy for five years still has a one-in-four chance of not ending up married to him. As always, the odds for minorities are even longer.

Just as we saw with marriage, the educated middle class fares much better than everyone else. Young people without high school degrees are three times as likely to cohabitate as those with college degrees; people below the poverty level are twice as likely to cohabitate as those 300 percent above it.[49]

This is somewhat counterintuitive. If you had to guess where cohabitation came from, you'd probably think that it originated with the countercultural revolutions of the '70s as college radicals turned their backs on bourgeois '50s morality and embraced sexual liberation—and that this enlightened, sophisticated movement gradually spread to the rest of society.

But the exact opposite is the case. The rise of cohabitation actually began in 1935.[50] It was a slow-rolling wave inaugurated by people without high school degrees shacking up. By 1950, about 18 percent of people under 25 who hadn't graduated from high school were living together. After 1950, their rate shot up to 50 percent in just 10 years and went even higher in the 1970s. Meanwhile, rates of cohabitation for college graduates lagged far, far behind: In 1950, less than 10 percent of them cohabited. The cohabitation rate for college graduates actually *declined* from 1955 to 1960. By the time cohabitation hit the college crowd in the 1970s, it was already a fact of life among the lower classes. Seen in this light, cohabitation looks less like an enlightening social change and more like a spreading social pathology working its way up the culture from society's have-nots.

The Breakup

The final piece of America's disappearing-marriage puzzle is divorce. Divorce isn't new, of course. America's divorce rate has been wobbling around since the Civil War.[51] During the early part of the twentieth century, divorce was rare. But in the ensuing years the divorce rate grew slightly before experiencing a dramatic spike immediately at the conclusion of World War II—and then falling off sharply for the 1950s and 1960s, when it remained quite low.

How low? In 1960, there were only 9.2 divorces for every 1,000 married women. After 1970, the divorce rate began climbing, hitting 22.6 in 1980.[52] Rates per thousand can be a little bit opaque, so here's another way to understand the statistics. The chance that a person in 1910 who was married would someday be divorced was around 15 percent; by 1960 the odds rose to around 32 percent; and by 2000 to around 45 percent.[53]

The only good news in this story is that since the 1980s, America has hit a plateau—we've never gone over the 50 percent failure mark for marriages and have mostly hovered above 40 percent. And, like anything else, there are risk factors for divorce. The biggest is simple longevity: The longer a marriage lasts, the better the chance it will continue to last. With each passing year of marriage, a couple's chance of divorce drops. Another factor is a person's age at time of first marriage: 60 percent of people who marry before age 20 get divorced, while only 40 percent of those who wait until after 22 do.[54] Education matters, too. Couples with college degrees get divorced at about half the rate of couples without a high school degree. And, as always, blacks have it especially bad: 70 percent of black marriages eventually end in divorce.

The worse news is that our divorce plateau may be a statistical illusion. Part of the plateau is explained by a "tempo effect," meaning that as the age of first marriage keeps creeping upward, it pushes back the age of divorce, skewing the numbers. The other part is that the rise of cohabitation may be keeping the divorce rate low because it keeps higher-risk, unstable relationships off the books, so to speak. The people who, 40 years ago, would have gotten married and then quickly gotten divorced, today just move in together and then split—thus keeping their failed unions from showing up in the box score.

The origin of the divorce epidemic is, like the fertility decline itself, something of a mystery. There are small-bore causes such as cohabitation, which, in addition to everything else, also hurts marriage. (People who live together before they get married—no matter what their social class—are more likely to divorce than people who do not.[55]) And beginning in the mid-1960s, there was a sea change in divorce law as states began reforming codes to make it easier for couples to split.[56] The old laws made it difficult to divorce unless one party could prove serious cause. For instance, until its laws were reformed in the 1960s, New York state permitted divorce only on the grounds of adultery.[57] The controlling law, if you can believe it, was written by Alexander Hamilton, in 1787.

Over the years, unhappy spouses began flouting the law by admitting to whatever they had to in order to get out of their marriages. (The joke in New York was that there were actually two grounds for divorce: adultery and perjury.) By the mid-1960s—before the no-fault reforms came into existence—more than 90 percent of divorces were uncontested, even though this meant that one party was admitting (often untruthfully) to fault. Perturbed by this incongruity between fact and law, small groups of judges and lawyers worked to change the statutes, making it possible for couples to divorce for any reason whatsoever. Or no reason at all.

As a result of this new legal regime—which was deemed so uncontroversial that there was barely any contemporaneous discussion of it—divorce rates increased even further. The research is murky on exactly how much of the increase in divorce is attributable to the new laws. Studies on the effect of no-fault suggest that it increased the divorce rate somewhere between 5 percent and 30 percent.[58] That's an awfully wide range, but the point is that every study shows there to be at least *some* measurable effect.

As for other factors in the rise of divorce, you don't have to be a Puritan shrew to notice all the converging trend lines—the Pill, the premarital sex, the cohabitation, the increasing age of first marriage, the increasing number of people who never marry. Taking the very long view, James Q. Wilson blames Milton, Locke, and the Enlightenment in general.[59] His argument is typically fluid and persuasive. The short version is that when reason replaced religion and custom as the lodestars for human thinking, it became natural for the sacramental view of marriage to be replaced with a contractual view. This understanding of marriage as a contract elevated the two individuals over the idea of the joint unit—the family—and then gave them the implicit freedom to modify or terminate the contract according to their own pleasure.

But whatever the root causes, one of the effects of divorce is that it depresses fertility. After all, married couples have more kids than singles. And the less time a couple is married, the smaller their window to have babies.

The Big Chill

The takeaway from all of this is that the contours of male-female relationships have changed in subtle, but unfathomably important, ways over the last 40 years. Today an adolescent boy and girl are likely to have sex while they're still in high school. It won't be "premarital" sex, because neither of them has any intention of getting married to the other. They're likely to move in with another boyfriend or girlfriend down the line in their early twenties. If they're lucky, they'll eventually get married. And if they're really lucky—which is to say, if they're far enough up the middle-class ladder to have graduated from college and gotten good jobs—they'll have a fighting chance to stay married for 10 years. If they are unlucky—if they haven't finished college or are members of a minority group—then moving in with their significant other will probably turn out differently. They'll have a child out of wedlock, and they probably won't get married. If they do tie the knot, they'll probably get divorced in reasonably short order. There are plenty of bad outcomes for society that have arisen from this new regime of dating and mating, but the one that concerns us most here is that as a result, everyone—both the lucky and the unlucky—will wind up having fewer babies.

This change is particularly stark in contrast to the period that immediately preceded it. It's fashionable to carp about all the hidden misery and hypocrisy of the post-war era. But the numbers don't lie. During the 1950s and 1960s, men and women waited longer to have sex, cohabitated less, had fewer children out of wedlock, got married earlier, and stayed married longer. All of which contributed to the explosion in fertility we saw during those Baby Boom years.

The trials and tribulations of marriage in America are something of a synecdoche for our fertility problem. Both phenomena are, as analytical matters, incontrovertible. And some causes—like the effect of cohabitation on marriage or the effect of women going to college on fertility—are obvious. But a whole host of other causes remains shrouded in mystery.

When it comes to marriage, the biggest question is the one of class leadership: Why did the lower-middle class decide, en masse, to stop emulating the elites and start patterning their sexual and marital behaviors on the lower classes? This is a big, important question, upon which turns the fate of a 5,000-year-old Western institution. And as it turns out, this question—or rather, a bizarre variation of it—is at the heart of America's one-child policy, too.

CHAPTER FOUR

What You Can, and Cannot, Measure

In the 1990s an international team of 23 geneticists began study-ing a peculiar marker on the Y chromosome.[1] The team, led by Tatiana Zerjal, was studying one of those trace bits of DNA signature that is passed down through families. This particular marker was odd because it appeared in several population samples that were localized in broad, but distinct, geographical areas. When all was said and done, the geneticists found the marker present in 16 different populations stretching across Asia, from the Pacific to the Caspian Sea.

What's more, Zerjal's team found that fully 8 percent of all the males in these populations carried the marker—an extraordinarily large number. As the team studied the data, examining the locations and migration habits of men carrying the marker, they determined that this little bit of DNA most likely originated in Mongolia, roughly a thou-sand years ago. The 8 percent of men who carried it were all descended from a single man whom, incidentally, you've probably heard of: Zerjal and her team concluded that he was almost certainly Genghis Khan.

Today the Great Khan has 16 million living descendents. Or to put it somewhat more grandly, 0.2 percent of the world's total population is descended directly from him. He is the most spectacular example of a sometimes forgotten historical fact: Having a large number of children was once a symbol of great prestige. This stands in stark contrast to the status of children in modern times. Today, the number of children people have declines as their level of economic, financial, and social achievement rises. The bearing and raising of children has largely become the province of the lower classes.

To be sure, Genghis Khan did not "raise" his progeny in the traditional way. He raped and pillaged his way across a continent. Nonetheless, he is one of several figures from long ago who spawned so many children that we can still see their genetic footprints. In 2005, another squad of geneticists identified a marker present in many Chinese men which was traced back to Giocangga, the grandfather of the first emperor of the Qing dynasty.[2] Similar testing revealed that 20 percent of the men in Ireland are descended from a fifth-century chieftain, the wonderfully named Niall of the Nine Hostages.[3]

None of these *patres familias* could be considered family men by any modern standard. Yet the tendency of society's elites to have large numbers of children once extended beyond warlords and emperors. Massimo Livi-Bacci reports that from the fifteenth to eighteenth centuries, the number of children Italian women bore correlated directly with their social status.[4] The poorest women in Florence, for instance, averaged 3.0 children, while the richest women averaged 4.9 children.[5] Another demographer, Jean-Pierre Bardet, examined the fertility of seventeenth- and eighteenth-century French women and found that in 1670, upper-class women bore an average of seven children, while lower-class women had an average of six children.[6] As France began to modernize, the fertility of both groups decreased. By 1789, the lower classes dropped their average to five children. But the upper class cut back even more—dropping to just four children.

At some point, this shift happened all across the globe. Everyone started having fewer babies, but the elites, who had traditionally led the way in childbirth, began having noticeably fewer babies than people on the lower end of the social spectrum. Children went from being a marker of success to an indicator of failure.

A Curious Maladaptation

In 2008 an Austrian researcher at the International Institute for Applied Systems Analysis published an extraordinary study. Vegard Skirbekk assembled all of the available data on fertility by socioeconomic status. There were a total of 909 data sets spanning 700 years—beginning in 1270 and ending in 2006.[7]

Skirbekk's findings were fascinating. In the early fourteenth century, elites (that is, people with greater wealth, education, and social status) had nearly twice as many children as people in the lower classes. But over time that percentage dropped steadily. By 1600, elites were bearing only 25 percent more children. In the Western world (Europe and North America) the trend lines crossed in 1750. After that year, reproduction among elites went below that of the lower classes for the first time. And it never returned.

Sifting through the data, Skirbekk uncovered a few universal truths. For starters, education has *always* depressed fertility (by an average of 26.5 percent).[8] Which means that our little charts showing how the accumulation of bachelor's and graduate degrees mean fewer babies for modern women is not a condition unique to today's America.

Skirbekk summarizes the various claims that elite status makes on people's lives somewhat succinctly:

> Status in modern societies requires time; higher education attainment . . ., finding a job and climbing the career ladder, buying a car and a house, identifying a spouse and attaining financial security can take many years of reproductive life.[9]

Yet the key finding of Skirbekk's research is that the fertility choices of elites have historically driven the fertility choices of the lower classes.

In other words, poor people have always modeled their baby-making on rich people. When the lords and ladies had big families, the peasants aspired to have as many children as they could afford. But when the poor saw the elites having fewer children, they tended to have fewer children themselves in an attempt to emulate what they took to be successful behavior. This dynamic has been broadly true for several hundred years now. Skirbekk quotes another scholar who found that

> fertility decline was "led" by the middle and upper classes. Social elites apparently did act as leaders in modifying this most basic of activities—human reproduction.[10]

This may seem like a small point, but it leads to a much larger one. Because if (1) the elites really do influence the baby-making behaviors of the lower classes, and (2) the economic environment is arranged to reward people who do not have children, then we have a self-reinforcing loop:

> If actual fertility for one generation is lower, the fertility prefer-ences of the next generation will also be lower. Moreover, par-ticularly for the upper social echelons, increasing consumption aspirations and wealthier reference groups can imply higher opportunity costs of childbearing and reduced fertility.[11]

As it turns out, biologists have a term for this: It's called "evolu-tionary maladaptive behavior." Out in nature, maladaptation works something like this: A particular breed of female birds has a preference for males with elaborate sexual ornaments. (Don't get excited—this typically just means fluffy or elongated tail feathers.) Over time, the female birds choose the more elaborately ornamented male birds and so, the species develops even more elaborate ornamentation. The problem is that in the long run, those big, floppy feathers become an impediment to practical things, like flying and catching food. At that point, you have a selection process that helps the least fit members of the species breed the most.

That's always been the worry of the eugenicists like Margaret Sanger. It's even the premise for Mike Judge's 2006 cult classic *Idiocracy*. But it's not quite the problem we face today. In fact, our maladaption is much worse. Reproduction has become an impediment to material success, but the lower classes aren't mindlessly popping out babies. No, they're trying to adapt their behavior and have fewer children so that they, too, can climb the social ladder. Our maladaption regarding fertility—the creation of a system where economic and social success are largely dependent on *not* having children—is a result of many factors, some of which we will discuss in the next chapter. And as I said at the beginning, this isn't a grand conspiracy. Rather, what we have are disparate parts of modernity evolving independently, but, taken together, in such a way that unquestionably discourages childbearing. There are hundreds of such tiny evolutions. To take just one very small example, consider the car seat.

Car Seat Economics

When it came time for my wife to deliver our first child, we left Old Town Alexandria and headed north to Washington. All babies—especially first babies—must have The Best and it is generally acknowledged that Sibley Memorial Hospital is The Best place to have a baby in the nation's capital. During our mandatory pre-delivery parenting class, the nurse made a big show of hammering home the hospital's rigorous discharge policy: At Sibley they won't let your baby out the door until you demonstrate that you have a federally certified infant car seat. After you've been discharged, hospital policy gives way to D.C. law, which stipulates that children less than a year old and under 22 pounds must ride in a rear-facing, infant car seat, installed in the back of your car. Children between one and four years old may ride in a forward-facing child safety seat, installed in the back of your car. And from ages five to eight, children must use a federally approved child booster seat, also in the rear of the car. These are primary offense laws, mind you, meaning that if a police officer spots you illegally transporting children—if, for instance, you buckle your seven-year-old into the front seat for a trip to the corner store—they can pull you over and issue a citation giving you a choice of a $25 safety class or a $75 fine.[12]

This was all news to me, but it turns out that every state in the union now has laws on the books mandating the use of car seats for infants and toddlers. Thirty-eight states have laws mandating the use of booster seats for older kids, too. And if anything, the laws in the District of Columbia are on the lax side. In Massachusetts, once eight-year-olds graduate from their booster seats, they must remain in the back seat of the car, using normal seatbelts, until age twelve. In Maine, children over 40 pounds must be in a booster seat until they reach eight years of age or 80 pounds—whichever comes last. The penalty for violating these laws varies from state to state, ranging from $10 to $500 per infraction. (The District of Columbia also tacks two points onto your license for good measure.) In Nevada, you can be sentenced to up to 50 hours of community service, on top of everything else.

Enforcement can be quite zealous. A few years back, the District of Columbia took to setting up roadblocks and pulling aside vehicles with car-seat-age children in order to perform random checks. The officers handed out mock summonses, instructing bad parents to attend car seat safety classes. In 2000, Arkansas judge Doug Schrantz made an example out of a mother who had foolishly secured her three-year-old with a normal seatbelt in the back of her car. Schrantz fined her $125 and ordered her to write an obituary for her daughter. You know, to teach her a lesson.

Funnily enough, parents are compelled to buy car seats but are discouraged from installing them on their own. Instead they are urged—by doctors, public safety advocates, even the car seat manufacturers themselves—to have the devices professionally installed at a car seat inspection center—usually a local firehouse or police station. Although the installation is free, it can aggravate other problems. For instance, car seats now have expiration dates. If you used a car seat for one child and want to re-use it for another, you may be out of luck. And if the car seat installation inspector determines that your seat is past its "use by" date, they will likely refuse to install it. On parenting message boards, some people claim to have had their out-of-date car seats confiscated by the officials who were supposed to install them.

The Doctors, the Bible Thumper, and the Legislature

How in the world did we get here? If you were born before 1975, chances are you were never buckled into a car seat. Infant car-carrying devices have been around since the 1930s, but the vast majority of children rode sitting in an adult's lap or higgledy-piggledy in the back seat. How loosey-goosey was parenting back in the '30s? In 1937, a product called "The Baby Cage" hit stores.[13] Whatever you're currently imagining, it's much worse. The Baby Cage was marketed to people who lived in tenements and didn't have yards or balconies. It was a wire box designed to be mounted *outside* of your apartment window, so that your baby could sit in this little mesh box, dangling several stories above the pavement, and enjoy the fresh air and scenic views.

Such barbarities were well on their way to extinction three decades later when, in 1965, Seymour Charles founded Physicians for Automotive Safety, a Nader-style public advocacy group. Charles was a New Jersey pediatrician, and in the early 1960s one of his young patients was killed after being thrown from a car during an accident. Charles began attending auto safety conferences and started to see the issue as one of public health. By 1971, Charles succeeded in getting the federal government to begin issuing "standards" for child safety seats—a product which barely existed. At the time, the safest of the car seats was the Ford Tot-Guard; it sold a total of 75,000 units in seven years.

Enter another pediatrician, Tennessean Dr. Robert Sanders. Bob Sanders was involved in the Tennessee Pediatric Society, where by chance, he ended up chairman of the Accident Prevention Committee. As a consequence of this position, when the state formed a task force on highway safety, Sanders was invited to join. It was on the state task force that Sanders met another committee member, a fellow named Ed Casey.

Casey was not a physician, but he thought child safety seats were mandated from a power above even government. Specifically, he believed they were enumerated in Deuteronomy 22:8: "When you build a new house, you shall make a parapet for your roof, that you may not bring the guilt of blood upon your house, if anyone should fall from it."[14] As Sanders's son wrote in a biography of his father, "Casey thought of the parapet, or low wall or railing around the edges of a roof, as being analogous to a child restraint device itself, including its anchorage inside the car."

Sanders never shared Casey's fundamentalist views, but he nonetheless became convinced of the dangers of automobiles and the need to protect children from them. Rather like Charles, he came to see traffic accidents as a disease in need of a cure. Sanders would eventually call them the "epidemic of our time" and liken them to polio. He soon began petitioning the Tennessee state legislature to pass a law requiring the use of car seats.

In 1977 he succeeded. Tennessee passed a law mandating car seat usage until age four, but with an exception for newborns, who were allowed to be held in their mothers' arms. Sanders, now known as "Dr. Car Seat" (later activism would change his nickname to "Dr. Seat Belt") was triumphant. He understood that the ratchet only turns one way and that someday, compulsory car seat usage would force mothers to give up the foolish practice of cradling their infants as the family car rocketed toward danger and death. As it happens, the ratchet turned even faster than Sanders had hoped: Four years later the "babes in arms" exception was rescinded. Once the first domino tipped, other state legislatures began to fall in line. In 1981, Rhode Island became the second state to put a car seat law on the books. Four years later, all 50 states and the District of Columbia had some form of a law mandating their use.

Once states required the use of car seats for infants and toddlers, there was pressure to expand the zone of protection as other dangers presented themselves. In 1993, the increasing prevalence of airbags created concern that this new safety feature for adults created a hazard for children. Advocates requested that children be relegated to the back seat, where they would be safe from airbag trauma. They were. In Washington State in 1996, four-year-old Anton Skeen was killed after being ejected from his car during an accident, even though he was secured by an adult seat belt. Four years later, Washington passed the first booster seat law—the "Anton Skeen Act"—introducing a new class of required child safety seats for older children.

Safety über Alles

And we're still not safe enough. One NTSB expert explains that "In the advocacy world, they're really pushing the 'Five Step Test.'" This standard de-emphasizes age in favor of an evaluation of the child's body positioning in an adult seatbelt. Typically, children have to be somewhere above 4 feet 9 inches and 80 pounds to pass the Five Step Test. (Thereby making them eligible to leave their booster seat behind and use a normal, grown-up seat belt—though only in the back of the car. Of course.) According to growth-chart data from the CDC, a 50th-percentile child would not meet the height and weight requirements until around the age of 11. A move to the Five Step Test would probably result in a further extension of the car seat regime, since a quarter of 12-year-old girls weigh less than 80 pounds.

The moral of the story is this: While the car seat is objectively pro-child, it is also vaguely anti-family. If you had five small children in 1977—a situation not at all rare back then—few vehicles could accommodate enough car seats to transport the entire brood at the same time. (This was actually one of the chief objections to the Tennessee bill back at the time.) Today it is nearly impossible to fit more than two car seats in most cars. Which means that transporting a family of five—two adults and three children—necessitates either a larger, more expensive vehicle or two cars and drivers. The days of piling a gaggle of five-year-olds into the family station wagon for a jaunt to the park are over.

The role car seats play in depressing fertility is minuscule—so minuscule as to be immeasurable. But it does add costs to the price of children. Those costs are invisible if you have one or two kids. But you need an entirely different, and more expensive, class of vehicle if you have three or four or (perish the thought!) five children. In 1976, when car seat laws were sweeping from sea to shining sea, 16 percent of women had four children and 20 percent had five or more.[15] Today, the percentage of women who have five or more children is 1.8 percent.[16] I'm *not* suggesting that car seat laws caused this change. What I'm saying is that they didn't make life any easier for parents with lots of kids. (As a side note, they didn't radically transform auto safety, either. The most optimistic estimate is that between 1975 and 2005, car seats saved a grand total of 7,896 lives. Every one of them is a miracle for which we should be thankful. But saving 263 lives a year isn't exactly conquering polio.)

Now, nobody involved in the car seat movement *wanted* to make life harder for families. To a man, every one of them cared deeply about the welfare of children. And by the same token, nothing about the car seat revolution was foreordained by the culture. The story of the car seat is like the story of the Pill: History unfolded in a certain way because of happenstance and the peculiar ambition of one or two people. And as with the Pill, there were unintended effects.

While the effect of car seats on fertility may be immeasurably small, there are plenty of other "freakonomic" influences on fertility that *are* quantifiable. Recall Steve Sailer's "dirt gap" theory, in which fertility increases with housing affordability.[17] Well, the dirt gap is real. But when you look more closely, the picture becomes even more interesting: Because it turns out that fertility varies not only by where you live, but by what kind of house you live in.

Our House Is a Very Fine House

As a formal matter of classification, there are three basic kinds of housing: tenements (meaning large apartment buildings or condominium complexes), attached-family homes (meaning townhouses, row houses, or duplexes), and detached, single-family homes. The data in America show that single-family homes produce more kids than the other kinds of housing. For example, in 2000, the average single-family home had 1.01 school-aged children, which was more than twice as many as the average townhouse and three times as many as the average tenement unit.[18] If you control for the size of the units by keeping the number of bedrooms constant the difference shrinks, but it doesn't disappear. Nationally, this gap has been observable since at least 1947, when row houses had 9 percent more children per unit, and single-family homes 17 percent more children per unit, than tenements.[19]

Amazingly, this trend is universal. When sub-replacement fertility first appeared in Europe after World War I, demographers went into something of a panic. In Sweden, researchers quickly discovered the effects of housing on fertility. They noticed that the small, modernist tenements that had sprung up across the country were pushing couples to have fewer children.[20] Demographers in the United States came to similar conclusions, namely that the preponderance of apartment buildings in dense, urban locales was stunting American fertility.[21]

Subsequent research has demonstrated the effects of housing type on fertility across the globe. Studies show the same results—fewer babies in apartments or condominiums, more babies in single-family homes—everywhere from Colombia to Great Britain to Iran.[22] An Iranian study in 1995 found that married couples living in single-family homes not only had higher actual fertility, but even higher *desired* fertility, than married couples living in apartments.[23] How much does housing type matter? A 1988 Canadian report showed that even when you control for education, income, and other factors, married couples who lived in tenement-type buildings had 0.42 fewer children over their lifetimes than married couples in single-family homes.[24]

And wouldn't you know it, over the last 40 years, the percentage of single-family homes has generally decreased in America while the percentage of townhouses and condominium units has increased. In fact, there's a fairly obvious correlation. From the 1940s until the 1960s, there was a boom in the construction of detached, single-family homes as mass-produced housing communities sprang up across the country.

By 1960, single-family detached homes represented their biggest share of housing stock ever.

Percentage of Total Available Housing by Type			
Year	Single-Family Detached	Townhouse/ Row House	Apartment/ Condominium
1940	63.6%	7.6%	10.5%
1950	63.3%	6.1%	11.0%
1960	68.8%	6.3%	10.7%
1970	66.2%	2.9%	14.5%
1980	61.8%	4.1%	17.8%
1990	59.0%	5.3%	17.7%
2000	60.3%	5.6%	17.3%
Source: U.S. Census Bureau, Census of Housing (http://www.census.gov/hhes/www/ housing/census/historic/units.html).			

During the Depression and throughout World War II, very few new homes were built in America—over a span of 16 years, housing starts averaged less than 100,000 per year.[25] In his classic survey of the suburbs, *Crabgrass Frontier*, Kenneth Jackson notes that "there were virtually no homes for sale or apartments for rent at war's end." The housing shortage was so acute that six million families lived with relatives or friends and another half-million lived in temporary Quonset huts.

Into the breach stepped Abraham Levitt and his two sons, William and Alfred. They had been small-time home builders before Pearl Harbor, but once hostilities commenced they began taking on larger government jobs building housing for war workers. William picked up some ideas while serving with the Navy's Seabees. (He would later quip, "No man who owns his own house and lot can be a Communist. He has too much to do.") By the time Japan surrendered, they had perfected something like mass-produced home construction using flat, concrete-slab foundations and pre-fabricated home sections. The Levitts broke the construction process into 27 steps and crews were trained to perform only one of them, moving from lot to lot, as if they were on an assembly line. In 1946 the Levitts acquired 4,000 acres of potato farms on Long Island and set about building "Levittown"—the largest privately-built housing development in American history.

When Levittown was finished it included 17,400 housing units, every one of them a single-family home. It was a smashing success. The houses sold like crazy and other builders rushed to imitate the Levitt model. The effect on the housing supply was almost immediate: 114,000 new homes were built in 1944; that number jumped to 1,183,000 four years later. Just as important, 97 percent of the units built between 1946 and 1956 were single-family homes, a dramatic departure from pre-war building.

It is not a coincidence that this timeframe happens to coincide with the Baby Boom. The single-family home was engineered to make family life easier. Situated on lots with grass on all four sides, the houses made it easy to send kids out to play. The Cape Cods in Levittown were designed with the kitchen in the front of the house and a window overlooking the yard—so that mothers could keep an eye on the children while they cooked. Development planners made sure to include plenty of playgrounds and parks. Levittown became home to so many children that locals jokingly referred to it as "Fertility Valley" and "The Rabbit Hutch." Such was the awesome power of the single-family home.

But in the 1960s the tenement began making a comeback. The condominium came into vogue along with high-rise apartment buildings. The percentage of tenements as a part of the total housing stock increased by 40 percent from 1960 to 1970 and by another 23 percent from 1970 to 1980.[26] Surprise! It's the precise timeframe during which America's fertility numbers went into steep decline.

The Rise of Capitalism
Some of the influences on fertility that we've discussed are minor (like car seats), some are not (like urbanization). However, all of them are

in their own turn products of larger cultural forces, such as economics or religion. And by "economics" here, we really mean "capitalism."

Now, to be clear: I'm not anti-capitalist, exactly. Capitalism deserves, as Irving Kristol put it, two cheers: It's a good system, better than what came before, and no one has yet come up with an improved alternative. But, like other good things, such as car seats, capitalism is good for people, but not so great for the family.

To backtrack a little bit: we've talked a lot about plummeting fertility rates in the '60s and '70s. However, as we've seen, American fertility has actually been falling since the Founding. And, as I mentioned at the beginning of the chapter, if we step back even *further*, the fertility rate among the educated classes has been falling for a little bit longer. As we've seen, the year 1750 roughly marks the point at which educated people in Europe and North America stopped having as many children as uneducated people. This time coincides with many major historical developments, such as greatly increased lifespans, and we'll get to those in the next chapter. But perhaps the biggest historical development that took place at this time was the rise of capitalism.

In 1776, the Scottish philosopher Adam Smith wrote *The Wealth of Nations*. It didn't "begin" capitalism, exactly—capitalism emerged out of a movement called "mercantilism," which began some two hundred years before. But it set out some of the principles of what we would call capitalism. One central point of *The Wealth of Nations* was that governments and communities should avoid passing protectionist policies, and should allow individuals to act in their own self-interest, even at the temporary expense of local businesses. Allowing this would, over time, enrich everybody, including the original community. But if you're paying attention, you might notice that the end of protectionism means, in a sense, the end of community loyalty.

Now, capitalism is a good thing—maybe even a great good thing. And it's undeniable that acting in one's self-interest is an aspect of human nature that has always profoundly shaped history. But by treating individuals as autonomous actors, capitalism began to set them apart from and even against their communities. If you were a feudal serf, you knew what you were and what you would be. Your life was miserable and had no chance for improvement, but at least it made sense.

A man born into in a capitalist system has no such constrictions and no such security. He has to fend for himself and create himself. Most of all, he has to keep moving; he can't stagnate or bank too much on the stability of the future. The man with a family has more obligations, which means less freedom to move and take risks. In this way, having a family is in a very real sense never in someone's self-interest. He might *desire* a family; people certainly still *have* families. But the family itself is now in his way. In time, as women began to work in serious numbers in the twentieth century, they, too, became individuals who had to keep moving—so today we have two self-interested individuals, and they both know it's not to their advantage to start a family. It might not even be to their advantage to commit to marriage at all.

I'd say "so what do they do?" but we already know what they do. They stop having children and they stop getting married.

Viewed through this lens of economic theory—which is grossly oversimplified—some developments seem inevitable. The rise of divorce, urbanization, the car seat, perhaps even the creation of the Pill, all come from the slow collapse of the idea of "community" and the treatment of each individual as a single entity acting alone for himself or herself. Other influences all slowly resolve themselves into one basic truth: It is not in most people's self-interest to have families, and without something else pushing them to procreate, they simply aren't going to.

If, as we keep saying, demography is not destiny, then neither is economics. There are other forces at work in the culture that are as important as money. One, for instance, is religion. And the counterbalance religion can provide to such individualistic incentives is an important one. Unfortunately for Americans, it is also fading away fast.

The Fall of Religion
Of all of the evolutions in twentieth-century America, the most consequential might be the exodus of religion from the public square.

I'm not going to recapitulate the collected works of Richard John Neuhaus, but I think we can take it as given that over the course of the last century—and particularly the last half-century—religion has been slowly tugged further and further from the center of modern American life.

This movement has had a number of consequences for American fertility. But let's start with its effects on relationships. When it comes to demographics, there are two important dimensions to religion: belief and practice. Studies generally differentiate between different religious sects (the belief part) and religiosity, or how often you worship (the practice part). Belief has small effects on relationship behavior—Catholics and evangelical Protestants are less likely to cohabitate and more likely to get married than non-evangelical Protestants and unbelievers, for instance.[27] But the big effects are determined by whether or not people actually show up at church.

How powerful an influence can religion be on behavior? So powerful that even if you're not the churchgoing type yourself, you'll be affected if your parents are. For instance, let's pretend you're not a churchgoer. If your mother never goes to church either, then you're twice as likely to shack up with a boyfriend (or girlfriend) than you would be if your mother went to church more than once a week. That's the second-order effect of church. The first order is even stronger. For instance, a young woman who attends church infrequently—say, once a month—is three times more likely to cohabitate than one who goes to church weekly. And a woman who never goes to church is seven times more likely to move in with her boyfriend. (Remember, cohabitating also makes you less likely to get married and, if you marry the person you're living with, makes it more likely that you'll get divorced.)

Religion makes a difference once people tie the knot, too, because couples who go to church enjoy their marriages more than couples who don't.[28] If you attend church regularly when you're married, you're more likely to be happier both with your relationship and your spouse. Married couples get happier the more often they go to church and happier still if they share the same faith and pray together outside church. (Again, religious affiliation matters a little, but not nearly as much as practice.[29]) It follows that something which causes people to get married more quickly, to stay married, and to be happy while married, also results in more babies.

Demographers have been obsessing about the effect of religion on fertility in the United States since the early 1900s. Back then, studies concentrated on the difference between Catholics and Protestants because, for most of the century, Catholics had higher fertility rates. In 1960, for instance, Catholic women averaged 0.5 more children per lifetime than their Protestant counterparts.[30] So there was a time when the belief component of religion mattered quite a lot.

Practice mattered back then, too, though in an expected way. For Protestants, church attendance was of very little consequence: a Presbyterian woman who went to services every week was likely to have just as many babies as one who went every few months. But religious practice was very important for Catholics: Catholic women who attended church more regularly could be expected to have more children—up to 1.1 more, depending on frequency—than those who did not.

Over the years, the fertility difference between Protestants and Catholics narrowed. Demographers claimed that America was witnessing the "end" of Catholic fertility.[31] But "Catholic fertility" wasn't really ending. What was happening was that *practicing* Protestants were beginning to act like *practicing* Catholics—and the new difference that emerged was between those who regularly went to church and those who were more passive in their faith, regardless of their sect.

We talked earlier about "desired fertility." Well, today surveys show that just 21 percent of non-religious Americans view three or more children as being the ideal family size. Yet 36 percent of Protestants and 34 percent of Catholics view three or more children as ideal.[32] And this disparity increases with church attendance. Among those who attend church every week, *41 percent* say that three or more children is ideal.

Those desired fertility numbers don't project out perfectly to the real world, but the shape of the curve does. Using data from the 2002

National Survey of Family Growth, researchers found that women with no religious affiliation had a fertility rate of 1.8, while women who said that religion was "somewhat important" to them were at 2.1. Women who said religion was "very important" had a gaudy 2.3.[33]

Pile up enough of this data and it's there for anyone with eyes to see: Religion helps marriage and marriage helps fertility—the end result being that religiosity winds up being an even better predictor of fertility than either education or income.[34] And as Americans have become more secular, they've cut back on having children. The good news is that while each of these three worlds—marriage, church, and fertility—is incredibly complicated, the interplay among them is somewhat straightforward. The bad news is that these realms are so foundational that it's difficult to see how society might consciously nudge them in a positive direction. Sure, it makes sense that we could increase American fertility if we could (1) strengthen the institution of marriage, so that more people got married and stayed married; and (2) make America more friendly to religious belief than it is now. (I'm not asking for a Yankee version of Afghanistan; something like the balance we had in the 1950s would be dandy.)

But how do you influence marriage and religion in the public square? They're pulled along by massive, invisible cultural undercurrents. There's no policy solution; you can't even consciously assemble a countercultural movement. You might as well try to alter the tides. And that's where we get to the really scary stuff. Because there are people out there who don't *want* to reverse the tide. There is an entire school of thought that believes America's demographic conundrum isn't a problem to be solved, but rather a key part of our evolution to a higher state of being. The people who vibrate with excitement at this prospect call it the Second Demographic Transition.

CHAPTER FIVE

Very Bad Things

B efore we explain what the Second Demographic Transition is all about, let's fast-forward to its terminus. On November 14, 2009, three gondolas escorted an empty red coffin through the canals of Venice.[1] The drab little floating parade concluded at the town hall, where the coffin was laid to rest in a mock funeral, symbolizing the death of the once-mighty city-state. Venice, you see, is undergoing a demographic crisis. In 1960, Venice had a population of 145,000.[2] By 2009, it had dropped to 60,000. For some context, Venice averages about 60,000 visitors a day. So at any given moment, half of the people in Venice are tourists.[3]

Some local businesses keep population clocks for the city, because the population decline is only getting worse. Twenty-five percent of Venetians are over the age of 64, which means that (1) The city's low fertility has inverted its age structure, giving it many more old people than people in their reproductive years; and (2) As fewer and fewer babies are born in Venice, more and more Venetians will die without being replaced. Remember our imaginary town, when we talked about what happens as demographic momentum gives out? Venice is midway through the Big Shrink.

The population of Venice will continue to contract and could approach nothingness within about 40 years. Listen to Matteo Secchi, part of a local group dedicated to bringing attention to Venice's demographic disaster: "There are no more people, there is no more culture, there is no Venetian way of life," he laments, "and the city is every day more like a museum." A museum, Secchi says, "like Pompeii." The difference is, the poor people of Pompeii were wiped out by a volcano. The people of Venice simply decided to stop having children. [*] Amazingly enough, there is a group of demographers which sees this as positive development.

The Second Demographic Transition

Paul Ehrlich's overpopulation hysteria aside, serious demographers have spent most of the last four decades studying the phenomenon of falling fertility. Most of these academics gravitated toward causal models. For instance, they'd hypothesize that changes in a given set of economic conditions would lead directly to people having fewer babies. Such theories date all the way back to the period before the Baby Boom, when demographers such as Kingsley Davis[+] and W. S. Thompson[5] suggested that America's falling fertility was a rather straightforward matter. Progress (with a capital "P") was creating eco-

---

[*] The same fate befell Sparta, believe it or not. In his 2011 book *How Civilizations Die*, David Goldman notes historical accounts of Sparta shrinking from a population of 10,000 men to just 1,000, shortly before the city-state's fall to Thebes. After Sparta went into eclipse, its military traditions lived on in a ceremonial state, mostly for the delight of visitors from other parts of Greece. Goldman quotes two other historians (Paul Cartledge and Antony Spawforth) who depict Sparta's decline into a kind of living museum: "The prestige of the 'revived' training and the tourism which it generated helped this otherwise fairly typical provincial Greek city to maintain a place in the world and allowed the Spartans to feel that they were still 'special.'" Goldman concludes, somewhat less charitably, that modern Italy is becoming not a museum, but a "theme park." Ouch.

nomic structures—city living, industrialization—which lowered the incentives for couples to have children. This created, in Davis's words, "a ripening incongruity between our reproductive system (the family) and the rest of modern social organization." Since Davis's time, many demographers have expanded on this general theory as the world has accelerated in the direction Davis first reported: We are more industrialized and more globalized, with the costs of child-rearing ever increasing and the benefits constantly declining.

We've already talked about some of these factors. The 1,000 percent increase in college tuition, the $800,000 in forgone wages for a mother who stays home, the low fertility we see in densely urban states. In a sense, these causal explanations are comforting because they suggest that if we could just pull the right lever, or create the right inducements, we might be able to fix America's fertility problem.

But there is another school of thought, which explains our falling fertility as something more than the mere consequence of economic change. This school believes low fertility is the result of modernity itself and represents the next evolution in human society. And these demographers see this evolution as a good thing. A very good thing, indeed.

In 1986, two European researchers, Ron Lesthaeghe and Dirk J. van de Kaa, took measure of the decline in fertility rates across the industrialized world and put together a grand unified theory. They called it "The Second Demographic Transition" (or SDT).[6] To explain it, though, we have to step back a moment, to the "First Demographic Transition." And to understand *that*, we should go back to the beginning. The very beginning.

A Brief History of Population

It took nearly 500,000 years for the world's population to hit the 5 million mark, which it did sometime around 8000 B.C.[7] Human life was plenty nasty and brutish back then, but it was its shortness that mattered most. It took so long to get to 5 million because it was devilishly hard to keep 5 million people alive all at once. But the advent of agriculture improved access to food, which produced gains in health and longevity, which led to a pick-up in the rate of population growth: From 8000 B.C. to the age of Julius Caesar (45 B.C., give or take) the world's population grew to somewhere in the neighborhood of 300 million. (It should go without saying that these are academic estimates. The important thing here isn't the exact number, but the general rates of growth.)

That growth rate continued on basically the same line from Caesar, through the Middle Ages, until about 1750, bringing the total number of people on our little blue ball of mud to 800 million. But in the eighteenth century, the pace of population growth increased again. This time by a lot. We crossed the threshold of 1 billion around 1825. And while it took thousands of years to get a billion people alive at the same time, it only took another hundred years to get to 2 billion, which is where we stood in 1925. The third billion was added even faster: We hit that milestone in 1960 and have been off to the races ever since.

What happened after 1750 to cause the rate of population growth to accelerate? Lots of things, but the most important was the decline of the mortality rate. As nutrition, sanitation, and medicine improved, people began living longer and demographic momentum built up in our population profile. In ancient Rome, life expectancy was about 25 years.[8] In nineteenth-century England it was 40 years, an increase of barely 60 percent over the course of two millennia.[9] Since then, the average life expectancy in the First World has just about doubled in under two centuries. As one sociological study from the 1960s put it ironically, the explosion in population after 1750 was "due to death control's exceeding birth control."[10]

All of this led to the First Demographic Transition, which began manifesting in various countries in the 1800s in response to this radical change in mortality. At the moment when a country's death rate slowed noticeably, its fertility rate also began to slow. As people lived longer, they had children only within the confines of marriage, and began to master some forms of contraception. In the textbook case of the First Demographic Transition, the fertility rate goes from being high, but relatively constant, to gradual decline, until it reaches the replacement rate—all in response to declining mortality. This transition is tied closely to industrialization and it has happened for different countries at different times. In America the transition took place between 1860 and 1960, which is roughly when Europe experienced it, too. The developing world is going through it now.[11] Today, only 3 percent of the world's population lives in a country whose fertility rate is *not* declining.[12]

One of the side effects of the First Demographic Transition is that parents became more child-centric. Children were once free-range and—this may sound horrible—somewhat disposable. But as the number of children born to each couple decreased, the little dears became much more dear. Writing 30 years ago, the French medievalist Philippe Ariès theorized that as people cut back on their progeny they concentrated more care and energy into each one.[13] Ariès labeled this interregnum the "child-king era." It's important to understand that he wasn't talking about our Peaceful Power karate camp world, but about the early twentieth century, after the First Demographic Transition had been completed. But the age of the child-king was short-lived, according to Ariès:

> The decline in the birth rate that began at the end of the eighteenth century and continued until the 1930s was unleashed by an enormous sentimental and financial investment in the child. I see the current decrease in the birth rate as being, on the contrary, provoked by exactly the opposite attitude. The days of the child-king are over. The under-forty generation is leading us into a new epoch, one in which *the child, to say the least, occupies a smaller place.*[14] [emphasis in original]

The end point of the First Demographic Transition was a world in which parents tried to maximize resources and opportunities for their children, resulting in fewer children overall. But when fertility rates began collapsing in the late 1960s, another demographic transition was occurring, the result of a fundamental restructuring: People no longer put children at the center of their lives. Instead, they put themselves there. Here it's best to let Ron Lesthaeghe explain his theory of the Second Demographic Transition in his own words:

> [We] posited that new living arrangements, and cohabitation (premarital or postmarital) in particular, were not solely the outcomes of changing socioeconomic conditions or rising female employment, but equally the expression of secular and anti-authoritarian sentiments of better-educated men and women who held an egalitarian world view, placed greater emphasis on Maslow's "higher order needs" (i.e., self-actual-ization, individualistic and expressive orientations, need for recognition), and . . . had stronger "postmaterialist" political orientations.[15]

So the First Demographic Transition displaced the family and put the child at the center of society. In the Second Demographic Transition, then, the individual pushed both children *and* family aside, and became the axis around which all life revolved. The "bourgeois family model" was giving way to, in van de Kaa's view, an "individualistic family model," which valued freedom for contraception, abortion, cohabitation, and divorce.[16] This does not mean that people have stopped having children—merely that in the Second Demographic Transition, procreation became an act of self-actualization. And because raising children is difficult, resource intensive, socially inhibiting, and (if we can be candid) often unpleasant, it is not an exercise many people want to put themselves through multiple times.

The theory of the Second Demographic Transition has some weaknesses. For instance, as we've seen in America, the rise of cohabitation was *not* the product of enlightened guys and gals from Berkeley shacking up and sticking it to the man. It was a pathology born of the underclass, which gradually worked its way up through society, until it affected everyone *except* the highly educated—who still marry (and stay married) at very high rates. Another weakness of the SDT theory is that its proponents claim that one of the factors contributing to the transition is liberalized contraception and abortion regimes, which give couples full control over their fertility aspirations.[17] But as we'll see later, actual fertility now lags far behind aspirational fertility.

Yet despite its weaknesses, the SDT theory also has compelling strengths. For one, it predicts that cohabitation, widespread contraceptive use, and liberal abortion policies will materialize in all developed, democratic countries, the result of people valuing their self-actualization and individualism over more traditional moral precepts. These three horsemen have indeed ridden across the entire liberalized world.[18] What's more, SDT theory predicts that the sub-replacement fertility we now see in every industrialized nation will be structural and permanent. So far, it has been. Also, SDT theory predicts that *all* countries will tend toward the same fertility declines as they liberalize. And so they have. But the most compelling aspect of SDT theory is that in some places in America, the transition Lesthaeghe and van de Kaa predicted *hasn't happened yet*. And those places are exactly the ones you would expect.

Two Americas (Again)

Some American researchers have pushed back against the Second Demographic Transition and its universalist claims about how the world is heading toward a secular, enlightened, self-actualized paradise that—by the way—has no children. After all, unlike Europe and Japan, America's fertility rate isn't so awful and our high levels of religious belief and practice set us apart from the rest of the industrialized world. Maybe we're the exception that disproves the rule.

But when you break America into its component parts, we may not be as exceptional as we look. Remember, if you go by the fertility numbers, there's a bigger spread between the American states than there is among the countries that make up Europe. And when you break down our individual states by metrics that signify a Second Demographic Transition—low fertility, late marriage, high rates of cohabitation—you find that the states sort into two distinct clusters. Liberal, secular, SDT-type states include New York, Massachusetts, Rhode Island, New Jersey, Connecticut, and California. States with higher fertility, early marriage, and lower rates of cohabitation—basically, the anti-transition states—include West Virginia, Tennessee, Kentucky, the Carolinas, Alabama, Mississippi, Oklahoma, Arkansas, Texas, Utah, and Idaho. Culturally, economically, and demographically, these two groups represent very different things.

For instance, the states that conform to the SDT pattern are wealthier. Also, when you strip out minorities and look only at non-Hispanic whites, you see that the more secular, Northeastern states (and California) also lead the way in late childbearing. And childlessness. In fact, in nearly every demographic indicator, these states look very much like Western Europe. It's the states of the South, Plains, and parts of the Mountain West that look exceptional. It's possible that these regions really are exceptions—rocks sticking out and resisting the pull of a great undertow. But it's also possible that they just haven't succumbed yet and that, sooner or later, they'll transition too and become as barren as the rest of the Western world.

Mind you, proponents of the Second Demographic Transition don't see the move to permanent sub-replacement fertility as a bad thing. Quite the opposite: They view it as a grand evolution to a higher way of being. "Bourgeois postmodernists"—as van de Kaa called the populations ushering in the SDT—"do not accept authority without question, are tolerant of the behavior of others, seek to express themselves freely, support emancipatory (human rights, ecological, gender) movements, favor diversity, and look without prejudice at developments leading to multiculturalism."[19] What's not to like?

But wait—there's more! When a country makes the transition, it also means that the little bourgeois postmodernists have stopped believing in God, too, as religious belief and practice numbers drop. (And in America, this means they'll vote more Democratic.[20]) Because of their low fertility, countries that have made the transition will often rely on mass immigration to keep their population profile minimally functional—which creates greater racial and ethnic diversity. Each of these is a substantial moral good from a certain perspective. One of the most revealing endorsements of the Second Demographic Transition came from Duke sociologist Philip Morgan in a 2003 paper evaluating the costs and benefits of population contraction and the SDT:

> Low fertility produces rapidly aging populations and possible country-level population decline. It will reduce the proportion of the global population living in Europe and North America. . . . For whom is this a problem? It clearly depends on one's perspective. An African American colleague recently questioned my research agenda: "so you're studying the disappearance of white folks." I was taken aback; this is not how I prefer to characterize my work. But he had made his point: for many, "fewer white people" does not sound like the greatest crisis of the twenty-first century.[21]

Morgan ultimately agrees with his African American colleague that whatever problems may be associated with a Second Demographic Transition, they probably aren't *so* bad in the end.

We can't say with certainty whether the old-fashioned "causists" or the SDT "transitionists" are right. And to be sure, this isn't an either/or proposition: There's enough evidence to suspect that both are correct to some degree. But what we can be relatively certain about is that the sunny view of our sub-replacement future—a happy, ecologically pure, multiracial, morally tolerant, peaceful, and prosperous utopia in which the whole world looks like Seattle writ very large—is a mirage.

Very Bad Things

As we've seen, in the 2010 revision of its population projections, the United Nations put a happy face on our future by assuming that every country now seeing lowest-low fertility will rebound to replacement fertility in the next 70 years. Maybe that will happen. But let's suppose, just for the sake of argument, that it does not. Let's pretend that fertility rates basically maintain their current levels, without getting better or worse. Then what?

Demographic momentum is a two-way street. Just as it causes population to grow even after fertility has fallen below replacement, momentum eventually causes population to contract, even if fertility rates increase. Halving times mirror doubling times. So for instance, if current fertility rates remain constant in Europe, the total population of the continent will go from 738 million in 2010 to 482 million by the end of the century.[22] That's a scary scenario, but there's spookier stuff out there. Remember, just 3 percent of the world's population lives in countries that *are not* seeing fertility decline.[23] And all evidence suggests that once fertility decline sets in, it does not stop until the TFR is below the replacement rate. So it's entirely possible that Europe's future is the world's future.

There are two demographic consequences of prolonged sub-replacement fertility. The first is that the age profile of the country—the proportion of young people to old people—inverts. (We talked about this earlier: the nib of the fountain pen compared with the upside-down pyramid.) As the age profile shifts, the average age increases, making the society, on the whole, more elderly. Which leads to the second consequence: the overall population eventually begins to shrink as the fat cohorts of old people die off and there are too few young people left in the skinny cohorts to make enough babies to replace them.

Each of these developments carries its own set of problems. Consider Germany. With a TFR of 1.36, Germany has a population today of 82 million people.[24] The Germans experienced not one fertility collapse, but two: In the West they suffered the same drop that Europe, America, and Japan experienced after 1968. But then the East experienced its own fertility drop after the Wall fell. Germans now refer to this second collapse as "the Kink." But this nickname doesn't quite do it justice. In terms of sheer magnitude, it was on the scale of what you'd expect in a country suddenly plunged into war. "For a number of years East

Germans just stopped having children," explains Reiner Klingholz, director of the Berlin Institute for Population and Development.[25]

If Germany's fertility rate remains constant, its population will fall to 44 million by the end of the century.[26] Today, 20 percent of Germans are over the age of 65. By 2050, 34 percent will be over 65. By 2100, it will be 39 percent and German geriatrics will outnumber children under the age of 15 by 4-to-1.[27] The wolves have come for Germany.

Take the example of the town of Hoyerswerda, near the Polish border. Sociologist Fred Pearce reports that Hoyerswerda had a population of 75,000 in 1980 and the highest birth rate in East Germany.[28] When the Wall fell, the people in Hoyerswerda stopped having children. In the former East the fertility rate fell to a nearly impossible 0.8. (Since then it has rebounded to 1.2.) Within 30 years, Hoyerswerda lost half of its population. The number of children under 15 declined by 80 percent. The town began to close up shop.

The main job of Hoyerswerda's government these days is demolishing abandoned buildings. With so few people, they have loads of vacant housing structures—more than a third of the housing stock has already been torn down.[29] There's lots of empty commercial real estate, too, because as the citizenry died out or left town, stores and offices shuttered. And don't even think about industry. Formerly an industrial hub for mining and power, the coal mines in Hoyerswerda are shut down now and scheduled to be flooded in the hopes that a lake might attract some tourism. A giant chunk of German urban planning is now concerned with how to shrink cities.[30] (German demographers refer to the fatherland's condition as the *schrumpfende Gesellschaft*, or "shrinking society."[31]) As one report from the University of Cologne explains,

> Shrinking so that the cities can operate in an economic and
> sustainable way is . . . urgent for managing the development in
> East German cities successfully but it is necessary, too, in West
> German cities in the medium run. In other words: the trends
> of shrinking cannot be reversed by just some measures, but
> the whole idea of city and urban planning has to be adjusted

to the shrinking process and that means the concepts of urban development have to be rethought.[32]

That means tearing down buildings and turning industrial and commercial sites into parks. The new German urbanism features lots and lots of parks where buildings used to be, although occasionally a building can be repurposed instead of destroyed. For instance, turning an office that was once an obstetrics clinic into a retirement home. It's hard to find uses for all of these abandoned buildings, though, because there are just so many of them. Since 1989, for example, 2,000 schools in the East have closed down simply for lack of students.[33]

In the big eastern cities—Chemnitz, Görlitz, Halberstadt—populations have already shrunk anywhere from 15 percent to 25 percent.[34] When I said a moment ago that the wolves have come for Germany, I meant it literally, too. In the eastern part of the country, depopulation has lured wolves out of the forests in numbers not seen in two centuries. Wolf packs are now frequently seen around small towns and dwindling population centers such as Spreewitz.[35]

On the western side of the country, the state of North Rhine-Westphalia is suffering similar problems: It has been struggling to find enough workers to care for its bumper crop of retirees, forcing the state to take some radical steps. For instance, the government instituted a program to convert local prostitutes into elder-care nurses. As one official told the *British Medical Journal*, it's "an obvious move [since prostitutes possess] good people skills, aren't easily disgusted, and have zero fear of physical contact."[36] Old men never had it so good.

You see freakish developments like these across the industrialized world, wherever the consequences of low fertility are finally being felt. In Japan, more than half the country is now categorized as "depopulated marginal land." One such area is the village of Ogama, on Honshu island.[37] Once home to 250 people, in 2006 the handful of folks left on Ogama—there were only eight elderly Japanese remaining—decided to sell the village to a waste management company, which planned on turning the town into a landfill.[38]

Don't Trust Anyone Over 65

All of which is why you constantly hear academics and government officials and blue-ribbon committees worrying about our "graying" population. There's a raft of reports and studies on the subject published by outfits ranging from the European Commission to the Center for Strategic and International Studies.[39] The bottom line is this: In 1950, the median age in America was 30.[40] In 2000, it was 35. By 2050, it will be 40. Which is the median age in Florida today.[41]

Let's think through the consequences of America becoming Florida Nation for a moment. There are the superficial changes, of course. As in Germany, former obstetrics clinics might be converted into nursing homes while "anti-aging cafés" spring up, like weird, sci-fi versions of Starbucks (they're already numerous in South Korea, which is ahead of America on the road to fertility collapse).[42] The structural economic changes are more significant. An older population means a shrinking labor force. For a time, you can make up that shortfall by importing labor from other, younger countries. But fertility rates are falling even faster in the developing world. As demographer David Reher points out, "in a few short decades there is a good chance that labor shortages will become a problem affecting most of the world and not just one of the developed nations."[43] And from there, the problems cascade.

With fewer people working, the tax base declines just as demands on the government (in the form of pensions and medical coverage) increase. But that's just about the only kind of demand that will increase, because old people tend to consume most everything else at a lower rate. Everything, that is, except for healthcare, which we'll get to in a moment.

For instance, one thing old people tend not to demand is investment opportunities. Their focus is on preserving money in low-risk vehicles and drawing down their investments to substitute for lost income. So capital pools will shrink, too. Which is just as well, because as our society ages there will probably less creative, technological, and industrial dynamism, too. Nicholas Eberstadt notes that there is "a clear social pattern to the age of innovators and discoverers . . . Significant innovations and big discoveries tend to be made between the ages of 30 and 50, with the peak of creativity coming somewhere between 35 and 40 years of age."[44] We may already be seeing the blunting of our creative force.

"Total-factor productivity" is the metric economists use to measure dynamism. Roughly speaking, it's the total economic output *not* caused by inputs. Think of it as the value added by people and ideas, as opposed to raw materials. From 1890 to 1913, America's total-factor productivity rose annually by 1.3 percent.[45] From 1913 to 1950—a period marked by the invention spurred by the two world wars—it grew at an astounding 2.3 percent annually. After the war it slumped, but still remained extraordinarily high. From 1950 to 1973 it was 1.7 percent annually. And then, with the end of the Baby Boom, it collapsed. Our total-factor productivity increased barely at all—just 0.1 percent for each year until 1980. After 1980, it crept upward a little: from 1980 until 1995 it averaged around a 0.7 percent annual increase.[46] And from 2000 to 2006 it was a more robust 1.2. Hooray for us: We have nearly returned to the level of innovation and forward progress of the 1890s.

Maybe you don't trust "total-factor productivity" (many economists do not) and you'd like another metric. The nonprofit group Global Entrepreneurship Monitor compiles data on private business start-ups across the world. When you look at their data, the results jump out at you: Countries with younger median ages tend to have greater percentages of entrepreneurship than countries with older median ages. So Italy (median age 43.5 years) has a new business ownership rate of 1.0 percent, while China (median age 35.5 years) has a rate of 10.0 percent.[47] This isn't a straight apples-to-apples comparison, of course. Every country blends a unique mix of factors that influence entrepreneurship—access to capital, government regulation, corruption, and so on. And a country's developmental stage matters, too. Countries that are efficiency-driven will tend to have higher rates of entrepreneurship than more advanced countries, whose economies are innovation-driven. Yet in every country, the bulk of entrepreneurs are between 18 and 34 years old.[48] And in advanced, innovation-driven economies, such as ours, very few entrepreneurs are over the age of 45.

Economists don't know anything for certain in the best of times. Since the rapid aging we're seeing across the world is unprecedented, they're even more in the dark than usual. So we shouldn't take their predictions as fatally binding. Still, just about no one who studies the subject thinks that very old populations are likely to make economic life *better*. Instead, the projections range from "it might not be so bad (if we adapt well, change our patterns of behavior, and entirely revamp the social welfare system)" to the very dire assessment of Kieran McMorrow and Werner Roeger, who say that the consequences of older populations

> will be significant in terms not only of a slowdown in the growth rate of output and living standards but also with regard to the fiscal and financial market trends . . . [such as] falling rates of capital accumulation and a slowdown in productivity growth.[49]

McMorrow and Roeger conclude by predicting that the future "bodes ominously." Mind you, these are the concerns of rich, First World countries, like America. If you're a poor, developing country, the prospects of population aging are much, much worse. There will be 1.2 billion people over 65 in the developing world by 2050 and they will need others to feed and keep watch over them.[50] There are no Life-Alert systems in Bangladesh. A decline in lifestyle for a middle-class American retiree might mean canceling cable, moving to a smaller apartment, and not eating out. A decline in lifestyle in a place of abject poverty is something altogether different.

Shrinkage

After a country gets old, it gets smaller. We've already talked about some of the population declines for countries with lowest-low fertility.

If Italy, Spain, Germany, and Greece maintain their current fertility levels and don't import lots of immigrants, then by the end of the century their populations will shrink by 86 percent, 85 percent, 83 percent, and 74 percent, respectively.[51] If this scenario takes place, population historian David Reher writes, "urban areas could well be filled with empty buildings and crumbling infrastructure . . . surrounded by large areas which look more like what we might see in some science-fiction movies."[52] Europe would become Hoyerswerda, writ large.

The key variable in that scenario is immigration. Such enormous declines assume zero immigration—which almost certainly will not happen. Each of those countries already has a reasonable yearly inflow of migrants; there's no reason to assume that this spigot will suddenly shut off. If anything, the demographic vacuum created by a shrinking population demands *more* immigration: The economy, the labor force, the infrastructure, all of those empty buildings, practically beg for a substantially increased number of immigrants. Where would those immigrants come from? In Europe, the supply mostly comes from North Africa and the Middle East—which creates its own set of cultural problems. There's an old joke among demographers: *Democracy, immigration, multiculturalism. You may pick two.* But even this might be a high-class problem to have because, remember, those sending countries are going through their own demographic transitions. The supply of even these imperfect (by European reckoning) immigrants might not last to 2050.

For the sake of argument, though, let's assume that something in between these two scenarios happens. Sub-replacement European countries take in some large measure of immigration; it's enough to keep their population from falling by 80 percent, but not enough to stave off a serious contraction altogether. What then? The short answer is: We don't know. Since the Industrial Revolution (at least) there is no model for a country experiencing a sustained, structural shrinking of its population.[53]

A few years ago the scholar Ben Wattenberg[*] conducted a little thought experiment on the subject using a fictional industrialist, Jack Jones:

> As the American population grew by 130 million people from 1950 to 2000, there was one thing Jack Jones had going for him: a customer boom. If widgets were your game, there were 130 million new customers for widgets. Acme would make them. True, your wily competitors might gain a good share of new widget buyers, but there was a margin for error. . . .
>
> But what's going to happen to Jack Jones's European counterpart, Heinz Hoerst, and his employees, and the European economy in which he participates, when the number of customers shrinks, substantially? Consider real estate again. Over a period of decades in Europe there will be fewer buyers for existing properties. Less demand for a constant supply yields lower prices. Lower prices yield lower values upon which to finance loans to provide for investment capital, diminishing both jobs and profits.[54]

Still, it would be nice to have something a little more concrete than thought experiments. The closest thing we have to data is Japan, which began flirting with sub-replacement fertility around 1960. Japan's demographic momentum petered out in 2006 and in 2008 the country began contracting. So far, its population has dropped by about a mil-

---

* Wattenberg, by the way, deserves your respect. In the 1970s, he was a lone voice in the wilderness pointing out that Paul Ehrlich's "Population Bomb" theory was ridiculous. For his trouble, he was often used as a punching bag by the overpopulation crowd. In 1970, this meant nearly all of the media, the policy elite, and academia. It was so bad that on August 13, 1970, Johnny Carson brought him onto the *The Tonight Show* to "debate" Ehrlich, on whose side Carson was firmly planted. History shows without a scintilla of doubt that Wattenberg was right.

lion.[55] Because Japan has no immigration to speak of, and its fertility rate shows no signs of increasing, there is no reason to expect that the country's contraction will abate in the foreseeable future. So let's look at what's happened to the Japanese.

Even in the 1980s, when Japan's economy seemed invincible, Japanese demographers were already worrying about what the country's aging and eventual shrinking would mean for the future. Demographer Naohiro Ogawa told a reporter in 1984, "Owing to a decrease in the growth rate of the labor force . . . Japan's economy is likely to slow down, approaching an annual rate of one or even zero percent, in the first quarter of the next century." Guess what: From 1950 to 1973, Japan's total-factor productivity increased by an average of 5.4 percent per year. From 1990 to 2006 it increased by 0.63 percent per year.[56] Since 1991, Japan's rate of GDP growth has exceeded 2.5 percent in only four years and the annual rate of growth has averaged 1.03 percent.[57]

We keep saying that correlation is not causation, and it's true. The economic story of Japan's last two decades is enormously complicated. There was a national real-estate bubble and a national banking crisis to go along with a regional, and then a global, financial crisis. Lots of economists have tried to explain what went wrong in Japan and it's not clear how much a part demographics plays. But there are signs that seem to implicate demographics pretty clearly: The household savings rate, which was 15 percent in 1990, is down to 2 percent today, as the increasingly elderly population has moved from asset accumulation to retirement drawdown.[58] The Japanese state pension fund is now a net seller of bonds, as it begins its own drawdown and tries to pay for the flood of retirees using a smaller pool of workers. While the size of the impact is open for debate, age is clearly affecting the Japanese economy.

It could be that Japan is headed for a doomsday scenario of default and collapse. Or it's possible that matters won't get completely out of hand. (One economist argues interestingly, if not convincingly, that with a declining labor force, even Japan's low growth actually results in pretty good per-capita gains for Japanese workers.[59]) Yet no one surveying Japan's situation envisions a sunny economic future, because even if the country does bounce back from what were essentially two lost decades, its aging population, increasing public burdens, shrinking workforce, and dwindling population will continue to be a drag on every area of the economy. This relentless undertow is the best-case scenario. It assumes that all the pillars of Japanese society remain relatively stable and that no structural crisis is precipitated—such as the failure of the welfare state.

Even though we're in much, much better demographic shape than Japan, this is what we're up against in America. We don't have to worry about towns being turned into landfills and acres of depopulated cities being bulldozed. (Except for Detroit.) What we're in danger of is having the government safety net disintegrate.

The Decline and Fall of Social Security (and Medicare)

Entitlement talk is deadly dull, so I'll keep this short—but it's necessary to understand how the American welfare state works so that you can understand why it's in danger. And on this score, we owe a small debt to Al Gore and his lockbox. During the fall of 2000, Vice President Gore bored America to death talking about his plan to save Social Security. Gore promised to take incoming tax revenues from FICA and secret them away into a "lockbox" where they would be reserved solely for Social Security payouts and not for use in the general budget. Gore's plan was faulty—money is inherently fungible and his lockbox would have been no better at conserving dollars than the UN's oil-for-food program was at keeping international assistance out of the hands of dictators.

But Gore got one thing right. By droning on (and on and on) about his lockbox, he awakened the public to a signal fact about our Social Security regime: *We do not pay for our own Social Security benefits.*

For decades, Americans believed that the Social Security Trust Fund—the official name of the repository of your FICA taxes—took your tax money and squirreled it away until your retirement, at which point it was disbursed back to you. That couldn't be further form the truth. There is not—and has never been—such a savings pool. What really happens is that the taxes deducted from workers' paychecks by the government are placed into the Trust Fund, and then immediately doled out to the current batch of retirees. Once today's generation of workers retires, their children will pay for their Social Security checks with *their* taxes.

In his disquisition on Social Security, Gore pretended that what threatened the program was a giant accounting problem. If only the government could keep Social Security funds securely locked away from the rest of the budget, then our government-run pension system could survive in perpetuity. In reality, Social Security is threatened by a much simpler dynamic: More retirees and fewer babies.

Social Security is, in essence, a Ponzi scheme. Like all Ponzi schemes, it works just fine—so long as the intake of new participants continues to increase. When Social Security was started in 1937, only 53,236 Americans received benefits. The entire output of the program totaled under $1.3 million.[60] Social Security's growth, however, was nearly geometric. By 1950, 3.5 million Americans were receiving payments. By 1980, 35 million retirees were getting checks. By 2006, as the first Baby Boomers were taking retirement, that number shot up to more than 49 million people who were being paid $546 *billion* in benefits, all of which came directly from taxes paid by current workers.

The problem is that while the number of workers paying into Social Security has risen, it has not risen nearly as fast as the number of retirees. In 1940 there were 35.4 million workers supporting 222,000 retirees—that's a ratio of almost 160 workers for every pensioner.[61] By 1950 that ratio was 16.5 workers for every retiree. By 1965, it fell to 4.0 workers for every retiree. By 2010, just 2.9 workers were paying for the benefits of each retiree.[62]

Ratio of Workers Paying FICA Taxes to Retirees Collecting Social Security Benefits			
Year	Workers (in millions)	Beneficiaries (in millions)	Ratio (number of workers supporting each retiree)
1940	35.390	0.222	159.4
1950	48.280	2.930	16.5
1960	72.530	14.262	5.1
1970	93.090	25.186	3.7
1980	113.656	35.118	3.2
1990	133.672	39.470	3.4
2000	155.295	45.166	3.4
2010	156.725	53.398	2.9
Source: Social Security Administration (http://www.ssa.gov/history/ratios.html).			

The Social Security Administration predicts that by 2034, the ratio of workers-to-retirees will fall to just 2.1 workers for every retiree as a result of (1) roughly 80 million Baby Boomers retiring and (2) the declining fertility rates having failed to produce a proportionate number of new workers.[63]

As the worker-to-retiree ratio dropped over the years, the tax burden increased. When Social Security began, taxes for the program were only 1 percent of earnings, up to $3,000.[64] By 1960, it was 3 percent of earnings up to $4,800. By 1971, when the demographic problem first revealed itself, the rate had jumped to 4.6 percent up to $7,800. Today it stands at 6.2 percent of earnings all the way up to $106,800. If I make one prediction that's a stone-cold, mortal lock, it's this: Social Security taxes will keep increasing. They have to.

With Medicare, the picture is even more bleak. At least Social Security is a defined benefit. We know how many payees there are, and how much they'll each get. The only variable is how long they'll live. But Medicare has no ceiling. We can guess, based on past performance, how much each retiree will use in Medicare benefits, but that's about it. We don't know what new treatments will develop, how the epidemiological profiles will change as people live longer, or what the price tags on medicine will look like 20 years from now.

In 1975, 24.8 million people were enrolled in Medicare and each of them cost $1,985 a year.[65] By 2010, the enrollment was 47.5 million and each beneficiary cost $9,828 (for a total cost of $523 billion).[66] Medicare, like Social Security, is run on a "trust fund" that doesn't exist. And like Social Security, it's unsustainable in its current form. In 2010, the program spent $32.3 billion more on benefits than it took from taxes. By 2020, 63.9 million people will be receiving Medicare and by 2040, after the Baby Boom wave has crashed, 88.3 million people will be enrolled and both the total and per-person costs will continue to rise.[67] By 2040 it's predicted that each Baby Boomer retiree will eat up $17,156 per year, for a grand cost of $1.5 trillion, annually. (Remember, that's just a guess. The number could easily be greater.) At that point not only will the cost of the program be higher than ever, but the funding will be at its low point: Because of our fertility rate, there will be just two workers to pay for each beneficiary.[68] Good luck with that.

Repent Now, the End Is Nigh!

Since the 1980s, policy wonks have been telling us how our social welfare programs are about to implode. *The system is not sustainable! Either benefits or taxes must be changed—something's got to give!* And that's all true. But this harangue ignores the root cause of why the system isn't sustainable. Social Security and Medicare were conceived in an era of high fertility. It was only after our fertility rate collapsed that the economics of the programs became dysfunctional. Yes, these programs could be salvaged by drastically altering the tax and/or benefit structure. But they could also be saved if Americans started having more babies. The only problem is that, as we discussed earlier, the system makes it *harder to have* babies, creating a negative feedback loop.

As Massimo Livi-Bacci once said, children are not just a matter of personal consumption and preference, but also one of social investment. Yet you never hear the fertility rate mentioned in discussions of Social Security and Medicare. You know why? Because the government believes that our unspoken one-child policy is so immutable that an increase in the fertility rate is not even considered a possible outcome. How do we know this? From looking at the actuarial assumptions the government makes. For Medicare, it assumes that America's TFR will stay somewhere between 1.7 and 2.3 for the next 70 years. For a median projection, it assumes our TFR will be a nice, even 2.0.[69]

As with the United Nations 2010 projections, there's no real reason for this assumption. It just sounds good. But if the green eye-shades at the Medicare Trust Fund can't envision a world where American fertility rebounds, neither can they imagine a world where our fertility follows the path of Japan, Italy, and Germany. Which means that, for whatever it's worth, our government does not subscribe to the theory of a Second Demographic Transition.

If the only real danger low fertility posed to America were a rickety entitlement system, then we'd be in pretty fair shape. And the truth is, if our fertility rate were to settle in at 2.0 for the long haul, we'd be okay. Sure, there would be problems. Sustaining Medicare and Social Security would require an increasing share of the government's revenues, which would mean less money for items such as defense and infrastructure. And you don't have to be a doomsayer to imagine how this restructuring could cascade into other, larger problems: say, geopolitical instability, or sustained economic doldrums, or even a tightening of the pressures that push fertility down in the first place. But we'd still be a long way from civic funeral processions, the demolition of abandoned buildings, and hookers being converted into nurses for old-folks homes.

Which brings us, finally, to a wee bit of good news. Because, despite all of the above, America still has two big things going for it.

CHAPTER SIX
The Bright Side

The Forum Theater opened its doors in New York City in February 1923.[1] Situated in the Bronx, the Forum was one of those grand old theaters, with seating for more than 2,000 and a stage big enough to showcase both films and live performances. But times and competition were tough, and between the neighboring chain cinemas and the Great Depression, the independent Forum closed down after a few years. In 1948, the Forum was resurrected—not as a traditional theater, but as a gathering place for a new class of immigrants who were pouring into the city. Rechristened as the "Teatro Puerto Rico," it was the first big American symbol of the Puerto Rican wave.

The theater booked acts from the home island and brought them up to the city, where a community of Puerto Rican immigrants was congealing. Puerto Ricans had started trickling into America (mostly to New York City) in the 1920s at a slow pace, typically fewer than 2,000 immigrants per year. But those numbers added up over time. By 1930, there were 50,000 Puerto Ricans living in the city.[2] In 1946 the community reached critical mass: Suddenly there were enough Puerto Ricans in New York that people back on the island felt as though they wouldn't be settling into a strange land. Overnight the rate of immigration shot up to 30,000 *per year*.[3] And it kept growing from there.

"I like to be in America! Okay by me in America!"

The '50s were a golden age for Puerto Ricans in America. The Teatro Puerto Rico became not just an immigrant gathering place, but a venue of real cultural importance, attracting big acts from all over Latin America. It was a reference point in the wider, mainstream culture, like the Apollo Theater and the Cotton Club. In 1957, *West Side Story* debuted on Broadway and its tale of Puerto Rican New Yorkers in love became a runaway success. By then, Puerto Ricans were a major subculture in New York—so much so that in 1958, they took over what had previously been the city's "Hispanic Day Parade" and renamed it the "Puerto Rican Day Parade."[4] That first year, the parade was held in Harlem. The next year it moved front and center to Fifth Avenue. Three years later the film version of *West Side Story* introduced the rest of America to Puerto Rican culture. It grossed $43.6 million at the box office—that's $446 million in today's dollars—and won the Academy Award for Best Picture.[5]

This vibrant era was the result of massive immigration between 1946 and 1964. Yet today, Puerto Rican culture is practically invisible, largely because Puerto Ricans themselves have basically stopped coming to the United States. In 1955, 80,000 Puerto Ricans immigrated to America; in 2010, the number was 4,283.[6]

That steep drop wasn't caused by new restrictions on immigration: emigrating from Puerto Rico to the United States actually became *easier* in the intervening half-century. And while the economic situation in Puerto Rico brightened somewhat, it didn't improve dramatically: people living in Puerto Rico still have many fewer opportunities and a much lower standard of living than people in America. And the population of Puerto Rico kept growing. What makes that drop in immigration—from 80,000 to 4,000—even more striking is that during that during the same period, the population of Puerto Rico nearly doubled, going from 2.25 million to 3.99 million. The big fundamental change in Puerto Rico since 1955 is that the country's fertility rate collapsed. In 1955, Puerto Rico's TFR was 4.97.[7] But over time the Puerto Rican fertility rate diminished considerably. By 2000 it had dropped to 1.99; in 2012, it was 1.64.[8]

The case of Puerto Rico suggests that whether you view immigration as a blessing or a curse, you should understand that it may be temporary. As their fertility rates drop below replacement, sending countries cease to become sources of migration. Some day, all of Latin America will probably have a fertility rate like Puerto Rico's. And that day is coming sooner than you think.

Immigration: A Love Story

Our feelings about immigration tend to follow our political leanings, which is fine: immigration is a political issue. But it can be useful to think about it in demographic terms, too.

Migration to America has historically tracked the country's economic health. In the early 1800s, it boomed, peaking at 427,833 immigrants in 1854. When the Civil War broke out, immigration dried up, dropping to 91,918 immigrants in 1861.[9] After the War Between the States ended, it sprang back to life. By the turn of the century, people flocked to America as the Industrial Revolution created unprecedented wealth: Between 1901 and 1910, 8.8 million immigrants arrived. In 1914 alone, 1.2 million immigrants came, seeking refuge from the brewing conflict in Europe. In bad times, immigrants stayed away. During the whole of the 1930s, only 528,431 people came to America. (Every era had its own quotas and legal strictures on immigration, but in general, supply has always outstripped demand.)

After the Great Depression abated, immigration returned in force until, in the 1980s, a new dynamic emerged: people began immigrating in large numbers *illegally* from Mexico and Central and South

America. There had always been stray illegals as part of our migrant mix, but in the 1980s, it became a wholesale industry. Today there are 26.6 million legal immigrants living in America—and (we think) about 11.3 million illegals.[10]

Part of America's immigration story is grounded in economics. But fertility rates play a role, too. As much as other countries are exporting excess labor, we import foreigners to take the place of the workers we didn't make the old-fashioned way. Just as a thought experiment, imagine what the immigration picture would look like today if *Roe v. Wade* hadn't led to 54 million abortions since 1973.[11] Surely, not all of those aborted babies would be in the workforce. But some large portion of them would be, leaving fewer jobs for the 37.9 million immigrants (that's legals plus illegals) who have come in their stead.

America needs immigrants to prop up the entitlement programs we're not having enough babies to fund. In order to keep Social Security and Medicare in operation, we need a stable ratio of workers to retirees. In 2003 a United Nations study suggested that, with the Boomers reaching retirement and our fertility rate quite low, America will need to add a whole lot of immigrants in the coming years. In order to keep the ratio at three workers for every retiree—about where we are now—the UN estimated we would need to add 44.9 million new immigrants between 2025 and 2035.[12] If we wanted to keep the ratio at 5.2 workers for every retiree—about what it was in 1960, before the collapse of the American fertility rate—we'd need to import 10.8 million immigrants a year, every year, until 2050. At which point the U.S. population would be 1.1 billion people, 73 percent of whom would be the descendents of recent immigrants.

Needless to say, this would be a cure worse than the disease. Putting aside questions of culture, cohesiveness, and politics, it would be *logistically impossible* to add 10.8 million immigrants a year. We do not have the housing, the schools, the roads, the sewer capacity, or any other infrastructure necessary to accommodate so massive, and so unrelenting, a wave. As Phillip Longman notes, "such a flow would require the equivalent of building another New York City every ten months or so."[13]

And it's important to remember that immigration—particularly illegal immigration—has other side effects. To pick just one, illegal immigration is often a boon for the middle and upper classes. It provides a steady source of cheap labor—child care and lawn care and strawberries cost less than they would otherwise. But for people in the lower classes, immigration expands the labor pool and depresses wages.[14] (If you're going to welcome illegal immigration, you should do so with your eyes wide open.[15])

Yet at the same time, it's sobering to imagine what America's fertility rate would look like today *without* all of our recent immigrants, both legal and illegal. The TFR for native-born American women was 2.0 in 2011; the TFR for foreign-born women was 2.6.[16] Margaret Sanger and the Malthusians had it wrong: It's not that immigrants are "outbreeding" the natives—it's that the natives would be depopulating themselves into oblivion without the help of immigrants. As I said before: Immigration, at least as America has experienced it, presents many problems—but they are high-class problems. (Europe is a different case; see Christopher Caldwell's definitive book on the subject, *Reflections on the Revolution in Europe*.)

Yet there's a catch: Ultimately, it matters very little whether you think mass immigration is a good or bad thing, because what America thinks about immigration will ultimately be immaterial. You see, there is a supply side to the immigration story, too. Illegal immigrants began streaming over America's southern border in the 1980s for several reasons. America was safer and freer than their homelands. There were more, and better, jobs in the United States. But there was also an enormous surplus of labor in Latin America as a result of high fertility rates. In Mexico, for instance, the fertility rate was 6.72 in 1970. It dropped to 4.71 in 1980; 3.40 in 1990; and 2.58 in 2000.[17] Since 2007 it has hovered around replacement, finally dipping to 2.07 in 2009.[18] You see this trend across the entire Latin American world, from El Salvador to Guatemala. Some South American countries, such as Chile, Costa Rica, and Trinidad and Tobago, are already well below the replacement level.

There is no reason to believe that the example of Puerto Rico will not translate to the rest of Latin America. Fertility rates are generally still higher to our south than they are in America. But the *rate of decline* is steeper. The average fertility rate for Latin America in the 1960s was 6 children per woman; by 2005 that average had dropped to 2.5.[19] Within a decade or two, every single country in Latin America will likely have a fertility rate below that of the United States. And at that point, these countries will have their own labor shortages, meaning emigration from the region may significantly diminish.

The Power of America's One-Child Policy

So in sum: Immigration isn't as good for your demographic profile as baby-making—and it causes lots of problems.[20] Yet we are lucky to have it for as long as it lasts. Think of it as a hedge against our native fertility rate, should we continue down the slope toward Italian or Japanese levels (as Second Demographic Transition theory suggests we will). If the Japanese had immigration, they might not be turning depopulated villages into landfills. Yet there's something demographically disconcerting about America's recent experience with immigration. For all the concerns about Hispanic immigrants not assimilating, in at least one way, they are pulled very quickly into American culture: our one-child regime pushes down their fertility, too.

In 2005 the Center for Immigration Studies released an interesting report: Immigrants to America tended to have higher fertility rates than the countrywomen they left behind. For example, in 2002 the Mexican fertility rate was 2.40. But the fertility rate of Mexican immigrants in America was 3.51.[21] This phenomenon manifested for many source countries. For example, the Canadian fertility rate was 1.51, but Canadian immigrants had a higher rate, too (1.86). Ditto for immigrants from China, Korea, Cuba, El Salvador, and the United Kingdom. *

But here's the trick: The influence of American life on fertility is so irresistible that even these abnormally high-fertility immigrants quickly fall toward the national average. A 2008 study by Emilio Parrado and Philip Morgan shows that Hispanic immigrants start acting like natives pretty quickly.[22] For example, for native non-Hispanic white women, every year of education they attain reduces the average number of children they will have by 5.5 percent. This education effect holds roughly true for Hispanic immigrant women, too—for the first and second generations. But by the third generation, Hispanic Americans are *even more* susceptible to the education effect—each additional year of schooling reduces the number of children they'll have by 6.8 percent. To see the clearest evidence of Hispanic immigrants rushing back toward the mean, you have to look at cohort results, and not cross-sections (a difference I won't burden you with here because I promised we were done with math). Yet the effect is big enough that you can sometimes see it in the cross-sections, too. From 2007 to 2009, the fertility rate fell for all groups of women in America. But it fell fastest for Hispanics.[23] Some subgroups have been dropping faster than others. Among Mexican-born Americans, the birth rate (a cruder measure than the total fertility rate) dropped between 2007 and 2010 by 23 percent. And that's after it had already fallen by 26 percent between 1990 and 2007.[24] The Hispanic fertility rate is still higher than the non-Hispanic white fertility rate. But while the white TFR declined by 3

---

* There are two interesting asides which don't bear directly on our discussion, but are worth mentioning anyway. First, the above numbers are for legal immigrants. Illegal immigrants had an estimated TFR of 3.06. When you control for education and ethnicity, the fertility rate of illegals looks very much like that of generic Hispanic immigrants—meaning that legal status alone does not seem to be much of a factor influencing fertility. Second, immigrants from the Philippines, India, and Vietnam all had much lower fertility rates than their compatriots back home, so the phenomenon is not universal.

percent in two years, the Hispanic rate dropped by 9 percent—three times as fast.

Estimates about how long it will take for Hispanic immigrants to reach the national average vary. The Census Bureau projects that their rates will be indistinguishable from the native rates by 2100.[25] Other demographers peg the Hispanic American fertility rate at 2.1 by 2050.[26] Still others suggest that Hispanic immigrant fertility is *already* close to replacement and the numbers put out by the Census Bureau greatly exceed the observed "completed fertility rate" for Hispanic immigrants, which is already quite close to the national average.[27] (Remember: The total fertility rate is a statistical construct dependent on data, estimation, and mathematical manipulation; the completed fertility rate is a much firmer number, based on tabulated birth records.)

All of this is a good reminder of the limitations of social science. But the objective isn't to predict the precise moment when the fertility of immigrants will have been ground down to native, middle-class levels. It's simply to point out that, sooner or later, that moment will arrive.

Who Wants a Baby?

Immigration is one of the two things we have going for us when it comes to our fertility rate. The other is even better, because it has no downside whatsoever: Americans still want to have babies. This sounds like such a simple thing—who doesn't love babies? They're cute and precious and wonderful. (Even more so if they're not yours.) But it's a much bigger deal than you can imagine.

When sub-replacement fertility was first observed in the West, demographers believed that the situation wasn't as dire as it looked. Since prolonged sub-replacement fertility had never been seen before, the eggheads found it hard to believe that people had simply stopped *wanting* babies. Instead, they thought that modern life, with higher education, employment opportunities for women, and all its consumptive glory, had enticed couples to postpone parenthood until later in life. This postponement, they believed, created a statistical mirage: numbers for the total fertility rate would be lower than actual completed fertility, because women would have babies later in life and closer together, fooling the old TFR models. Demographers assured one another that once this "tempo effect" was fully taken into account, it would be revealed that in Western baby-making, the situation was, more or less, business as usual.

It turns out that the tempo effect is real enough. Women do wait longer to have babies than they used to and, when they have more than one child, they space them closer together. And, yes, this does somewhat distort TFR numbers, making them appear slightly lower than they should be. But the tempo effect does not fully (or mostly, or even in significant part) explain sub-replacement fertility in the industrialized world. At the crudest level, the real explanation for why people no longer have babies is this: They don't want to.

A good indicator of fertility is desired fertility. In many industrialized nations, the notion of the ideal number of children is quite low. (More on this in a moment.) But in America, it is not. As we mentioned earlier, the number of children Americans say is "ideal" has been falling since the 1930s, but since the 1970s it has been reasonably stable and it is—at least in comparison to other first-world countries—still high.

Before we proceed, a couple of notes on fertility ideals: First, men and women have surprisingly similar ideas about how many children are ideal. Studying Americans born between 1957 and 1964, Philip Morgan and Heather Rackin determined that while this group's sense of what constituted "ideal" changed over the course of their lives, men and women had substantially similar ideas at every point.[28] At age 24, for instance, the women thought the ideal was 2.22 children; men thought it was 2.17 children.

Second, there's a difference between "ideal" and "expected" fertility. "Ideal" fertility can be a little mushy. When people are asked in surveys what "ideal" fertility is, they sometimes get pushed down a rabbit hole. Does the question mean "ideal" for the person answering? Or what the person answering thinks *everyone else* thinks is ideal? "Expected" fertility is a much more concrete metric—it means how many children the woman being asked expects to have, when all is said and done. Even so, the two measures typically generate responses that are quite close to one another. But there is a distinction, and expected fertility is, as you'd expect, a more accurate indicator of actual fertility. As one final caveat, consider this: ideal fertility changes for individuals over time. In any given population sample, people at the beginning of family formation will have different ideals and expectations than people toward the end of their childbearing years. For example, in industrialized nations, women aged 35 to 49 have slightly higher ideal fertility numbers than women aged 20 to 34.[29] (This may be something like window-shopper's remorse, as women idealize the children they didn't have.)

So here's the good news: The ideal family size in America is really high. As measured by both Gallup[30] and the General Social Survey[31] Americans think around 2.5 children is ideal. The even better news is that this ideal has been fairly steady for 40 years.[32]

That doesn't mean that our picture of "ideal" hasn't changed, though, because beneath the top-line number, the data have moved around quite a bit. Two children has been the plurality preference since 1970, when the GSS started measuring. Back then, 40 percent of Americans said two kids was ideal, while 25 percent preferred three children and 21 percent wanted four of them.[33] In the 1980s and 1990s, the percentage of people who viewed zero or one child as ideal more than doubled, while the percentage who idealized four (or more) kids dropped by more than half. But these changes were offset by growth in the numbers of people who thought that two kids were ideal. All of that aside, the fact that we still want to have more children than the replacement rate is encouraging—as is the fact that this desire has persisted for nearly half a century, even as modern life was conspiring to make family life more difficult and more costly.

And not only are our ideal fertility numbers encouraging—so are our expected fertility numbers, which match up almost exactly with our actual fertility. Americans expect to have just about two kids each, and they get just about two kids each.[34] I know what you're thinking—this is the dumbest statistic you've ever heard. *Of course* actual fertility is going to be closely related to expected fertility. Except that it doesn't work out that way for everyone. In the United Kingdom, ideal is 2.5, expected 2.3—and actual is 1.9. In Greece, ideal fertility is 2.3, expected fertility is 2.1, and actual fertility clocks in at a ghastly 1.4.[35] In most developed countries, both ideal *and* expected fertility are far ahead of the actual numbers. This is a symptom of deep structural problems with family formation and childbearing—even deeper than the lowest-low TFRs suggest by themselves.

Statistical Hocus Pocus

Unfortunately, every silver lining has a cloud. In 1979 a unique survey, the National Longitudinal Survey of Youth, began. The study used a sample of almost 13,000 American kids between the ages of 14 and 22 and asked them all sorts of questions. The survey then followed this same group through the years, revisiting them and asking follow-up questions, to see how their attitudes had changed and their lives had turned out. The survey opened a window into what our ideal fertility numbers really mean at the individual level.

What the survey showed was that the sync between Americans' expected and actual fertility numbers is really a just a trick of mathematics. Yes, on *average*, American women have almost exactly the number of children they expect to—on average women fell just 0.25 children short of their target and men 0.40 children short. But that's because most people were either having more, or fewer, children than they intended. Nearly 60 percent of people missed their mark. And it's only the *averaging* of all these mistakes that makes it look like everything is going according to Hoyle.

For example, the completed fertility numbers in the survey were about what we'd expect: Women with less than a high school education had 2.55 children; women with a bachelor's degree or more had 1.67 children. But both these groups largely missed the number of children they intended to have. The less-educated women wound up with more children than they had hoped for. The more-educated women wound up with fewer. How many fewer? If a woman went to college, she had 0.54 fewer children than she said she wanted.

The study results bore out pretty much every lesson we've learned so far about how college, delayed marriage, delayed childbirth, and increased divorce have impacted fertility. A woman who had a child before the age of 24 was likely to achieve or exceed her fertility goal. By contrast, a woman who was childless at 24 was 8.4 times more likely to have fewer children than she wanted. As you would expect, marriage is an important driver, too. People who were married by 24 were likely to hit their targets, so long as they stayed married. Divorce made it twice as likely that women would not have as many children as they wanted.

So all of that happy talk about our ideal and expected fertility numbers needs to be tempered a bit by the realization that it's a precarious achievement. It's based on a statistical illusion and all the trends in modern life—more college education, cohabitation, later marriage—will probably broaden the rift between intentions and results.

Leading? Or Lagging? (Plus, more doom.)

There's another caution about ideal fertility and it points toward the possibility of real doom. It's long been assumed that people's notions of ideal fertility lead and shape behavior when it comes to having their own children. After all, that's the obvious assumption. But it's possible that, at the societal level, the "ideal" numbers might actually be *lagging* indicators, which are *shaped by* actual fertility. If this turns out to be the case, it would mean that the trap of lowest-low fertility is even more insidious than we first thought.

Demographers have always believed that as societies developed, people downsized their ideas of how large a family should be. It was these reduced expectations, the thinking went, that led people to have fewer babies. Yet while actual fertility might sink quite low if people were unable to attain their family goals, demographers believed that ideal fertility would always be at (or just above) two children per woman. The reasoning behind this (enormous) assumption was that for as long as sociologists had been asking the ideal question in the developed world, two children was always the most common response.

But in 2001, demographers were shocked to find that in two European countries, Austria and Germany, the ideal fertility rate had fallen to 1.7.[36] Like lowest-low fertility itself, a sub-replacement ideal had never been seen before. Europe was in uncharted territory again.

Searching for an explanation, researchers examined the sub-replacement ideals in Austria and Germany. None of the usual suspects fit. It wasn't driven by bad economics—Austria and Germany had lower unemployment rates than most other European countries. It wasn't delayed family formation—the age of first birth in the two countries was younger than it was for most of the rest of the continent. And it wasn't total fertility—while Austria and Germany had very low fertility rates, they were still higher than Spain, Italy, and Greece, all of which had lower TFRs and higher ideals than Austria and Germany. There was, however, one thing that stuck out.

While Austria and Germany's fertility rates weren't the lowest in Europe, these two countries were the *first* European countries to fall below the replacement rate. Which led demographers to a disturbing hypothesis: What if people derived their "ideal" family size by looking around them and intuiting the societal norms? After a country has seen lowest-low fertility for a generation, people might view sub-replacement as normal, because it's everywhere around them. And they might then adjust their own ideals downward. Perhaps the reason Austria and Germany saw their ideal numbers go below replacement was simply because they had been sub-replacement the longest. If this theory was correct, then we would eventually expect ideal family size to go sub-replacement in other European countries, too.

Since then, we've seen mixed data. A 2006 Eurobarometer study claimed that everything was just fine. Germany's ideal family size number had miraculously jumped back up—all the way to 2.18—in just five years.[37] But other European nations have been slowly slipping, with the Czech Republic, Italy, and Romania joining Austria in having sub-replacement ideal numbers. Another trial conducted around the same time showed drastically different results. The Population Policy Acceptance Study reported that Germany and Austria still had sub-replacement ideals.[38] But now Belgium, Italy, the Czech Republic, Lithuania, and Slovenia did, too. (Fun fact: In the PPAS poll, 23 percent of German men said that "zero" children was the ideal family size.)

So depending on which data you believe, lowest-low fertility in Europe is either slowly undermining notions of ideal fertility or dragging it off a cliff. Pick your poison. Either way, it looks as though our understanding of ideal fertility may have to be reassessed. We used to think of it as a potential savior. *If we could just help people achieve their ideals, then even a country experiencing lowest-low could dig itself out of a hole.* But the loop might actually run in the other direction. When people grow up in a world without babies, they might stop wanting babies for themselves. Even in the abstract ideal.

The whole concept of "ideal" fertility suggests a certain remove from the real world, a realm of vague, half-expressed ideas and desires. But it's having a very real effect on American life. For good or for ill, fertility is shaping nearly everything in our national conversation.

CHAPTER SEVEN

Domestic Politics, Foreign Policy

On Halloween night in 2004, my wife and I strolled lazily through Old Town. The coffee shops had cobwebs strewn across their doorways. Lee Street, site of the town's oldest and fanciest houses, was closed to traffic so trick-or-treaters could marvel at the elaborate decorations and haunted-house installations. There were trees that looked alive. Fog floated down to the sidewalk from front porches. Bach's *Toccata and Fugue in D Minor* was piped in from speakers inside one house; others had a playlist of screams and groans and haunting sounds emanating from open windows. Ghouls merrily guarded large baskets of candy on the doorsteps. The only things out of place were the signs: "Kerry-Edwards: 2004." They were everywhere. In windows. On doors. There were—I'm not making this up—several jack-o-lanterns with the slogan carved into them. Dressed as Clark Kent and Supergirl, my wife and I walked Old Town nearly end to end that night. We saw one placard posted for George W. Bush, who would, if you'll recall, win the election by more than 3 million votes.

He didn't do so well in our neck of the woods. John Kerry carried Old Town 67 percent to 32 percent.[1]

There's no structural reason our neighborhood, a suburb of the nation's capital, should be such a Democratic stronghold. Washington, D.C. is a company town, and no matter who's in power, there are always about an equal number of elephants and donkeys roaming the metropolis. The close-in suburbs, in particular, are havens for the kinds of political transients who come and go with the government. In 2004, Virginia was a reasonably Republican state. George W. Bush won the election by 2.4 points nationally, but he was up by 8 in Virginia.

Yet somehow Democrats had found one another in Old Town, and transformed it into a little gated community of their own. And it turns out that in this regard at least, Old Town is quite ordinary. For the last 30 years, people across America have been turning their cities and towns into politically monolithic sanctuaries. This development is a striking departure from our country's history. And it has a lot to do with fertility.

Sticking With Our Own Kind

In their 2008 book, *The Big Sort*, Bill Bishop and Robert Cushing crunched the numbers on places like Old Town.[2] They looked at election data at the county level, searching for counties where one party was dominant over the other. In 1976, only 26.8 percent of the counties in America went for either Jimmy Carter or Gerald Ford by a margin of 20 points or more.[3] That's a pretty remarkable statistic: The 1976 election was an incredibly polarized moment, with the country shaken by Watergate and Nixon's resignation. Carter won, 50 percent to 48 percent, and in three out of every four counties, the vote was reasonably close, which meant that Republicans and Democrats were, for the most part, pretty evenly interspersed at the local level, even if, in the aggregate, their state tilted one way or the other.

But after 1976, something happened. As people began graduating from college at higher rates they became increasingly mobile and willing to put down roots far away from where they were raised. And they began to cluster around other like-minded people. So much so that in 2000, America had one of the closest presidential elections in the nation's history: George W. Bush won the race despite losing the popular vote to Al Gore, 47.9 percent to 48.4 percent. Yet in nearly half of the counties in America (45.3 percent of them) the vote wasn't close at all: Either Gore or Bush won by more than 20 points. In 2004—another very close election—the percentage of what Bishop and Cushing refer to as "landslide" counties increased to 48.3 percent. The end result is fewer neighborhoods that are ideologically mixed and more places that look like Old Town (or its Republican doppelgänger). Bishop and Cushing's conclusion is inescapable: We are sorting ourselves into little communities of the saved.

This sorting is not an accident. It is the result of conscious migration. Every year, more than 10 million Americans move from one county to another.[4] (In the last five years, the number of people moving has declined, but it's unclear how much of this is real behavioral change and how much is simply due to the housing market collapse and subsequent recession.[5])

Over time, our increased mobility allowed people to find islands of those with similar lifestyles and, consequently, politics. Between 1976 and 2004 the margin of victory for the winning party increased in two-thirds of America's counties—far more than you would expect if people were migrating randomly.[6] But very few people consciously look for political camaraderie when they move. What they look for is, for lack of a better word, culture. They want to be near people who share their interests and values. Do the neighbors use environmentally conscious lawn products? Do they go to yoga? Or to church? Are there golf courses or playgrounds, mass-transit options or hipster gastropubs? What are the schools like? Drive around a neighborhood tallying up these little cultural markers and you can get a pretty good sense of the politics of the people living there. You didn't need to see the John Kerry signs in Old Town to know it was a Democratic bastion—the coffee shops and doggie salons gave it away.

In that sense, voting patterns are really just a lagging indicator showing what people are doing for other reasons. Because this sorting happens even in what you might think of as already homogenous places. For instance, Utah is a wildly Republican state. Yet in recent years, downtown Salt Lake City has slowly been sorting itself out. Even though Mormons make up a majority in the Salt Lake area, they've been gradually leaving the city core as it's become more religiously diverse. What happened is this: The few non-Mormons in the area clustered in Salt Lake, prompting the Mormons to move out. The city core area lost a net of 5,000 Mormons in five years.[7] Those formerly urban Mormons have moved to the suburbs, making these outlying areas even more homogenous than they already were. (As a result, voting has followed the same pattern: Suburban counties have become even more dominantly Republican, while Salt Lake City itself actually went Democratic in 2008—by 300 votes—for the first time in almost half a century.[8])

But we still must go deeper. After all, what cultural marker do the yoga studios and pet boutiques and macrobiotic bistros really signify? More than money or education or religious affiliation they mean one thing: *childlessness*. And perhaps the biggest lesson of the Big Sort is that people with larger families seek each other out, just as surely as people with small (or no) families find each other, too. Family formation drives not just political differences (as we saw in Chapter 1) but also geographic preference. It's probably not a coincidence that the Big Sort began after 1976, just as the effects of the fertility bust were manifesting.

In a paper exploring the electoral effects of the Second Demographic Transition, Ron Lesthaeghe and his colleague Lisa Neidert looked at America's 3,141 counties using 22 markers of family formation, including mean age at first birth, the percent of never-married women aged 30 to 34, and the total fertility rate.[9] They found that, at the county level, these markers correlate with the percentage of the vote George W. Bush received in 2000 and 2004 in precisely the way

Bishop and Cushing saw: The greater the family formation scale, the more likely the county was to be a landslide for Bush and vice versa. When you get to the state level, the data are even more striking: in 2000 and 2004, you could predict whether a state went for Bush almost entirely by looking at the white fertility rate. Steve Sailer found a 0.86 correlation between the two.[10]

A House Divided

All of this geographic and ideological sorting has real-world consequences in American politics. Back in the years after World War II, Congress was filled with politicians who were, by objective measures, fairly moderate.[11] There were conservative Democrats and liberal Republicans, and until the early '60s, more than 40 percent of House members counted as moderates by their voting records. That number stayed at about the same level until 1976, when it began dropping, hard. Politicians began rallying around the two ideological poles until, by 2005, only 8 percent of House members were moderate.[12]

Goo-goo idealists like to shake their heads over the terrible, awful, no-good polarization of America. They look wistfully at the golden past, as if the '70s were an era of thoughtful, sober, mature politics. Which is nonsense, of course. Our political culture is, at the *individual* level, basically what it always was. But as an electoral matter, it's undeniable that changes at the *aggregate* level have affected our elected politicians.

As William Voegeli writes, "Throughout the 20th century many politicians and scholars considered the ideological heterogeneity of America's two main political parties both offensive and absurd."[13] Political debate was often as vicious as it is today, but there were conservative Democrats, liberal Republicans, and everything in between. The difference is that today we have one purely liberal party and one purely conservative party. This change is not the result of a conspiracy or some coarsening of modern life. It's because of Bishop's Big Sort: As counties became more monolithic, they elected more ideological representatives.

We don't have as many moderate congressmen as we used to because we don't have as many politically balanced neighborhoods. It's not that individual people have become more stridently ideological than they used to be. It's that they've grouped themselves geographically in such a way that the poles no longer cancel one another out when it comes time to vote.

Changes in fertility have altered the fundamental dynamics of American politics. We have always had ideological divides on questions such as war or abortion. But now these divides are both ideological *and* partisan. There are no more pro-life Democrats or Republican doves. This evolution makes it harder to achieve consensus and allows our fights to drag on and on, without resolution. And if you think fertility has changed how we conduct domestic affairs, wait until you see how other people's fertility is shaping our foreign affairs.

When You're a Superpower, Other People's Fertility Matters, Too

The forces of demography are pushing every nation on earth in the same direction: fewer and fewer children. You see some causal factors—such as education, divorce, and cohabitation—at work in many nations. Other factors—such as alcoholism in Russia, of which more anon—are country-specific. And in addition to our own problems, America has to worry about these foreign fertility trends, too.

In June 2009, Iran held what was universally predicted to be a sham presidential election. Radical Islamist incumbent Mahmoud Ahmadinejad was pitted against the slightly-less-radical Islamist Mir Hossein Mousavi. To the surprise of no one, the ruling regime announced highly suspect results two hours after the voting was completed. Yet people across the world were surprised the next day when hundreds of thousands of disaffected Iranians took to the streets to protest the outcome. Befuddled by the display, Western governments were caught flat-footed. They shouldn't have been. Because if you view the world through the lens of fertility, Iran showed every sign of being a powder-keg.

Iran's Youth Bulge

The Iranian fertility story reads like the rest of the world's, only more so. Thirty years ago, Iran's fertility rate was 6.5. Today, not even two generations later, it is 1.88.[14] This dramatic reduction has a number of consequences. First, it means that Iran will experience population decline within 40 years. Because the fertility rate did not fall slowly, the country has no demographic momentum to keep population on the slow growth line that most Western countries are seeing. Demographic momentum can buy a country time to devise a strategy for managing contraction. But in Iran, the trap will spring shut around 2050, when the country will begin to shed millions of warm bodies.

Second, Iran's demographic momentum has created a grossly distorted age structure within the population. Today, Iran's median age is 27 years. A gargantuan 24.1 percent of its population is under 14; only 5.0 percent is over 65. This is what German demographer Gunnar Heinsohn calls a "youth bulge." And Heinsohn makes a compelling case that youth bulges are historically linked to conflict.[15]

Heinsohn's theory goes something like this: A surplus of young adults—particularly adult males—leads to rampant competition for jobs. This in turn leads to higher levels of unemployment, downward pressure on wages, and poverty. All of which leads to social failure—specifically the inability to marry. Throughout history, unemployed and unmarried young men have always been trouble. If there are a handful of them, they turn to crime. When they comprise a giant cohort, they resort to revolution. One study shows that between 1970 and 1999, 80 percent of civil conflicts occurred in countries where 60 percent or more of the population was under the age of 30. Countries with youth bulges were twice as likely to experience civil violence during the 1990s.[16]

History is rife with examples of youth bulges gone bad. From eighteenth-century France to the Balkans in 1914 to Japan's invasion of China in the 1930s to the Marxist insurrections in Latin America during the 1970s and 1980s—all were fueled in large part by too many young men without enough work.[17] Iran is a case study in the youth bulge. Heinsohn calculates that a society is in danger when 15- to 30-year-olds make up 30 percent of the population. Thirty-six percent of Iran's population is in that cohort right now.[18]

These young Iranians do not have particularly bright economic prospects. Oil is, far and away, Iran's leading industry—it accounts for 80 percent of the country's exports and something like a fifth of every Iranian's income. But Iran's output of crude has plateaued while its demand has risen. With questionable reserves, it's possible that as soon as 2020, Iran may no longer have an oil export business.[19] The country's other leading exports are fruits, nuts, and carpets. Its only industries of note are textiles, cement, and food processing. Already, Iran's economy is fraying at the seams. In 2002, 40 percent of the population was below the poverty line. The Iranian government's own (rosy) projection puts unemployment at 15 percent. (It is likely double that, and even higher among the young.) Inflation was at 12 percent in 2006 and has, by all accounts, risen since.

Once you understand Iran's demographic instability, the post-election uprising makes a great deal of sense. As do the ruling regime's strategic moves over the last several years. Much has been made about Mahmoud Ahmadinejad's outlandish presidency, full of threats and provocations. In particular, Westerners seem beguiled by Iran's seemingly irrational pursuit of nuclear weapons. From the Iranian perspective, however, this course makes perfect strategic sense.

Iran's current youth bulge will be its last. By 2050, 30 percent of Iran's population will be composed of elderly dependents. A dwindling number of younger workers will be forced to support them. In wealthy, First World countries, such situations lead to earnest discussions about pension benefits and tax rates. In Third World countries, they lead to violence. It is one thing to be old and rich; being old and poor is quite another.

This is why President Ahmadinejad went to great trouble relocating millions of Iranians from rural villages to cities, where they can be more easily controlled (as evidenced by how efficiently the 2009

uprising was put down). From a geostrategic perspective, Iran's leaders surely understand that the country's weak position will become
progressively weaker, leading to ruin. Its only hope lies in the prospect
of expansion: Southeast Iraq, Saudi Arabia (where Shiites dominate
the oil-rich eastern region), and the United Arab Emirates all present
attractive targets, with ample oil reserves and potentially sympathetic
populations. Empire is Iran's most logical path to salvation.

After all, with economic ruin on the horizon, and a demographic
catastrophe in progress, they have nothing to lose in a conflict, other
than several million military-aged men who, left to their own devices,
might become revolutionaries instead of soldiers. Iran must either use
its youth bulge to conquer a neighbor, or use war with a neighbor to
thin out its youth bulge.

Of course, if Iran were to attempt to establish regional hegemony,
it would face the wrath of the United States and (what remains of) the
Western powers, much as Saddam Hussein did in 1990. That is, unless
they have a nuclear deterrent. When you game it out, Iran would be
foolish *not* to try for nuclear weapons. Its fertility rate and economic
reality practically demand it.

It is impossible to understand the workings of the Middle East
without taking into account youth bulges. The chaos of the Palestinian territories is partly due to an enormous youth bulge. The *median*
age in the Gaza Strip is 15.8 years and 49 percent of all adults in the
territories are between 15 and 30 years old. And there is an even larger
youth cohort coming up behind them—*42 percent* of the entire population is under 15.[20] Anyone who has negotiated with a teenager will
understand, then, why seeking a peaceful reconciliation between Israelis
and Palestinians is maddeningly difficult.

Look for youth bulges in other Middle Eastern countries and
you'll see a Who's Who of problem states: Yemen's median age is 18.1
years, with 43 percent of the population under the age of 15.[21] Little
wonder the country is a hotbed of radical extremism and violence.
Making Yemen even more worrisome is the fact that its fertility rate
is still booming, clipping along at 4.63. Syria's median age is slightly

older, 21.9 years, and only 35.2 percent of its population is under 15.[22] This explains why the country is in a constant state of belligerence toward its neighbors: If the autocratic regime doesn't give its young men an object to work against, they might look inward. By contrast, the pacific United Arab Emirates has a median age of 30.2 years.[23]

China: A Paper Dragon

The Middle East may be America's perpetual problem, but China is our largest strategic challenge. Increasingly urban and advanced, China is an economic power with expansive military ambition. It's not just the mind-boggling public works projects and glittering modernist structures. The People's Liberation Army has been building out its submarine force for decades. Once upon a time the Chinese purchased Russian *Kilo*-class subs, but in recent years they birthed their own program. In the last decade they've also quietly developed the J-20, a fifth-generation fighter plane, which is an enormously expensive undertaking. (There are only three other serious fifth-generation fighter programs in the world; the R&D price tag for two of them, the F-22 and F-35, was upward of $65 billion each.[24]) A fifth-generation fighter in the Far East has only one purpose: to act as a counterweight to American air power. And China has finally embarked on the costliest of all military endeavors—the creation of a blue-water navy to project power. In June 2011, China announced that it had begun construction on its first aircraft carrier.[25] Each of these moves suggests that China has the economic and military capital to compete with America in the medium-term future.

But the structure of China's human capital is a very different matter. We've talked already about how China's population will soon get very old and then begin to rapidly contract: By 2050, the country's population will be falling by 20 million every five years; one out of every four citizens will be over the age of 65.

If you keep the fertility rate as your lodestar, China's challenge for America takes a very different form. Far from worrying about the

Chinese economy overtaking America's, or China becoming a regional hegemon, we should be preparing to manage a suddenly weakened and unstable China. We mentioned it earlier but it's worth restating: China didn't get around to setting up a pension system until 2000. The Chinese entitlement scheme is even worse than America's: It covers only 365 million Chinese citizens and it is already unfunded to the tune of 150 percent of the country's GDP.[26] Remember the dictum that as the age distribution of a society inverts, labor shortages are created? China is already experiencing its first labor shortages in the manual labor sectors and is preparing for a coming crunch in manufacturing.

In addition to all of the other problems China's One-Child Policy has wrought, it has created a dangerous sex imbalance. Normally, 105 boys are born for every 100 girls. But in China (and certain other countries, mostly in the Far East) sex-selective abortion has played havoc with that ratio. China now has 123 boys born for every 100 girls.[27]

The inevitable result of this is a large cohort of men who—as a matter of mathematics—cannot marry. The world has seen sex imbalances before. From ancient Athens to Bleeding Kansas to China's Taiping Rebellion, a skewed sex ratio has often preceded intense violence and instability.[28] So in addition to everything else, the Chinese will have a large cohort of military-aged, unmarried men—tens of millions of them—floating around at precisely the moment when the country is facing the burden of its uncared-for elderly.

As if all of this weren't daunting enough for China's leaders, there's no obvious way out of the trap One-Child has created. Even if the Chinese government dismantled this regime tomorrow, the Chinese people have fallen into the same habits Austrians and Germans have: After a generation of fertility rates near lowest-low, even the fertility *ideal* in China is now sub-replacement. In 2006 a study was conducted in Jiangsu province, one of the few areas where, under certain circumstances, women are officially allowed to have two children. When surveyed, 55 percent of the women there said that one child was best. The average ideal number of children was 1.46.[29]

All of which suggests that what America needs to prepare for in the coming decades is not a shooting war with an expansionist China, but a declining superpower with a rapidly contracting economic base and an unstable political structure. It's not clear which scenario is more worrisome.

The Sick Man of Europe

Like the election protests in Iran, the emergence of Russia's Vladimir Putin in 2000 also took the Western foreign-policy establishment by surprise. At the time, it was widely assumed that that while Russia was poor and sometimes corrupt, it was nevertheless on its way toward economic modernization and political harmony. In 1999 you would have been hard-pressed to find a policy analyst who thought that Russia would shortly be headed back toward authoritarianism and confrontation with the West. But the underlying demographics of Russia should have been warning enough.

Russia has experienced population decline three times during the last century. Each period was marked by crisis. The first depopulation came from 1917 to 1923, as the Russian Empire was overthrown and the Soviet Union was forged.[30] The second came during 1933 and 1934 as Joseph Stalin collectivized the country's farmers, resulting in millions of deaths. The third came during World War II, which cost the lives of 25 million Russians. (Remember: No nation has experienced long-term prosperity in the face of contracting population.)

As demographer Nicholas Eberstadt reports, after the Soviet Union collapsed in 1991, something completely unexpected happened to Russian fertility. During the last 16 years of Soviet power, there were 36 million Russian births. As soon as Russians became free they suddenly, and without any explanation, stopped making babies. In the first 16 post-Soviet years, there were only 22.3 million births.[31]

Fertility rates were already low in the dying days of the Soviet Union, hovering around 2.0. So by the time the Wall fell, the country had very little demographic momentum. For a brief moment under

Gorbachev, the fertility rate surged to 2.2, but after 1989 it imploded. By 1999 it was 1.17; since then it has ticked upward to 1.3. Today, the country's population is falling by 200,000 a year, and that loss rate is speeding up. In 2005, Russia had 143 million people; by 2025, it's projected to be down to 136 million.[32] Or worse—the low-ball projection sees the nation falling to 121 million.

No one knows what is driving Russians toward national suicide. It seems to be a combination of factors. On the fertility side of the equation, patterns of family formation have changed dramatically since the end of the Soviet Union. Many couples choose long-term cohabitation as an alternative to marriage. In 1980, only 11 percent of births were to unwed mothers; by 2005 that number had shot up to 30 percent.[33] Divorce has skyrocketed—Russia has the world's highest divorce rate.[34] Abortion is rampant, with more than one abortion performed for every two live births. Even that's an improvement over recent history: for decades, Russians had *more than twice as many abortions as births*.[35] This might be the most grisly statistic the world has ever seen. It suggests a society that lacked the will to live.

But mixed with Russia's fertility problems are mortality problems. The Russian people are, literally, sick. The average life expectancy in Russia is only 66 years, behind Azerbaijan and just ahead of North Korea. It is lower for Russians now than it was in the 1950s.[36] A 20-year-old Russian man today has less than a 50–50 chance of living to age 65. The causes of death in Russia are so numerous as to suggest social catastrophe. From infant mortality to AIDS to heart disease to violent death, Russia doesn't resemble Eastern Europe so much as sub-Saharan Africa. But Africans have to contend with civil conflicts and infectious diseases; in Russia a colossal factor driving the mortality rate is simple alcoholism.[37]

Such countries are not led by polite technocrats. If Vladimir Putin did not exist, the Russian people would have invented him. Russia faces something like extinction, or at least transformation into a society that will be unrecognizable to the Russian people. The country has very little to lose, which is why, far from letting himself be lectured at by the "community of nations" on matters we deem bad behavior, Putin has been aggressive and confrontational. Whether it is the assassination of journalists, or wars in Chechnya and Georgia, or Putin's brazen return to the presidency, Russia has behaved like a wounded bear. Strong countries do what they can; the weak do what they must. However, Russia's fertility problem has been around for a very, very long time.

CHAPTER EIGHT

Losing Battles (What Not to Do)

In 1944, the Soviet Union was boot-deep in war, its young men being ground up at a gruesome rate. Over the course of six years the Russians lost some 10 million servicemen and 15 million civilians. Joseph Stalin knew that even if Russia survived the confrontation with Nazi Germany, it would bleed to death demographically in the years that followed. That is, unless he could coax babies—lots and lots of babies—from the wombs of Soviet women. So on July 8, Comrade Stalin announced the creation of the Motherhood Medal, given to any woman who bore at least six children. The medal was easier to win in theory than it was in practice.

Mothers became eligible for the medal only on the first birthday of their sixth child. And the first five children needed to be alive at that moment, too—no small miracle in a backward, war-torn country. (Stalin allowed that if a child died in service to the state, he still counted as being alive.) Amazingly, 4 million first-class Motherhood Medals were handed out before the Soviet Union collapsed, along with 8 million of the second-class versions, which required only five children.

The Motherhood Medal was merely the beginning of the Soviets' glorious people's fertility revolution. In 1955, Nikita Khrushchev called Western worries about overpopulation a "cannibalistic theory" invented by "bourgeois ideology."[1] He went on:

> Their concern is to cut down the birth rate, reduce the rate of population increase. It is quite different with us, comrades. If about 100 million people were added to our 200 million, even that would not be enough.[2]

The Politburo offered lump-sum payments for the birth of children. Then it increased state benefits for families with children, including bonuses for housing and work allowances.[3] In 1981 it offered women a full year of partially paid leave for having a baby.[4] In 1986 it upped the ante to a year-and-a-half's worth of leave.

None of which helped. The fertility rate in the Soviet Union declined throughout the 1950s and 1960s. By the 1970s it was sub-replacement.[5] The only upward spike came in the late 1980s. But even as the end of communism lifted the Iron Curtain, it blew the bottom out of Russian fertility.[6] As noted earlier, by 1999 it was 1.17, a cataclysmic level.

The new, democratic Russia has also pushed women to have babies. In 2006, President Putin doubled the government's monthly support payments for children and created a $9,200 bonus payment to mothers who have a second baby.[7] (Keep in mind that Russia's per-capita GDP was $10,700 in 2006.[8]) That was just the start. Putin declared 2008 "The Year of the Family." September 12 was established as "Family Contact Day"—the idea being that young Russian couples skip work and make boom-boom in pursuit of fabulous prizes. The companion to "Family Contact Day" was "Russia Day," exactly nine months later. Women who "Gave Birth to a Patriot" on Russia Day were guaranteed a selection of gifts, including refrigerators, TV sets, and washing machines. The grand prize was a new SUV.[9]

Public-service announcements linking childbearing to patriotism are plastered across urban areas in Russia. National parks have been re-landscaped to include loveseat-like benches. Another holiday—"The Day of Family, Love, and Fidelity"—was established for July 8.[10] The result of Russia's 65-year campaign to encourage babies? An anemic fertility rate of 1.54.

Russia is not the first country to fail to convince its citizens to have more children. Social engineering long predates the modern state. In ancient Sparta, fathers who sired three sons were exempted from garrison duty and those with four lads to their name paid no taxes at all.[11] Caesar Augustus levied a "bachelor tax" on unmarried aristocratic men. The English briefly toyed with a bachelor tax of their own in 1695 (though this was more for the purpose of raising war funds than encouraging baby-making). Worried about German fecundity, the French levied a bachelor tax during the First World War. And in 1927 Mussolini imposed a tax—ranging from 0.5 percent to a whopping 5.0 percent of income—on all unmarried men between the ages of 25 and 65. His goal was to create a "demographic jolt" for the new fascist state.[12] None of these attempts was successful.

So influencing a country's fertility rate is awfully hard. People have been trying for 2,000 years, mostly with abject failure. If America is to solve its fertility problems, we should start by understanding what didn't work for other countries. The encyclopedia of pro-natalist failure is long, but, for our purposes, the modern examples of Japan, the European Union, and Singapore are particularly instructive.

Japan's Robot Babies

In Japan, they don't have Motherhood Medals. They have, of course, robots. In 2010, a group of engineers from Tsukuba University built Yotaro, the robot baby.[13] Yotaro has an oversize head with big, puffy cheeks and light-filled eyes. When you shake a rattle near him, he kicks his feet in response. Yotaro's silicone skin is warm and soft. You can cuddle him and his facial expressions change as he becomes cranky or content. His nose runs with body-temperature saline. The idea behind Yotaro is that he might help young Japanese couples discover how enjoyable and rewarding it is to care for an infant and, with a little luck, coax them into having children of their own. The entire Yotaro project would be hysterically funny if it weren't so sad.

Fertility concerns in Japan are long-running and acute. The country's population peaked in 2004 and is already contracting. By 2050, it will have fallen from 127.8 million to somewhere in the vicinity of 100 million.[14] And that's just the beginning. The UN's rosy scenario has the country hitting 91 million by 2100. But if Japan's fertility rate stays where it is now, the projection drops to 56 million, a decline of 56 percent. This contraction will bring a host of economic problems, beginning with the collapse of Japan's welfare state.[15] In 1975 Japan had eight workers for every one retiree. By 2005, that ratio fell to 3.3 workers for each retiree. In 2055, it will be a thoroughly unsustainable 1.3 workers for every one retiree. How rare are babies? In 2011, for the first time, people in Japan bought more adult diapers than they did diapers for babies. It will likely continue to be this way for the foreseeable future.[16] In 2040, there will likely be one Japanese citizen over the age of 100 for every baby born.[17] None of this has escaped notice in the Land of the Rising Sun.

In 1972, Japan's fertility rate was still above replacement, sitting at 2.14. But the government had a sense of what the country was up against and introduced a monthly per-child subsidy for parents.[18] Over the years, Japan has tinkered with this subsidy, altering the amount and raising the age allowance. None of which made much difference: The fertility rate fell at a steady pace, to 1.76 by 1985.[19] Five years later, it was lower still (1.54) causing the government to form a committee charged with "Creating a sound environment for bearing and rearing children." The following year, the government passed a Childcare Leave Act aimed at helping working mothers.

In 1994, the government announced another scheme, this one a four-year "Angel Plan" (officially known as the "Basic Direction for Future Childrearing Support Measures"). The primary goal of the Angel Plan was to establish a network of day-care centers. In 1995, the Childcare Leave Act was superseded by a "Childcare and Family Care Leave Act" and in 1999, the government trotted out a "New Angel Plan," which added more day-care centers and expanded after-school sports and activities programs. The sole goal of these measures was to keep kids looked after between the end of the school day and the end of the work day, when their mothers finally arrived home from the office.

In 2002, the government unveiled yet another scheme, the "Plus One Plan." It was the result of a study which concluded that women were having fewer babies because Japanese fathers weren't doing enough of the work. Among other things, Plus One insisted that fathers take a whopping *five-day* paternity leave upon the birth of a child. The next year, Japan passed the "Law for Basic Measures to Cope with a Declining Fertility Society," followed two years later by the "Law for Measures to Support the Development of the Next Generation." Among the initiatives encompassed by these laws was a provision that required any business with more than 300 employees to create a "plan" for raising the fertility level of its workers.

Japanese Pro-Natalist Policies		
TFR	*Year*	*Action*
2.14	1972	Establishment of child allowances
1.54	1990	Establishment of inter-ministry committee on "Creating a sound environment for bearing and rearing children"
1.53	1991	Childcare Leave Act
1.50	1994	Announcement of Angel Plan for 1995–99
1.42	1995	Enactment of Childcare and Family Care Leave Act
1.34	1999	Announcement of New Angel Plan for 2000–04
1.33	2001	Amendment to the Employment Insurance Law, specifying 40 percent of salary to be paid to regular full-time employees during childcare leave
1.32	2002	Announcement of "Plus One" plan
1.29	2003	Enactment of "Next Generation" law Enactment of law on "Basic Measures to Cope with a Declining Fertility Society"

Source: Robert D. Retherford and Naohiro Ogawa, "Japan's Baby Bust," East-West Center Working Papers (http://www.eastwestcenter.org/fileadmin/stored/pdfs/POPwp118.pdf).

This encyclopedia's worth of plans, laws, and measures was doomed to fail. For one thing, Japan's federal government was, in many cases, simply issuing mandates instructing local governments and private employers to figure out a way to raise fertility. But even on their own terms, these pass-the-buck mandates were useless, because they lacked either incentives or penalties. For example, the law that "required" employers with more than 300 workers to create plans for raising the fertility levels of workers had no penalty whatsoever for companies that ignored it. The only benefit for companies that did bother to comply—which, remember, meant coming up with a plan, not actually raising fertility—was that they were allowed to display an official pink government logo on company letterhead and advertising materials. (The cutesy logo looked a little bit like—I'm not making this up—the "Hello Kitty" icon.)

Today the Japanese are getting somewhat bolder in their policy choices. In Japan's 2009 election, the two rival parties tried to out-bid one another on pro-natalist policies. The ruling Liberal-Democrat party proposed making the day-care system universal and free. It was defeated by the insurgent Democratic party, which promised a dramatic and immediate increase in the child subsidy, from $100 a month to $280 a month.[20] It is too early to know if this plan will work, although Japan's fertility rate seems to have increased slightly to 1.39.[21] Even so, in the face of 40 years of failure, this latest inducement seems unlikely to succeed.

The futility of this cascade of action is striking: With each attempt to raise fertility, Japan's TFR actually dropped further. How could that be? Perhaps because nearly all of Japan's pro-natalist initiatives were government-driven and mind-numbingly, obviously, unserious. Look back over that list: after-school sports programs and five-day paternity leave. These policies are so beside-the-point that they border on parody. Not one of them addresses the central causes of Japan's fertility decline.

Attack of the *Parasaito Shinguru*

Like America's, Japan's fertility rate fell prey to a constellation of forces—some social, some economic, some political. For instance, after World War II, American advisors bullied Japan into enacting the "Eugenic Protection Law," which made it the first country in the world to explicitly legalize abortion.[22] The law had horrifying, far-reaching effects: By 1955 the country had more abortions—*30 to 50 percent more*—than births. Not coincidentally, Japan's fertility rate totally collapsed during this period. To pick yet another cause, Japan has almost no immigration, so its demographic system is hermetically sealed. There is no influx of people with different attitudes about fertility. The government could, in theory, change its immigration policies, but there's little political will for such action. Japan likes being Japanese.

But culturally speaking, Japan's fertility problem is also a marriage problem. As Japanese women began attending college at higher rates in the 1970s, they began to delay marriage—by 2010, the average age of first marriage for Japanese women was 28.8 years.[23] At first these women postponed childbearing; then they abandoned it. And because out-of-wedlock births are still very much frowned upon in Japan, the decline of marriage has resulted in an even bigger hit to the fertility rate than it has in places like America and Europe, where women are willing to have babies out of wedlock.

All of which has led to some new cultural stereotypes. Earlier we mentioned the "dog mommies"—women who parade around with tiny dogs in strollers. There have also been a steady stream of press reports about shut-ins and various kinds of unemployed freeloaders. But perhaps the most ballyhooed new demographic type is the *parasaito shinguru* or "parasite single."[24] These creatures are mostly college-educated, working women who live with their parents well into their thirties. Not because they lack the money to pay rent, but because they choose to spend that salary elsewhere: designer clothes, international travel, trendy restaurants. In 2001, the *New York Times* noted that despite their relatively modest salaries, the parasite singles are Japan's biggest consumer class. That's because, unlike real adults, their entire paychecks are available for discretionary spending.[25] Sociologist Masahiro Yamada, who coined the term in *The Age of Parasite Singles*, explains, "They are like the ancient aristocrats of feudal times, but their parents play the role of servants. . . . Their lives are spoiled. The only thing that's important to them is seeking pleasure."[26]*

And even when the *parasaito shinguru* do consent to marriage, the unions increasingly do not last. The culture of marriage and divorce has gone through many cycles in Japan. In nineteenth-century Japan, divorce was incredibly common—as many as half of all marriages dissolved.[27] But in the twentieth century, the divorce rate declined, reaching an amazing 0.73 divorces per 1,000 people in the late 1960s.[28] After that, though, Japan's divorce rate took off—251,000 divorces were recorded in 2008, a rate of 3.1 per 1,000.[29] (By comparison, America in 2008 had a rate of 5.2 divorces per 1,000.[30]) This sounds positively glorious compared with the American number, but for Japan it's a radical change—an increase of 300 percent—in just two generations. Even worse, it comes paired with a *decrease* in the marriage rate—which has declined by a third over the same period—so that there are many more divorces but fewer marriages.[31] The growth of divorce and death of marriage have so destabilized the culture that the Japanese have attempted to cope in some truly odd ways. It's not just the emergence of the *parasaito shinguru*. Many couples now take part in a public "divorce ceremony": Guests are invited, toasts are made, and then the couple uses a hammer to smash their wedding rings. Next to that, the robot baby looks entirely reasonable.

It's not surprising that Japan failed to stoke fertility with its "Angel Plans" and "Plus One" programs. None of them addressed the root problem—marriage. And while the government was spitting out its limp attempts at natalism it made the problem worse by creating incentives for women to join the workforce. In 2004, for instance, the government abolished the tax break for wives earning small salaries, which

---

* Other Japanese sociologists attribute the rise of parasite singles to economic difficulty and inflexibilities in the Japanese workplace. This strikes me as wishful thinking, because it suggests the phenomenon is either an economic or a policy problem and not a messy cultural conundrum. The former are relatively easily solvable. The latter are not. Whatever the case, the fact remains that a growing portion of Japanese youth is not entering society.

had previously given some encouragement to married women who wanted to work part-time, rather than full-time.[32] If there is any good news in Japan, it's that when asked, the Japanese have been reasonably consistent in their belief of what constitutes ideal family size: Since 1974, most Japanese have claimed that 2.5 children is optimal. There is a chasm between the children people *want to have* and the children they *think they can have*. But no one in Japan has figured how to bridge this divide. And they're running out of time.

The European Experiment

Demographic concerns in Europe long predate those in Japan. Over the centuries, the Continent has periodically picked its fingers and worrywarted about its demographic future, in both directions. During some periods Europeans fretted about overpopulation (Malthus in the 1800s), during others depopulation (Montesquieu in the 1700s).[33] Today both concerns exist, simultaneously. On the far left, environmentalists believe that the world has too many people and that population reduction should be an explicit societal goal.[34] Everyone else in Europe—liberal, moderate, and conservative politicians, demographers, and even the bureaucrats in the European Union—understands that low fertility rates and their attendant consequences are a much more serious threat.

The European response to falling fertility rates is important for Americans to understand for several reasons: (1) European culture vaguely approximates our own; (2) European countries have attempted a wide variety of solutions to their common problem; (3) the results, too, have varied greatly.

In 2007, the European Commission issued a "Green Paper" on the subject of the Continent's dismal fertility rate.[35] The Commission found that the average TFR in the European Union was 1.5 and proclaimed that increasing this number was critical. The report was followed by a giant statistical survey.[36] The two publications proved powerful enough to provoke the European Parliament to adopt a resolution on the EU's demographic future.[37] (The University of Oslo's Nico Keilman makes a convincing case that the Completed Cohort Fertility number—which is a more precise measure than total fertility rate—is slightly rosier for the European Union. For women born in 1955 and 1965, the latest generation for which data are available, the CCF is 1.94 and 1.77, respectively.[38])

In typical European fashion, however, the Green Paper offered little in the way of concrete advice. There were no recommendations on how to actually increase fertility. In fact, there weren't even any *goals* as to what fertility rate would be desirable. Instead the Commission called on Europeans to pursue "demographic renewal." Whatever that means.

We might chalk up this haziness to typical European silliness. Yet when the European Union tackles economic matters—as in the Lisbon Strategy, for instance—it has been rigorously specific about numerical targets and expectations. In this light, Europe's unseriousness about reversing its demographic decline looks less like perfidy and more like grim resignation.

The Europeans have good reason to despair of their future. None of the 27 EU member states is above replacement level in fertility and only 8 of them are even near it—Ireland (2.01), France (2.08), the United Kingdom (1.91), Luxembourg (1.77), Denmark (1.74), Finland (1.73), Sweden (1.67), and the Netherlands (1.78). Fertility rates elsewhere are truly gothic: Spain (1.48), Germany (1.41), Hungary (1.41), Italy (1.40), and the Czech Republic (1.27).[39]

As you can see, there is a divide separating France and the Nordic countries, which have had some success at sustaining higher fertility, from the rest of Europe (particularly the East and the Mediterranean regions), which has not. France and the Nordic countries have pursued similar policies with regard to families and natalism and these policies are worth examining.[40]

For purposes of simplicity, we'll focus here on France, because whatever the practical differences between the French and Scandinavian approaches, the underlying theory is the same. Family policy began in France in 1938, as the country was nervously eyeing a resurgent Germany.[41] The state created the Family Code (*Code de la famille*), which provided an annual stipend (colloquially known as the "Housewife's Allowance") to parents for each child. Beginning in the 1970s, France began to adapt its policies to encourage working motherhood. The Housewife's Allowance was abolished in 1978, replaced by state-run day-care centers and a National Family Allowance Fund. This stipend paid families just enough to cover the costs of sending their children to the new day-care facilities.

In 1997, France announced a "New Family Policy," creating a complicated system of tax incentives and subsidies, all depending on the working mother's salary and how many children she has. The primary policy here is a "Family Allowance," which is paid to families with *at least two children* under the age of 16, and which increases with each additional child—the idea being to encourage multiple births by defraying the costs of parenting. In addition, both mothers and fathers are offered paid leave following the birth of a child. Mothers are then able to take unpaid leave of up to three years after each child and still have their job waiting for them. Mothers who return to work have a choice between a large network of state-run day-care facilities or an allowance to pay an independent nanny or babysitter. The result: a TFR of 2.08.[42] Not bad at all.

France's success is impressive but comes with some caveats. For starters, it's worth noting that despite France's nearly century-long commitment to natalism, it still has not been able to sustain a replacement-level fertility rate. What's more, France's fertility numbers are helped by immigration. Like America, France has a large, fecund immigrant population, which masks the lower fertility of the natives. The similarities between the effects of immigration on French and American fertility numbers are acute: Native-born French women have a TFR of 1.7. Some estimates put the TFR for foreign-born residents at 2.8, others put them closer to *three times* the native rate.[43]

Further, it's not clear that France's natalist policies are actually responsible for the country's higher fertility rates. European demographers and economists have spent a great deal of time working the numbers over the last 10 years. The best-case results suggest that the natalist programs—which essentially pay parents enough to put their kids in day care so that they can go to work—have created a small, positive effect. A large body of the research suggests they've had no effect at all, other than to nudge the timing of births slightly later in a woman's life and closer together.[44] Remember, the United Nations and other demographers who think declining fertility isn't that big a deal premise their worldview on the idea that the French experience— massive state spending to achieve a native fertility of 1.7—works, and is reproducible in other societies. They see France as the Best-Case Scenario toward which, they hope, the rest of the industrialized world will inexorably trend.

Command Fertility

If France is the best-case scenario, Singapore may be the worst. At the risk of sounding like a prophet of doom, the fertility history of Singapore should scare the stuffing out of you. Superficially, Singapore's problem looks like Japan's, only worse. With a TFR of 1.11, Singapore has the one of the lowest fertility rates in the world. But Singapore's problem is actually quite different: They brought it on themselves.

Unlike Japan, with a culture that spans two millennia, Singapore is brand new. The area that would become Singapore was founded as a British trading port in 1819.[45] The native population, such as it was, consisted of small fishing communities. As the British hub grew in importance, it attracted immigrants, primarily from India and China, who mixed with the natives to create the ethnic mélange that exists today. After the Second World War (during which Singapore was occupied by the Japanese), British imperial ambitions faded. The last British troops left in 1959. In 1965 Singapore gained full independence under the rule of the authoritarian People's Action Party (PAP).

Singapore's government embarked on a massive program of industrialization designed to rapidly modernize the state. Among its initiatives were increased urbanization and an attempt to jumpstart women's rates of college graduation and workforce participation. Singapore's fertility rate was already in steep decline, plunging from 5.45 in 1960 to 4.7 in 1965.[46] As part of its modernization, the government initiated a campaign to drive fertility down even faster. Its leaders believed that a rapidly growing population would diffuse the country's economic progress and that slower growth would make the country, on a per capita basis, wealthier. Their first step was establishing, in 1966, the "Family Planning and Population Board," which used a combination of persuasive and coercive tactics. The government launched a propaganda campaign, using messages such as "Stop at Two" and "Small Families, Brighter Future."[47] The most popular slogan, recounted in numerous posters and public-service ads, was "Girl or Boy, Two Is Enough."

Accompanying this bright, cheery campaign was an array of less genial policies. Abortion was given free rein, sanctioned—and even encouraged—at every stage. Parents who had more than two children were penalized with no paid maternity leave and higher hospital charges for the delivery of the extra children. Couples were encouraged to volunteer for sterilization. Parents who were sterilized after one or two children were reimbursed for the medical costs of delivery and their children were given preferential admissions to the best schools. These tactics were frighteningly effective. In 1976—just 10 years after launching the campaign—Singapore reached its stated target, a fertility rate of 2.1. That's a reduction of 53 percent in a decade. The world had never seen anything like it.

It's a measure of Singapore's anti-natalist success that no one was more unnerved by it than the government that had put the train in motion. By the early 1980s it was clear to the country's leadership that the "Two Is Enough" policy had set off a chain of unintended consequences. The first thing they noticed was that the fertility rate didn't stop at 2.1. It kept diving, down to 1.74 by 1980. The second bit of alarming data was that the country's biggest fertility declines came from its elites: Like every other industrialized country, Singapore discovered that even without government prodding, the more education a woman had, and the better her job, the less likely she was to have children. Singapore's incentives had pushed the number of children born to upper-class women to a startlingly low number and the women who were still having children tended to be less educated and of lower social standing.

In 1983, Singapore's prime minister, Lee Kuan Yew, delivered a major speech on the country's new demographic problem. He spoke with a candor that is the luxury of autocrats:

> We shouldn't get our women into jobs where they cannot, at the same time, be mothers. . . . You just can't be doing a full-time, heavy job like that of a doctor or engineer and run a home and bring up children . . . we must think deep and long on the profound changes we have unwittingly set off. . . .
>
> Our most valuable asset is in the ability of our people, yet we are frittering away this asset through the unintended consequences of changes in our education policy and equal career opportunities for women. This has affected their traditional role as mothers.[48]

Lee went on to lament that it was too late to turn back the clock "and have our women go back to their primary role as mothers, the creators and protectors of the next generation. Our women will not stand for it. And anyway, they have already become too important a factor in the economy."[49] His solution was to embark on what would become known as Singapore's eugenics period.

In an attempt to boost fertility rates at one end of the scale while still suppressing them at the other, the government offered big tax breaks to highly educated women who bore three or more children. (Their kids were also given preferred admission to the more competitive schools.) A "Social Development Unit" was created to act as a matchmaking service for university graduates. Women with lower levels of education were given giant cash awards ($10,000) if they volunteered for sterilization after their first or second child. None of it worked. Elite women still shunned motherhood. After three years,

Singapore's fertility rate had fallen to 1.62 and showed no signs of stabilizing.

In 1986, the government began marching the other way, initiating a "New Population Policy." In a national address, Prime Minister Goh Chok Tong gave a clear-eyed view of the danger Singapore was in:

> The constraint of physical resources is not as difficult to overcome as the human resources problem. This type of problem requires us to change attitudes and tread on sensitivities. . . . I think the most serious challenge we are going to face is how to cope with the changing demographic profile—its size, composition, and age distribution. . . . I know this is a longer-term problem, but if we do not address it now, it can only become more serious.[50]

Goh dissolved the Family Planning and Population Board.[51] "Two Is Enough" was replaced by "Have Three Or More Children If You Can," a slogan broadcast on TV and radio, and pushed in print ads and on billboards.[52] Posters abounded proclaiming the joy and fulfillment of family life. And the government created a serious, multi-pronged campaign of incentives to encourage families to have more children.

At first, Singapore simply threw into reverse the machinery it had built to discourage births. Tax incentives were given to families with more than three children, as were the coveted primary-school admissions preferences. Unpaid maternity leave was increased from one year to four years for government workers. For a brief period between 1988 and 1990, the new pro-natalist measures seemed to be working: The fertility rate rose from 1.62 to 1.96 in 1988. It hovered around 1.70 for a few years, but then resumed its downward march. By 1999, it stood at 1.48.

So Singapore upped the ante. In 2000, the government announced a series of major new policies. The first was the "Baby Bonus" program, which paid families—straight cash—for having children: $9,000 for the second child and $18,000 for the third. The tax code was modified to give yet another incentive, this time a big break to mothers under the age of 31 who had a second child. The government also created "Child Development Accounts," which functioned like 401(k) funds for kids. Parents put money into a savings account that was reserved to pay for kid expenses. The government then matched their savings dollar-for-dollar—up to $6,000 for the second child and $12,000 for the third. To sweeten the pot even more, the government announced that working mothers would get 12 weeks of paid maternity leave for each child.[53]

The government also attempted to massage some of the external considerations that can factor into a couple's decision to have children. Singapore's housing market is largely government-run, so the Housing and Development Board offered better, larger houses to families with children. They made it easier for young married couples to buy a home. In an attempt to wrestle with the problem of childcare, the Housing Board helped grandparents find housing close to grandchildren, the idea being to recreate the web of intergenerational dependency.

At the same time, the government did its best to void the disincentives it had created earlier. The $10,000 sterilization bonus was discontinued. Leaders were reluctant to ban abortion outright, but launched a public campaign against it. Women with fewer than three children who sought either sterilization or abortion were required to attend counseling before any procedure would be performed.

In many ways, Singapore has become a natalist utopia, where traditionalist beliefs are now embraced in ways conservative American natalists can only dream about. In 1994, for instance, Prime Minister Goh spoke out against illegitimacy, calling single motherhood "wrong" and claiming that the "respectable part of our society" should never accept it because "by removing the stigma, we may encourage more women to have children without getting married."[54]

And yet, despite Singapore's traditionalist stances and heroic efforts to encourage family formation, the country has met with total and unremitting failure. In 2001, Singapore's fertility rate was 1.41. By 2004 it was 1.24. Today it is 1.11. Despite all the incentives, all the public campaigns, all the perks and payouts, the average woman in Singapore can barely be bothered to have a single child. If Singapore, with its authoritarian government and natalist bonanza—cash bonuses! tax credits! preferential housing! paid maternity leave! childcare from grandparents!—can't convince its modern, sophisticated population to have babies, what hope does anyone have?

The answer may well be, "not much." But I promised you I wouldn't get too wrapped up in doom. And it happens that there is a tiny glimmer of hope in a corner of the world where you'd never expect to find it. While no one was looking, people have started having babies again in a most unlikely place: war-torn, post-Soviet Georgia.

CHAPTER NINE

How to Make Babies

The Georgian people have had a rough couple of centuries. After being annexed by Tsar Alexander I, this tiny country on the Black Sea spent much of the nineteenth century with the Ottomans and Russians playing tug-of-war on its land. The Georgians finally got their own independent state in 1918. It lasted all of three years before a new group of Russians marched in and annexed them again, this time in the name of the Glorious Socialist People's Revolution. Life as part of the Soviet Union was even less pleasant than it had been under the tsars. Georgians were anxious to be free again, so when the USSR first started wobbling, they immediately held elections—the first fair and free elections to take place inside the Evil Empire *before* its fall. The vote was a precursor to the Georgians declaring their independence, which they did (again) shortly before the Soviet Union collapsed in 1991. Seven months later, Georgia's new government fell and the country descended into a civil war which lasted three years. When the war ended Eduard Shevardnadze—if you'll recall, he was Gorbachev's Kissinger—became president. In 2008, the Russian bear went marauding and invaded Georgia once more, with about 1,000 casualties.

Yet through it all, Georgia's fertility rate has been surprisingly resilient. Unlike most of the communist satellites, Georgia kept its fertility numbers healthy under communism and stayed over the 2.1 mark during the entire Soviet era.[1] It was only toward the end that fertility decline set in. Just as in Russia, freedom from Soviet tyranny did not help Georgian fertility. From a rate of 2.26 in 1985, it slid to 2.15 in 1990. Once civil war broke out, fertility collapsed: 1.72 in 1992; 1.55 in 1996; 1.46 in 2000. In 2003 it reached a nadir of 1.39.

In 13 years Georgia went from above replacement to lowest-low. But then something miraculous happened: Georgia's fertility started rising. Year after year, it ticked upward until, by 2009, it stood at 1.86—a mark that would make the French and Scandinavians proud. So what happened?

Behind the Numbers

The data offer some clues. Abortion has generally been on the wane in Georgia since 1980, when there were 99.1 abortions for every 100 live births.[2] Georgia's abortion rate stood at 61.3 per 100 live births just before the Soviet Union collapsed, but it increased dramatically during the civil war. In the rebound period since 2003 it has been relatively low, not going above 44.4. But this isn't dispositive—the abortion rate actually rose slightly from 2003 to 2006 during Georgia's fertility recovery.

The numbers on marriage and divorce, however, are more suggestive. Until 1980, Georgian marriages were both plentiful and healthy— with an annual marriage rate around 10 (per thousand people) and a divorce rate under 1.4.[3] But the marriage rate steadily eroded over the next 23 years, crashing at 2.9 in 2003—not surprisingly, the same year the country's fertility rate reached its lowest point. After 2003, the marriage rate recovered nicely, climbing all the way to a blissful 7.2. And at the same time, the divorce rate returned to very low levels, staying under 1.0.* Making matters even better, Georgian women started to marry slightly earlier. During the fertility collapse, while the marriage rate plummeted, the average age of first marriage increased, from 23.1 in 1992 to 25.6 in 2004.[4] But since 2005, the average age of first marriage has actually *decreased* slightly.

All of which set the table for Georgia's demographic comeback. When you look at the detailed breakouts of Georgia's fertility numbers, you see that its fertility decline was really a decline in fertility among women between the ages of 20 and 24. During the 13-year period when the Georgian fertility rate took a nosedive, women in other age brackets held their fertility relatively constant. It was women aged 20 to 24 who took the big hit, going from 165.6 births for every 1,000 women in 1991 to 93.8 births in 2003.[5] After 2003, young Georgian women began flocking back to motherhood. While the fertility rates of all cohorts increased after 2003, it was the 20 to 24 group that made up the lion's share, climbing to 128.2 births per 1,000.

The deeper meaning of those numbers is that the rise in Georgian fertility is the real thing, not a statistical ghost of the tempo effect. Georgian fertility suffered because Georgian marriage suffered — as a result of civil war and the political dislocation of the post-Soviet era. But even this doesn't fully explain Georgia's recovery.

"Go Forth and Multiply"

Patriarch Ilia II is the father of the Georgian Orthodox Church. Born in 1933, he has led Georgians since 1977. During his reign he faced

---

* Actually, Georgia's divorce rate fell to heroic levels (0.4 per 1,000 people — enough to make the Japanese jealous) during the country's fertility collapse and slightly increased during the recovery period. However, this does not necessarily suggest that divorce has no effect on fertility. The reason divorce levels were so low in the 1990s and 2000s is because the marriage levels were so low — there simply weren't all that many marriages to break up. And the reason the divorce rate climbed during the fertility recovery — from 0.4 to 0.9 — is because there were many, many more marriages. Since 2003, both the marriage and divorce rate increased by more than 100 percent.

down a generation of Soviet leaders committed to dismantling the state's religious heritage, but Ilia II outlasted the godless communists and today Georgia remains an intensely devout country. Eighty-four percent of Georgians belong to the Orthodox Church and they're religious, not spiritual, adherents.[6] Large majorities of both Georgian men and women attend church with some frequency and, counter to nearly every Western nation, the highest levels of church attendance are found among young adults, aged 18 to 29.[7]

After prayerfully considering Georgia's fertility collapse, Ilia II decided to take action. In late 2007 he promised that, going forward, he would personally baptize any child born to parents who already had two or more children.[8] This may sound like a small thing, but in a recent survey 96 percent of Georgians said it was important to baptize an infant.[9] (By way of comparison, in France just 57 percent of people agree that baptism is important.) The year after Ilia II's proclamation, the birth rate increased by 20 percent—four times the already substantial increase from the prior year. Ilia II's mass baptisms are now a staple of Georgian life.

Baby-Making 101

America is not Georgia. We have no national patriarch. And even if the Pope himself were to offer baptism to every family that popped out a third kid, it probably wouldn't move the needle on our fertility. But it's important to understand Georgia's successes for the same reason we study the failures of Japan, Europe, and Singapore. When you consider each of these in turn, you can come up with three golden rules for natalism, each of which applies to the United States:

(1) *Below a certain point, there's no turning back.* There is a temptation to view fertility as tomorrow's problem, a challenge to be dealt with at a future date—particularly when a country's fertility rate is near replacement. But fertility trends have the turning radius of a battleship, not a go-kart. (Georgia is the exception that proves the rule.) And the further fertility drops, the more unbendable the downward trend

becomes. It is difficult to change direction from a rate of 1.75. Below a sustained rate of 1.50 (Georgia only touched this briefly) there are no examples of a country returning to replacement level.

(2) Any efforts to stoke fertility must be sustained over several generational cohorts. The chief lesson of France and Scandinavia's modest successes is that a country must sign on for the long haul when crafting a natalist agenda. A four-year tax credit is useless. So is a long, but feckless, string of hopscotch initiatives, like Japan's. What you need is a serious, decades-long commitment to family growth.

(3) People cannot be bribed into having babies. Singapore's example demonstrates the futility of trying to bribe people into having children. And there's a good reason why: Having kids is, literally, no fun. Researchers have been studying the effects of children on their parents for decades and the results are nearly *always* the same. Having children makes parents less happy. You can slice, dice, and rationalize the data any way you like, controlling for age, church attendance, education, you name it. Doesn't matter. Take two people who are identical in every demographic way except for parenthood and the one with the kid will be 5.6 percent less likely to call themselves "very happy." Each additional child lops off another 1.6 points.[10] Why can't you bribe people into having babies? Because, for the most part, people aren't stupid.*

This last policy guideline is the most counterintuitive, because transferring money from the state to parents is where just about every

---

* A few words of caution: (1) The best case made for parental happiness is a 2012 study by Chris Herbst and John Ifcher which claims that the happiness measures of non-parents have been dropping in recent years to the point where they now approach that of parents.[11] We'll see if this result bears out over time. (2) I am not saying that children aren't the source of other virtues. (3) Most importantly, I am not suggesting that happiness is the virtue to be prized above all others. It is not, and no well-examined life can suppose it to be. (4) Finally, I am not saying that people can't be *argued* into having children because clearly they can—moral argument in favor of children is part of why religious practitioners have more babies than secularists. (5) What I *am* saying is that you can't bribe people into having a baby they don't want because no material incentives can possibly compensate for how parents' lives are upended and their happiness diminished. It's this rational calculation on the part of people who do not want children—or are ambivalent about them—that makes natalist bribery ineffective as a policy tool.

natalist discussion begins. And there is a sliver of support for it. For instance, in 1988 the Canadian province of Quebec instituted increasingly large payments that topped out with $8,000 for a family's third child. One researcher argues that the policy had a strong effect on fertility, increasing the chances of a couple having a first child by 16.9 percent and a third child by 25 percent.[12] In Estonia the government was able to goose its fertility by introducing a 15-month paid maternity leave.[13] This "mother's salary" was introduced in 2004 and it moved the country's fertility rate from 1.37 all the way up to 1.65.[14] Some research shows significant correlation between cash bonuses and fertility, but the list of failures is much, much longer. The consensus is that subsidies produce returns mostly at the margins: Studies of European countries show that for every 25 percent increase in benefits, fertility increases by 0.6 percent in the short term and 4 percent in the long term.[15] (And those are the baby bonus *successes*; remember how they worked out for Singapore.)

Of course, there are other ways to pay parents. France has its network of national day-care centers. Sweden gives mothers a full year of leave at 90 percent salary and an additional 13 weeks at a reduced salary.[16] The prominence of working mothers in Sweden versus homemakers in Italy prompts many left-leaning demographers to argue that we can augment fertility by encouraging *more* women to join the workplace—and then building an elaborate infrastructure for taking care of children. So that women can spend their days working to pay the state to take care of their kids.

Yet even if you take France and Sweden as the platonic ideals of gender relations and family policy, their examples are less than totally convincing: Even with plenty of high-fertility immigrants to boost their numbers, neither country is able to crack the 2.1 mark. Instead, it's more likely the case that, as demographer Jan Hoem concludes, fertility is "best seen as a systemic outcome that depends more on broader attributes, such as the degree of family-friendliness of a society, and less on the presence and detailed construction of monetary benefits."[17]

So what should America do? It's a big question, with hundreds of answers. But the overarching principle behind American natalism should always be this: The government *cannot* get people to have children *they do not want*. However, it *can* help people have the children *they do want*.

As I've tried to show, America's fertility decline was not caused by a grand conspiracy to eviscerate the family. Rather, it's been the result of a thousand evolutions in modern life. Many of these changes (the decline in infant mortality; the liberation of women into the workplace) have been enormously beneficial to us as a society. Some of them (the epidemics of divorce and cohabitation) have not. But even the changes we think of as beneficial have, as ancillary effects, created roadblocks to family formation. They delayed marriage and childbearing, or increased the cost of children, or decreased the return on that investment.

Effective pro-natalism is about removing those roadblocks. The following ideas aren't meant to be definitive solutions, but rather a starting point for discussion.

Undoing America's One-Child Policy

Social Security. After all my talk about the inefficacy of handing out money to parents, the first topic we're going to talk about is Social Security. There's a reason: The Social Security regime distorts the "market value" of children and forces fertility rates down. In the United States, researchers believe that Social Security has "crowded out" incentives to raise children to an amazing degree: Remember, its effects suppress the fertility rate by 0.5, on average.[18] This is a big problem. But it's also easily addressable and a variety of proposals exist in policy circles. Phillip Longman proposes a "Parental Dividend" system by which a couple's FICA taxes would be reduced by one-third with the birth of their first child, by two-thirds with the birth of a second, and then eliminated completely with the third (until the children turn 18).[19]

Other, more complicated, schemes abound. Cesar Conda and Robert Stein would increase the child credit to $4,000 while trimming the tax bracket to just two rates, 15 percent and 32 percent.[20] Ramesh Ponnuru advocates a massive simplification of the tax code coupled with an increase in the tax credit for children, upping it from $1,000 to $5,000.[21] But regardless of the means, all of these plans have the same goals: (1) Let parents keep more of their money. (2) Increase the relief with additional children. (3) Reduce the fundamental distortion that Social Security now creates. The existing system gives everyone welfare-state payouts in old age, regardless of whether they bore the cost of creating the taxpayers who fund the payouts. This last point is why reforming Social Security fits within our Golden Rules: these reforms don't hand out money to parents, they simply lessen the economic disconnect created by the government in the first place.

College. As previously discussed, higher education dampens fertility in all sorts of ways. It delays marriage, incurs debt, increases the opportunity costs of childbearing, and greatly increases the expense of raising a child. If you doubt that the economics of the university system are broken, consider this: Since 1960, the real cost of goods in nearly every other sector of American life has dropped, while the quality and utility of those goods has increased. College is exactly the opposite. Its real cost has increased by more than 1,000 percent. Meanwhile, the "value" of a college degree—that is, the wage difference between high school and college grads—has increased even in jobs where a college degree is not required and has no bearing at all on work-related knowledge.[22] And all of this has happened as the objective quality of the average college degree has, by most standards, declined.

If we were describing any other sector—say, the healthcare system or the financial industry—we would recognize college as a system that is either sub-optimal, bubblicious, or disfigured by some economic distortion. But because we're talking about The University, public debate has instead tended toward questions about how to get even *more* kids sucked into the maw of undergraduate life. (Try finding a politician, anywhere, who'll say, "What we need in the twenty-first century is to make it so that fewer of our children have to go to college!") Yet all bad things must eventually come to an end, and at some point there will be a serious discussion in America about reforming the college system. When we reach that moment, there are three natalist measures that would go a long way toward making it easier for parents to have the babies they want.

First, we could eliminate the need for college. The modern college degree functions less as an educational tool than as a credentialing badge—it's a marker that gives employers a vague estimate of a person's intelligence, social milieu, and work ability. Only in rare cases does it have any bearing on professional competence. (For example, 15 percent of U.S. Postal Service letter carriers have bachelor's degrees.[23]) The reason employers need this badge is because they aren't allowed to ask for test scores the way colleges themselves are. And that's thanks to an obscure 1971 Supreme Court case, *Griggs v. Duke Power*.

In *Griggs*, the Court held that employers could not rely on IQ-type tests if minorities performed relatively poorly on them. Blacks and Hispanics display a persistent underperformance on such tests, making it impossible for employers to ask for scores, unless the test has been guaranteed in advance not to produce disparate racial results. (And as the 2009 case *Ricci v. DeStefano* proved, even a test that has been sufficiently vetted for a lack of bias can cause trouble after the fact if minorities perform poorly on it.)

So what employers do is this: They launder their request for test scores through the college system, because colleges *are* allowed to use such considerations. The universities get rich, students and their parents go into hock, and everyone pretends that Acme Widgets is hiring Madison because they value her B.A. in sociology from Haverford, and not because her *admission* to Haverford proved that she is bright—a fact which a three-hour written test could have demonstrated just as well. If *Griggs* were rolled back, it would upend the college system at a stroke.

Second, we could encourage the university system to be more responsive to market forces. It's a peculiarity of the college market that schools are virtually indifferent to price. One suspects that Harvard and Yale could charge $100,000 a year and still fill their classrooms to capacity. By the same token, those two schools could probably drop their tuition to $10,000 without incurring all that many more applications than they currently do. But it isn't just the elite schools that have peculiar economics. In 2005 the thoroughly mediocre University of Richmond in Virginia raised its tuition by a gobsmacking 31 percent in a single leap.[24] Instead of prospective students shunning this higher price for what was an identical good—after all, the school itself did not change dramatically in three months—applications *increased* the following year.

One way to make universities more responsive to market dynamics would be to create a no-frills, federal degree-granting body, which would allow students to leapfrog the four-year system. Walter Russell Mead has advanced this idea, suggesting:

> The Department of Education could develop standards in fields like English, the sciences, information technology, mathematics, and so on. Students would get certificates when they passed an exam in a given subject. These certificates could be used, like the Advanced Placement tests of the College Board, to reduce the number of courses students would need to graduate from a traditional college. And colleges that accepted federal funds could be required to award credits for them.
>
> But the certificates would be good for something else as well. With enough certificates in the right subjects, students could get a national bac without going to college. Government agencies would accept the bac as the equivalent of a conventional bachelor's degree; graduate schools and any organization receiving federal funds would also be required to accept it.
>
> Subject exams calibrated to a national standard would give employers something they do not now have: assurance that a student has achieved a certain level of knowledge and skill.[25]

Such a move would force both private and public universities to fundamentally reexamine their businesses.

Finally, the government should stipulate that public universities become family-friendly. You can't—and shouldn't—try to force college kids to get married and have children. But for some students starting a family while they're in college is ideal. Consider the case of Brigham Young University.

Located in Provo, Utah, BYU is the flagship school of the Church of Jesus Christ of Latter-day Saints. It has 27,000 undergraduates, who come from predominately middle-class backgrounds. Fully one-quarter of these full-time students are married. And while the university does not keep records on it, school officials estimate that about a third of these married couples have children during their undergraduate years.

How does BYU incorporate thousands of babies into campus life? Obviously many of those young families have support from their own parents. But the critical factor is that BYU provides not just dormitory-style student housing, but also family housing: Located just off campus are blocks full of modest townhomes owned by the university which are reserved for married couples. There is no reason why state schools shouldn't provide a similar option. One suspects that relatively few students will want to avail themselves of it—but the point is to make life easier for those who do want to start their families early.

The Dirt Gap. Let's jump back for a moment to the Second Demographic Transition and its view of there being "two Americas"—one with high fertility and one with low. One of the drivers of this divide is the cost of land, which is a big factor in the cost of family formation. The price of real estate doesn't just determine your housing expenses, it also drives the costs of transportation, entertainment, babysitting, school, and, well, pretty much everything. Even worse, land constraints—be they physical boundaries or government-imposed regulations—not only make prices higher in normal times, but act as a multiplier during bubble times.[26] So while it was already costlier to have a baby in Manhattan in 1990 than it was in Indianapolis, it became disproportionately *even more expensive* with the real-estate boom of the early 2000s.

That said, the lesson of the Big Sort is that people live where they want to. There's no sense in telling Vermonters (who have the lowest fertility in America) that they should to pack up and head to Utah (which has the highest fertility). But since land costs contribute so much to family formation costs, the government has an interest in trying to open the field for parents who would have more children if they could afford them.

Many people make decisions on where to live based on employment. Intensely urban areas—Los Angeles, New York, Washington, Chicago—have high concentrations of jobs, but come with high land costs. We all know the middle-class stereotype: The happy young couple who move to the big, vibrant city for jobs, but then move to the soulless exurbs once they have kids. This gives them better housing options for the children, but places them further away from the concentration of good jobs. (Don't get me wrong, I'm a stereotype, too. After my wife and I had our first child, and started thinking about our second, we decamped from glorious Old Town and moved to a cookie-cutter subdivision with a backyard and a picket fence—the whole megillah. On the "when in Rome" principle, we even bought a minivan.*)

So how do we help families have access to large pools of jobs and live somewhere with a lower cost of family formation? Geography is regrettably resistant to social planning. There are only so many acres of land in Manhattan and there's nothing anyone can to do to make it less expensive. But the government *can* make the suburbs more accessible

---

* A brief note on the minivan, which is, I submit, deeply symbolic of the entire exurban experience: Living in Old Town was much more fun than our present circumstances. We could walk everywhere—to coffee, dinner, grocery shopping. We had running and bike paths along the Potomac River. Our commute into Washington took about 12 minutes. The only problem with Old Town was that it made actually raising children nearly impossible. Even a modest townhome there requires the salaries of two full-time professionals; childcare would easily have been $20,000 a year—or more, if you wanted a nanny who was in the country legally. The public schools were awful and the private schools were priced like colleges. I'm not romanticizing the exurbs into something they're not when I say the following: If you believe the primary task of family life is raising children, then the exurbs are fantastically utilitarian. In that way, the minivan is synecdoche for the exurbs themselves. It may not be sexy or fun, but it gets the job done.

to cities by improving our highway system. Since 1970, the "vehicle lane miles" (that's the metric traffic engineers use to count how much we drive) consumed by Americans have risen by 150 percent. During that period we added only 5 percent to our highway capacity.[27] Now you know why we have so much traffic these days.

The answer is not more public transportation. Light rail might work for the child-free. (Or it might not; there is a stark divide in the literature on mass transit.) But parents trying to balance work and children need the flexibility automobiles provide; they cannot easily drop a child at a babysitter or school, then take a train to work, then train home, and then fetch the child. (If you don't believe me, you try it.) The solution is building more roads. As Ross Douthat and Reihan Salam note wryly in *Grand New Party*, Dallas has twice as much pavement-per-person as Los Angeles. And half the traffic. And, not coincidentally, a higher fertility rate.[28] An improved highway system would make it easier for couples to access both the jobs cities provide and the housing affordability suburbs offer.

The dirt gap's silver-bullet solution, though, is telecommuting. Forty-four million Americans already telecommute for part of their workweek. The private sector has cottoned on to the benefits, but we can do better. Walter Russell Mead illustrates how nicely telecommuting scales: The average American spends one hour a day commuting to and from work. If you telecommute just one day a week, it's the equivalent of saving one week a year. Telecommute four days a week, and it's like getting a full month back.

Telecommuting points the way toward a revolution in American life. For starters, true telecommuting would virtually eliminate the dirt gap, letting an employee of a Silicon Valley company work and live in Montana, where land is one-hundredth the price. But as Phillip Longman argues, telecommuting also offers something more: the possibility of returning the home to the center of economic activity in America.

Parents who can live where they like and work from home will find it easier to care for children without organized day care. They can live near existing social and family networks. Suddenly the three-generation household—where grandparents care for kids while parents work, and then are cared for in later years by their own children—becomes possible again. Remember: The industrialized day care and retirement living which became the norm over the last 30 years are a historical aberration. There's no reason to think we can't go back to a world where the extended family is a part of daily life. Telecommuting wouldn't just make it easier for people to have families—it could return intergenerational family relationships to their traditional form.

Immigration. One of the lessons from Japan and France is that no wealthy, industrialized nation can prop up its fertility rate without large-scale immigration. America is, as we have seen, no different. A reasonably liberal program of immigration is necessary for the long-term health of our country. Yet at the same time, this liberal approach to immigration should be coupled with a staunchly traditionalist view of integration. America has been lucky in the way it has assimilated most of its immigrants. Europe—and France in particular—has not. "Europe" as we have known it for 15 centuries is almost certain to fade away in the next 50 years, replaced by a semi-hostile Islamic *ummah*. All that will remain of what we traditionally know as "Europe" is the name. This change was not inevitable; it is the result of a policy choice made by adherents of a truly radical faith: multiculturalism.[29] It is only now dawning on Europeans that their unwillingness to insist on standing for their own culture has been a terrible mistake. In 2011, the leaders of France, Great Britain, and Germany all publicly acknowledged that multiculturalism has been a societal failure.[30] Tolerance need not be surrender and a certain amount of cultural chauvinism is necessary for societal coherence. America should keep that in mind while simultaneously welcoming future tides of immigrants as they come to our shores.

The Church and the State. There is one final lesson to be drawn from the rest of the world. America is the most demographically healthy industrialized nation; it is also the most religiously devout. This is not a coincidence. People who regularly attend church have more children than those who do not. Look around the list of wealthy, first-world nations with plummeting birth rates and you see that, from Japan to Russia to Singapore to Spain, they all have one thing in common: an increasing tendency toward secularization.

Though America is a less devout country than it was two generations ago, we have, for the most part, resisted the secularist stampede. There is no reason for wishing the United States to be a theocracy. That said, it is important we preserve the role of religion in our public square, resisting those critics who see theocracy lurking behind every corner. Our government should be welcoming of, not hostile to, believers—if for no other reason than they're the ones who create most of the future taxpayers.

After all, there are many perfectly good reasons to have a baby. (Curiosity, vanity, and naïveté all come to mind.) But at the end of the day, there's only one good reason to go through the trouble a second time: Because you believe, in some sense, that God wants you to.

That's It?

All of the above suggestions are, in the scheme of things, incongruously modest in their ambition. After all, I've been arguing that America's fertility problem is the result of an enormous, interconnected web of factors that constitute something like the entire framework of modern life. If we are facing a cultural maladaptation, or part of a universal Second Demographic Transition, is telecommuting really going to save us? Probably not.

Not everyone thinks small-ball. As we saw earlier, over the years policy planners have tried all sorts of big projects, from planned housing to national day care. Some ideas are even bigger. In 1978, former French prime minister Michel Debré proposed altering the very fabric of his country's democracy. He wanted to start handing out extra votes to parents, an additional vote to each man for every son he fathered and an additional vote to each woman for every daughter she bore.[31] It isn't as crazy as it sounds. Debré understood that France's low fertility would eventually cause an age imbalance, increasing the proportion of older citizens. He believed that this army of retirees would put such a demand on the state's resources that the government would be forced to cut back on support for the young—and that politicians would be forced to obey the will of the gray-hairs, because of their voting power.

Debré's idea never took off in France, but it eventually found a place in the world of theoretical natalism. (It's now commonly known as "Demeny voting," after demographer Paul Demeny.) The only place Demeny voting has ever been even half-seriously considered is Hungary.[32] Hungary is a nascent democracy facing dire demographic problems—a TFR of 1.3 and a population that could shrink by half. If any country might be open to trying something nuts, it would be Hungary.[33] But even the Hungarians flinched in the end.

That's probably just as well. Demeny voting is one of those radical moves that could be a cure worse than the disease. (The mind reels trying to imagine the unintended consequences.) There have been other moon-shot proposals. The mass use of in vitro fertilization, for instance, has been held out as a way for parents to conquer the biological clock. Women freeze their eggs in their early twenties, toil away at their careers deep into their thirties, and then have technicians make their babies when they're ready. While this idea might be catnip to a certain kind of libertarian futurist, it strikes me as unrealistic. If we reach the point where people are so busy with their own lives that they outsource baby-making to a lab, then it's not clear why they'd be willing to yoke themselves to parenthood at all.

And what about the big cultural issues we spent so much time examining—divorce, marriage, cohabitation, contraception, women in the workforce? I'm afraid that, as a matter of policy, there's very little we can do to alter any of these stars in their courses. These are matters of enormous cultural consequence and government has never proved particularly adept at (consciously) influencing them.[*] On the

---

[*] The key word here is "consciously." The authors of *Roe* did not believe they were creating a national abortion mill. The inventors of the Pill thought they were making a tool to suppress the fertility of poor undesirables, not the middle class. The lawyers

big-ticket items, we are largely at the mercy of the culture. Our best bet, I suspect, is not to try to remake the culture with the levers of government, but to support those who want children and let *them* engage the culture with their lives.

And here there is some interesting news. One of the darker fears of liberal demographers is that, in the long run, the devout will inherit the earth. Second Demographic Transition theory rests on the idea that modern life will constantly drain the pool of religious believers, always luring believers away from their churches faster than they can reproduce. But some researchers suspect that the fecundity of orthodox believers might be more powerful than the modern pull toward secularism.

Demographers Eric Kaufmann and Vegard Skirbekk note that secular Americans have a TFR of just 1.66, compared with TFRs of 2.3 and 2.2 for observant Catholics and Protestants.[34] And while secular Americans are younger on average than devoutly religious Americans (regardless of their faith), by 2030 non-believers could peak at 18 percent of the population.[35] Meanwhile, since the majority of immigrants to America are practicing Catholics, the percentage of the population that is devout should increase. Here's what Kaufmann and Skirbekk have to say about faith and the Second Demographic Transition:

---

in California who created the modern divorce regime thought they were merely tidying up some clunky statutes. The list goes on and on. That said, there may be a handful of very, very modest moves the government might make. For instance, the current tax code discriminates against married couples in a rudimentary way by combining their incomes. For instance, imagine a man and a woman each making $80,000. If they marry, they are taxed at the top marginal rate of their combined $160,000, which is 28 percent. However, if they cohabitate, they are each taxed at only the $80,000 marginal rate, which is 25 percent. The government should not be in the business of rewarding cohabitation over marriage. The only obvious big-ticket policy change the government could make would be to restrict abortion. There are, to my mind, compelling and overwhelming moral arguments in favor of banning abortion. But I promised you I wouldn't delve into that and, as a matter of demographics, abortion is a modest factor in suppressing fertility in the United States (though it is much stronger among blacks). Georgia's experience suggests that higher abortion rates do not necessarily entail lower fertility rates.

In the context of the Second Demographic Transition, religious women tend to have more children than non-religious women. Conservative religious families are larger than theologically liberal families. Conservatives also are better at retaining their children within the fold than liberals. Seculars are growing through religious decline in much of the West but will be constrained by exceptionally weak demography. The net result is growing fundamentalism, an implosion of moderate religion and a short-run rise in secularism which will ultimately give way to decline over several generations.[36]

In fact, they go so far as to suggest that if secularism doesn't increase the pace at which it pulls believers from their path, the mere increase in numbers of religious Americans could actually push our fertility rate *upward*—to between 2.10 and 2.16 by 2043.[37] As always, I'm not suggesting that we can really predict a tenth of a point swing in 30 years. We have no idea how American religiosity will evolve in the coming decades and Kaufmann and Skirbekk's projections strike me as peculiarly optimistic. But even so, it's worth understanding that pathways for growth of our fertility rate do exist. Even if only in theory.

What It All Means

I said at the beginning that I wouldn't be selling doom and I'm going to keep my promise. Just because we're on one curve today does not mean we will continue on it indefinitely. As the financial services ads used to disclaim before the Great Recession, past performance is not indicative of future gains. (Or in the case of fertility, losses.) It's entirely possible that America will resist the trap of modernity, which pushes people to eschew children in favor of more pleasurable pursuits.

I also promised that I wasn't going to try to argue you into having babies. And there's no getting around the fact that if you have carefully ordered your life in such a way as to provide the maximum amount of pleasure for yourself, children won't just change your life. They will utterly and completely destroy it. A few years ago the writer Jennifer Senior caused a minor sensation with a story about being a parent in *New York Magazine*. Her essay was titled "All Joy and No Fun."[38] As another exhausted, downtrodden parent quipped to me after reading it, "Well, she has it half right."

Yet Senior's argument was more complicated than it looked. Her point was that in a world where pleasure is the highest value, children will *never* be attractive. But pleasure is a shallow goal and the well-examined life requires more. It demands seriousness of purpose. Nothing is more serious than having children.

My wife and I didn't leave Old Town because we disliked Yuppie paradise. We liked it very, very much. The morning croissants at the café around the corner, the evening jogs by the river, the nifty shops selling Florentine pottery, the coffee—my God, the coffee. We left not out of some perverted reverse snobbery, but because we believed that family life was more important. And if you believe in anything seriously enough—God, America, the liberal order, heck, even secular humanism—then eventually babies must follow.

It's this last bit, finally, that sits at the heart of the West's fertility crisis and America's One-Child Policy. Modernity has turned us into a deeply unserious people. Yet it's encouraging to note that while our fertility problem is more dire than it ever has been, neither the predicament itself, nor its root causes, are new. Here's Teddy Roosevelt making the case for natalism in 1905, in a speech to the National Congress of Mothers:

> There are many good people who are denied the supreme
> blessing of children, and for these we have the respect and
> sympathy always due to those who, from no fault of their
> own, are denied any of the other great blessings of life. But
> the man or woman who deliberately foregoes these blessings,
> whether from viciousness, coldness, shallow-heartedness, self-
> indulgence, or mere failure to appreciate aright the difference

between the all-important and the unimportant—why, such a creature merits contempt as hearty as any visited upon the soldier who runs away in battle, or upon the man who refuses to work for the support of those dependent upon him, and who though able-bodied is yet content to eat in idleness the bread which others provide.[39]

That Rough Rider was a real hard case. His indictment of the childfree doesn't sit very comfortably in our non-judgmental world. Today, we all make our own choices and every choice must be celebrated. But the core of T. R.'s concern—that having children is difficult but important work and that the main threat to fertility comes from a worldview that places the self at the center—is as on-point today as it was then. Ninety-nine years later, Joseph Cardinal Ratzinger made the same argument—albeit more charitably—in a speech to the Italian senate, saying "Children, our future, are perceived as a threat to the present, as if they were taking something away from our lives. Children are seen as a liability rather than as a source of hope."[40]

Perhaps, after wrestling for a century with the problems modernity has created, we'll figure out how to balance liberalism, modern economics, and family life.

I'm inclined to think not myself. But as always, hope must have the last word.

Acknowledgments

I owe many debts for this book, the first of which is to Tom Phillips. In 2008, Mr. Phillips awarded me a fellowship from his wonderful foundation, which began this project. The book simply would not exist without his generosity and support, along with that of John Farley, Vanessa Henderson, and the entire Phillips Foundation. I'm eternally grateful to all of them.

The next indispensable figure in the process was Phillip Longman. It was his sensational book, *The Empty Cradle*, which induced in me a numerological obsession with demographics. As a rule, you should never meet your heroes; but several years ago I ignored this sensible dictum and called to ask Phil if he might be willing to have lunch with me. He has been unfailingly kind ever since.

I am similarly grateful to the wonderful eggheads and academics on whom I have leaned throughout this entire process. I won't bore you with a list, but I will beg you to read through the end notes and consider exploring the primary sources, which are invaluable. They're not scary. I promise.

Academics and experts get a bad rap, but with only a single exception, every one I spoke with was friendly, helpful, and gracious. In particular, I'm grateful for the assistance given by Nicholas Eberstadt, Irina Badurashvili, Bill Bishop, Christophe Guilmoto, Brad Wilcox, Gabriel Rossman, Laura Lindberg, Vladimir Canudas-Romo, Clark Welton, Diane Rubino, Minja Choe, Pat Sanders, Hans Johnson, Joshua Brown, Michael Smart, Karlyn Bowman, Patricia Luevano, Jane Lawler Dye, Mark Lino, Elaine Weinstein, and Carl Haub.

I owe an enormous debt to the office where I go for my day job, the *Weekly Standard*. It's the only place I've ever worked, in large part because Bill Kristol and Fred Barnes manage to be both inspiring and accessible. And the magazine they built has been my second family for the last 16 years. Nobody else in journalism could possibly have it as good as I have had it working for them. Growing up at the magazine, my editors Richard Starr and Claudia Anderson have been sources of constant encouragement and wisdom. My heroes Andy Ferguson, David Tell, Chris Caldwell, Matt Labash, Tucker Carlson, Jody Bottum, David Brooks, and John Podhoretz taught me how to write. My two work wives, Vic Matus and Catherine Lowe, have been faithful companions. (It's another sign of Bill's and Fred's genius that they allow such office polyamory.) Philip Chalk helped with photos and offered keen design advice. And my dear friend Robert Messenger, no longer at the *Standard*, was this idea's Sherpa almost from its inception. Just once, every writer should get to work with him.

Many other friends pitched in: Susan Arellano, Christine Rosen, and Naomi Schaefer Riley were unfailingly generous and helpful. Christopher Levenick, Adam White, Douglas Patey, and Kaiti Saunders all read drafts of the manuscript and offered excellent advice. My friend Adam Keiper edits one of my favorite journals, the Ethics and Public Policy Center's *New Atlantis*. He edited this book with levels of elegance, care, and precision that leave me wordless. He is the kindest and best of men and the finished product is as much his as it is mine. Adam's *TNA* colleagues Caitrin Nicol, Brendan Foht, and Samuel Matlack were tremendously helpful. Brian Boyd and Steven Fairchild built the index while Adam's private collection of Baker Street Boys—Galen Nicol, Jonathan Coppage, and especially Barbara McClay—were perceptive, persistent, and helpful in the extreme as they did a metric ton of heavy lifting in getting the book ready for publication. My friend Emily Schultheis fact-checked the manuscript and fixed as many errors as it's humanly possible to find. Thanks, too, to Mark Adomanis, Ari N. Schulman, and James Taranto for suggesting corrections for the paperback edition. Whatever errors remain are my fault.

I'm especially grateful to Roger Kimball for publishing this small book. It couldn't have happened without him and his colleagues at Encounter. Heather Ohle, Sam Schneider, and Lauren Miklos were smart and sure and I'm glad to have saddled up with them.

Finally, there's my family. In truth, my two eldest children, Cody John Paul (now 4) and Cordelia Mary (now 2), were, at best, indifferent to the project. After weeks of asking every afternoon if I had finished the book, Cody eventually informed me that his special blanket, named "Bidi," had just completed *her* book. I told him that I was proud of Bidi, because writing a book is very hard. His look a mixture of accusation and baleful disappointment, he responded: "Yes, it *was* hard. Especially since she does not have arms"—here he paused—"but she finished it anyway."

Emma Elisabeth was less helpful still, though no less adored, arriving in the world as she did just a few weeks before the book was published.

And so it fell to my dear wife, Shannon, to provide all of the familial support and encouragement, in addition to being my editor of first, and last, resort. I can't possibly express my gratitude, admiration, and devotion in proper measure. I can only say thank you. And I love you.

Notes

Introduction: One Child for All!

1. American Pet Products Manufacturers Association, *National Pet Owners Survey: 2006* (Greenwich, Conn.: APPMA, 2006). http://www.americanpetproducts.org/press_industrytrends.asp

2. American Pet Products Association, *National Pet Owners Survey: 2008* (Greenwich, Conn.: APPMA, 2006).

3. Maureen Mackey, "The Pet Economy: Americans Feed the Beast, and Then Some," *Fiscal Times*, June 26, 2010. http://www.thefiscaltimes.com/Articles/2010/06/26/The-Pet-Economy-Americans-Feed-the-Beast-and-Then-Some.aspx

4. American Pet Products Association, *National Pet Owners Survey: 2011–2012* (Greenwich, Conn.: APPA, 2011), 128.

5. *Ibid.*, 127.

6. Mark M. Gray, "Family Pets and Fertility?" *Nineteen Sixty-Four* (blog), Center for Applied Research in the Apostolate, Georgetown Uni-

versity, February 21, 2011. http://nineteensixty-four.blogspot.com/2011/02/family-pets-and-fertility.html

7. **Pet Population:** Ann Hoevel, "U.S. Is a Nation of 360 Million — Pets," CNN.com, March 17, 2006. http://articles.cnn.com/2006-03-10/us/modern.pets_1_pet-industry-bob-vetere-pet-food?_s = PM:US

Human Population: U.S. Census Bureau, Population Division, "Table 2. Projections of the Population by Selected Age Groups and Sex for the United States: 2010 to 2050 (NP2008–T2)," August 14, 2008. http://www.census.gov/population/www/projections/summarytables.html

8. Jeffrey Toobin, "Rich Bitch," *New Yorker*, September 29, 2008. http://www.newyorker.com/reporting/2008/09/29/080929fa_fact_toobin

9. Rick Klein and Huma Khan, "Can Your Pet Save You on Your Taxes?" ABC News, October 13, 2009. http://abcnews.go.com/Politics/pets-save-taxes-congress-debate-happy-act/story?id = 8811927

10. Barbara Kohn, "Bill Proposed to Provide Tax Deduction for Pet Care," Examiner.com, August 7, 2009 (http://www.examiner.com/cats-in-national/bill-proposed-to-provide-tax-deduction-for-pet-care-expenses). *Humanity and Pets Partnered Through the Years (HAPPY) Act*, H.R. 3501, 111th Cong., 1st sess., July 31, 2009 (http://hdl.loc.gov/loc.uscongress/legislation.111hr3501).

11. DogTownMaryland.com.

12. Sophie Hardach, "Japan's Childless Turn to Canines," Reuters, August 27, 2007. http://uk.reuters.com/article/latestCrisis/idUKT33496920070826

13. U.S. Commercial Service, "Italy: The Pet Products Market Opportunities for U.S. Exporters," U.S. Department of Commerce, October 18, 2005. http://www.americanpetproducts.org/Uploads/MemServices/MarketSectorReportItaly.pdf

14. Central Intelligence Agency (CIA), *The World Factbook*. https://www.cia.gov/library/publications/the-world-factbook/

15. All these figures come from the U.S. Census Bureau's Fact Finder tool, located at FactFinder2.census.gov, relying on data from the 2000 census.

16. These data are also from the Census Fact Finder tool. I calculated the average number of children by looking at "average family size," which for Old Town Alexandria was 2.57 in the year 2000.

(Average family size is distinct from "average household size," which for Old Town was even lower, 1.78 — suggesting that Old Town is also a hotbed for singles.)

17. Joyce A. Martin, Brady E. Hamilton, Stephanie J. Ventura, *et al.*, "Births: Final Data for 2010," *National Vital Statistics Reports* 61, no. 1 (2012). http://www.cdc.gov/nchs/data/nvsr/nvsr61/nvsr61_01.pdf

18. J. Bongaarts and G. Feeney, "On the quantum and tempo of fertility," *Population and Development Review* 24, no. 2 (1998): 271–291.

19. Jane Lawler Dye, *Fertility of American Women: 2008*, Current Population Reports, U.S. Census Bureau, November 2010. http://www.census.gov/prod/2010pubs/p20-563.pdf

20. Marilynn Marchione, "Recession may have pushed U.S. birth rate to new low," Associated Press, August 27, 2010. http://www.d-transition.info/western-demographic-winter-2/recession-may-have-pushed-us-birth-rate-new-low-17/

21. CIA, *World Factbook*. https://www.cia.gov/library/publications/the-world-factbook/rankorder/2127rank.html

22. Jane Lawler Dye, "Fertility of American Women: 2008," *Current Population Reports* (Washington, D.C.: U.S. Census Bureau, 2010), 4. http://www.census.gov/prod/2010pubs/p20-563.pdf

23. Paul R. Ehrlich, *The Population Bomb* (New York: Ballantine Books, 1968), 12.

24. Mara Hvistendahl, *Unnatural Selection: Choosing Boys Over Girls, and the Consequences of a World Full of Men* (New York: Public Affairs, 2011), 96.

25. Paul R. Ehrlich and Anne H. Ehrlich, "The Population Bomb Revisited," *The Electronic Journal of Sustainable Development* 1, no. 3 (2009). http://www.ejsd.org/public/journal_article/10

26. D. Van de Kaa and K. Van der Windt, *Minder Mensn, Meer Welzijn* [Fewer People, More Welfare] (Utrecht: Het Spektrum, 1979).

27. United Nations, Department of Economic and Social Affairs, Population Division, *World Population Prospects: The 2010 Revision*, 2011. http://esa.un.org/unpd/wpp/Excel-Data/fertility.htm

28. Wolfgang Lutz, Warren Sanderson, and Sergei Scherbov, "The End of World Population Growth," *Nature*, 412 (August 2001): 543–

545. http://www.nature.com/nature/journal/v412/n6846/full/412543a0.html

29. United Nations, Department of Economic and Social Affairs, Population Division, *World Population Prospects: The 2008 Revision*, 2009. http://esa.un.org/peps/xls_2008\DB01_Period_Indicators\WPP2008_DB1_F01_TOTAL_FERTILITY.XLS

30. United Nations, Department of Economic and Social Affairs, Population Division, *World Population Prospects: The 2010 Revision*, 2011, File 1B: Total Population (both sexes combined) by five-year age group, major area, region and country, annually for 2011. *Nota bene*: I am comparing the cohorts aged 0 to 14 (5.626 million) with the cohorts aged 20 to 34 (9.335 million).

31. United Nations, Department of Economic and Social Affairs, Population Division, *World Population Prospects: The 2010 Revision*, 2011. http://esa.un.org/peps/Preliminary-Results/figures/figures_Total-Population_WPP2010-2008.htm

32. United Nations, Department of Economic and Social Affairs, Population Division, *World Population Prospects: The 2010 Revision*, 2011. http://esa.un.org/unpd/wpp/index.htm

33. Phillip Longman, *The Empty Cradle: How Falling Birthrates Threaten World Prosperity, and What To Do About It* (New York: Basic Books, 2004), 61.

34. Elaine Tyler May, *America and the Pill: A History of Promise, Peril, and Liberation* (New York: Basic Books, 2010), 20.

35. Interview with Zhao Bingli, Vice Minister, State Family Planning Commission, October 18, 2002. http://www.china.org.cn/english/2002/Oct/46138.htm

36. CIA, *World Factbook*. https://www.cia.gov/library/publications/the-world-factbook/geos/ch.html

Chapter One: America's Falling Fertility

1. Thomas L. Friedman, *Hot, Flat, and Crowded: Why We Need a Green Revolution—and How it Can Renew America* (New York: Farrar, Straus, and Giroux, 2008), 365.

2. Jonathan V. Last, "The Lost Girls," *Weekly Standard*, September 26, 2011. http://www.weeklystandard.com/articles/lost-girls_593650.html

3. Therese Hesketh, Li Lu, Zhu Wei Xing, "The Effect of China's One-Child Family Policy After 25 Years," *The New England Journal of Medicine* 353, no 11 (September 15, 2005): 1171–1176. http://www.nejm.org/doi/full/10.1056/NEJMhpro51833

4. Nicholas Eberstadt, "China's Future and Its One-Child Policy," World Economic Forum Address, September 7, 2007. http://www.aei.org/issue/society-and-culture/citizenship/chinas-future-and-its-one-child-policy/

5. Richard Jackson, Neil Howe, *The Graying of the Middle Kingdom: The Demographics and Economics of Retirement Policy in China*, Center for Strategic and International Studies (April 2004), 6.

6. Jung Chang and Jon Halliday, *Mao: The Unknown Story* (New York: Knopf, 2005).

7. Ben J. Wattenberg, *The Birth Dearth: What Happens When People in Free Countries Don't Have Enough Babies?* (New York: Pharos Books, 1987), 14.

8. Michael R. Haines, *Ethnic Differences in Demographic Behavior in the United States: Has There Been Convergence?*, National Bureau of Economic Research, July 2002, 22. http://www.nber.org/papers/w9042

9. *Ibid.*

10. *Ibid.*

11. *Ibid.*

12. Wattenberg, *The Birth Dearth*, 173.

13. National Vital Statistics System. http://www.cdc.gov/nchs/data_access/vitalstats/VitalStats_Births.htm

14. U.S. Census Bureau, *Statistical Abstract of the United States: 2011*. http://www.census.gov/compendia/statab/2011/tables/11s0083.pdf "Birth and Fertility Rates for States by Hispanic Origin Subgroups: United States, 1990 and 2000," *Vital and Health Statistics*, Series 21, no. 57 (May 2006), 24. http://www.cdc.gov/nchs/data/series/sr_21/sr21_057.pdf

15. U.S. Census Bureau, *Statistical Abstract of the United States: 2011*. http://www.census.gov/compendia/statab/2011/tables/11s0083.pdf

16. Brady E. Hamilton, Joyce A. Martin, and Stephanie J. Ventura, "Birth: Preliminary Data for 2009," *National Vital Statistics Reports* 59, no. 3, December 2010. http://www.cdc.gov/nchs/data/nvsr/nvsr59/nvsr59_03.pdf

17. Paul D. Sutton, Brady E. Hamilton, and T.J. Mathews, "Recent Decline in Births in the United States, 2007–2009," Center for Disease Control and Prevention, *NCHS Data Brief*, no. 60, March 2011. http://www.cdc.gov/nchs/data/databriefs/db60.htm#women

18. Betsy Guzmán, "The Hispanic Population," *Census 2000 Brief*, U.S. Census Bureau, May 2001. http://www.census.gov/prod/2001pubs/c2kbr01-3.pdf

19. Karen R. Humes, Nicholas A. Jones, and Roberto R. Ramirez, "Overview of Race and Hispanic Origin: 2010," *2010 Census Briefs*, U.S. Census Bureau, March 2011. http://www.census.gov/prod/cen2010/briefs/c2010br-02.pdf

20. U.S. Census Bureau, "Current Population Survey–March 2010 Detailed Tables," Table 3.17, "Year of Entry of the Foreign-Born Population by Sex and World Region of Birth: 2010." http://www.census.gov/population/foreign/data/cps2010.html

21. Haines, *Ethnic Differences in Demographic Behavior*, 24. http://eh.net/encyclopedia/article/haines.demography

22. CIA, *World Factbook*. https://www.cia.gov/library/publications/the-world-factbook/geos/us.html

23. Lydia Saad, "Americans' Preference for Smaller Families Edges Higher," Gallup News Service, June 30, 2011. http://www.gallup.com/poll/148355/americans-preference-smaller-families-edges-higher.aspx

24. U.S. Census Bureau, "Women by Number of Children Ever Born by Race, Hispanic Origin, Nativity Status, Marital Status, and Age: June 2006," U.S. Census Bureau, August 2008. http://www.census.gov/hhes/fertility/data/cps/2006.html

25. Robert Gutman and Clyde V. Kiser, "Differential Fertility in the United States," *Demographic and Economic Change in Developed Countries* (UMI, 1960). http://www.nber.org/chapters/c2383.pdf

26. Brady E. Hamilton, Joyce A. Martin, T.J. Mathews, Michelle J.K. Osterma, Paul D. Sutton, and Stephanie J. Ventura, *National Vital Sta-*

tistics Reports 59, no. 1 (December 8, 2010): 43, Table 12. http://www.cdc.gov/nchs/data/nvsr/nvsr59/nvsr59_01.pdf

27. CIA, *World Factbook*. https://www.cia.gov/library/publications/the-world-factbook/rankorder/2127rank.html?countryName=Ireland&countryCode=ei&regionCode=eur&rank=130#ei

28. National Vital Statistic System. http://www.cdc.gov/nchs/data_access/vitalstats/VitalStats_Births.htm

29. Gutman and Kiser, "Differential Fertility."

30. Steve Sailer, "The Dirt Gap: The Fundamental Cause of Red vs. Blue States," *American Conservative*, February 14, 2005. http://www.isteve.com/2005_Dirt_Gap.htm

31. *Ibid.*, 1.

32. National Exit Poll, November 4, 2008. http://www.cnn.com/ELECTION/2008/results/polls/#val=USP00p3

33. Elizabeth M. Grieco and Edward N. Trevelyan, "Place of Birth of the Foreign-Born Population: 2009," *American Community Survey Briefs*, ACSBR/09–15, October 2010. http://www.census.gov/prod/2010pubs/acsbr09-15.pdf

34. State of California, Department of Finance, *Population Projections for California and Its Counties 2000–2050*, July 2007. http://www.dof.ca.gov/HTML/DEMOGRAP/ReportsPapers/Projections/P1/P1.php

35. Clark A. Davis and J. Joshua Brown, "Trends and Differentials in California Fertility Rates 1970–2000," *California Journal of Health Promotion* 1, no. 3 (2003): 77–92.

36. *Ibid.*, 90.

37. Robert D. Putnam, *"E Pluribus Unum:* Diversity and Community in the Twenty-first Century: The 2006 Johan Skytte Prize Lecture," *Scandinavian Political Studies* 30, no. 2 (2007): 151.

38. Russell Shorto, "No Babies?" *New York Times*, June 29, 2008. http://www.nytimes.com/2008/06/29/magazine/29Birth-t.html

39. CIA, *World Factbook: 1995.* http://www.umsl.edu/services/govdocs/wofact95/wf950119.htm

40. National Institute of Statistics (Italy), "Resident Population and Population Change: Year 2010," May 24, 2011, 2. http://en.istat.it/sala-

stampa/comunicati/in_calendario/bildem/20110524_00/resident_popu-
lation_10.pdf

41. United Nations, Department of Economic and Social Affairs,
Population Division, *Replacement Migration: Is it a Solution to Declining
and Ageing Populations?* (New York: United Nations, 2001). http://www.
un.org/esa/population/publications/ReplMigED/Italy.pdf

42. S. Philip Morgan and Miles G. Taylor, "Low Fertility at the Turn of
the Twenty-First Century," *Annual Review of Sociology*, 32 (2006): 375–399.
http://www.ncbi.nlm.nih.gov/pmc/articles/PMC2849172/pdf/
nihms185225.pdf

43. United Nations, Department of Economic and Social Affairs,
Population Division, *World Population Prospects: The 2010 Revision*, 2011.
http://esa.un.org/unpd/wpp/index.htm

44. CIA, *World Factbook: 1995.* http://www.umsl.edu/services/gov-
docs/wofact95/wf950122.htm

45. CIA, *World Factbook: 2000.* http://www.photius.com/wfb2000/
countries/japan/japan_people.html

46. CIA, *World Factbook: 2006* and *World Factbook: 2007.* http://www.
theodora.com/wfb2006/japan/japan_people.html http://www.allcoun-
tries.org/wfb2007/japan/japan_people.html

47. CIA, *World Factbook: 2008* and *World Factbook: 2011.* https://
www.cia.gov/library/publications/download/download-2008/index.
html https://www.cia.gov/library/publications/download/download-2011/
index.html

48. United Nations, *Replacement Migration: Japan*, 51.

49. United Nations, Department of Economic and Social Affairs,
Population Division *World Population Prospects: The 2010 Revision*, 2011.
http://esa.un.org/peps/Preliminary-Results/figures/figures_Total-Popu-
lation_WPP2010-2008.htm

50. United Nations, Department of Economic and Social Affairs,
Population Division, *World Population Prospects: The 2010 Revision*, 2011.
http://esa.un.org/unpd/wpp/index.htm

51. United Nations, Department of Economic and Social Affairs, Population Division, "Future Expectations for Below-Replacement Fertility,"

Expert Working Group Meeting on Below-Replacement Fertility, Department of Economic and Social Affairs (October 7, 1997), Item 4, Section B. http://www.un.org/esa/population/pubsarchive/belowrep/belowrep.htm

52. United Nations, Department of Economic and Social Affairs, Population Division, *Replacement Migration: Is it a Solution to Declining and Ageing Populations?* (New York: United Nations, 2001), 11. http://www.un.org/esa/population/publications/ReplMigED/chap2-Litrev.pdf

53. S. Philip Morgan and Miles G. Taylor, "Low Fertility at the Turn of the Twenty-First Century," *Annual Review of Sociology* 32 (2006): 375–399. http://www.ncbi.nlm.nih.gov/pmc/articles/PMC2849172/pdf/nihms185225.pdf

54. United Nations, *Replacement Migration: European Union*, 90. http://www.un.org/esa/population/publications/migration/migration.htm

55. Shorto, "No Babies?"

56. CIA, *World Factbook: 1995*. http://www.theodora.com/wfb/1995/russia/russia_people.html

57. CIA, *World Factbook: 2011*. https://www.cia.gov/library/publications/the-world-factbook/geos/rs.html

58. David Johnson, "Russia Sees Drop in Population as Security Threat," *Russia Weekly*, Center for Defense Information, February 16, 2001. http://cdi.org/russia/141.html

59. Phillip Longman, *The Empty Cradle: How Falling Birthrates Threaten World Prosperity, and What To Do About It* (New York: Basic Books, 2004), 18.

60. *Ibid.*, 118.

61. *Ibid.*, 126.

62. *Ibid.*, 130.

63. *Ibid.*, 21.

64. Spengler (David P. Goldman), "The Peacekeepers of Penzance," *Asia Times*, August 22, 2006. http://www.atimes.com/atimes/Middle_East/HH22Ako2.html

65. United Nations, Department of Economic and Social Affairs, Population Division, *World Fertility Patterns 2007*, 2008. http://www.un.org/esa/population/publications/worldfertility2007/worldfertility2007.htm

66. Mara Hvistendahl, *Unnatural Selection: Choosing Boys Over Girls, and the Consequences of a World Full of Men* (New York: Public Affairs, 2011), 33.

67. *Family Planning* (film), directed by Les Clark, Walt Disney Productions, 1967.

68. Shorto, "No Babies?"

69. Hvistendahl, *Unnatural Selection*, 32–34.

70. Jeff Jacoby, "The Coming Population Bust," *Boston Globe*, June 18, 2008. http://www.boston.com/bostonglobe/editorial_opinion/oped/articles/2008/06/18/the_coming_population_bust/

71. Robert McClure, "Dalai Lama heads for Michigan after imparting enviro and other forms of wisdom here," SeattlePI.com (blog post), April 15, 2008. http://blog.seattlepi.com/environment/2008/04/15/dalai-lama-heads-for-michigan-after-imparting-enviro-and-other-forms-of-wisdom-here/

72. See http://www.unfpa.org/public/world-population-day/

73. Sue Dunlevy, "Babies a drag on the economy, report says," *Telegraph* (London), August 6, 2008. http://www.news.com.au/business/money/story/0,25479,24134255-5017313,00.html

74. Paul Murtaugh *et al.*, "Family Planning: A Major Environmental Emphasis," Oregon State University, July 2009. http://oregonstate.edu/ua/ncs/archives/2009/jul/family-planning-major-environmental-emphasis

75. Johann Hari, "Are There Just Too Many People in the World?" *Independent* (London), May 15, 2008. http://www.huffingtonpost.com/johann-hari/are-there-just-too-many-p_b_144065.html

76. Friedman, *Hot, Flat, and Crowded*.

77. Miss Ann Thropy [pseud.], writing in *Earth First!* in May and December 1987, cited in Chaz Bufe, "Primitive Thought," *Processed World* 22, Summer 1998, 16. http://www.archive.org/stream/processedworld22proc

78. Diane Francis, "The Real Inconvenient Truth," *Financial Post*, December 10, 2009. http://www.financialpost.com/story.html?id=2314438

79. Li Xing, "Population Control Called Key to Deal," *China Daily*, December 10, 2009. http://www.chinadaily.com.cn/china/2009-12/10/content_9151129.htm

80. Anne Applebaum, "Anti-Climate Change, Anti-Human," *Washington Post*, December 15, 2009. (Applebaum refers to Population Matters by the group's previous name: Optimum Population Trust.) http://www.washingtonpost.com/wp-dyn/content/article/2009/12/14/AR2009121402719.html

81. *Ibid.*

82. Stephanie Mencimer, "The Baby Boycott," *Washington Monthly*, June 2001. http://www.washingtonmonthly.com/features/2001/0106.mencimer.html

83. Annys Shin, "With City's Baby Boom, Parental Guidance Suggested," *Washington Post*, May 16, 2010, A01. http://www.washingtonpost.com/wp-dyn/content/article/2010/05/15/AR2010051503637.html

84. Jonathan V. Last, "There Goes the Neighborhood," *Weekly Standard*, September 13, 2010. http://www.weeklystandard.com/articles/there-goes-neighborhood

85. *Ibid.*

86. Shorto, "No Babies?"

87. Polybius, *The Histories, Book XXXVII*, trans. Evelyn S. Shuckburgh, 510. http://books.google.com/books?id=RnJiAAAAMAAJ&printsec=frontcover&dq=polybius+histories#PPA510,M1

88. Massimo Livi-Bacci, *A Concise History of World Population* (Italy: Loescher, 1989), 27, 73.

89. Daniel Gross, "Children For Sale," *Slate*, May 24, 2006. http://www.slate.com/id/2142366/

90. U.S. Census Bureau, "Historical Estimates of World Population." http://www.census.gov/population/international/data/worldpop/table_history.php

91. Mark Steyn, *America Alone: The End of the World as We Know It* (Washington, D.C.: Regnery, 2006).

Chapter Two: The Roots of One-Child

1. PinkandBrownBoutique.com

2. "Annual Cost of Raising a Child: 1960, North Central Region," U.S. Department of Agriculture. (A note on these numbers: Prior to 1989, the USDA did not produce cost estimates for the country as a whole. Rather, it produced estimates for different regions. According to Mark Lino, who runs the study for the USDA today, the North Central region—later renamed the Midwest region—from those earlier studies can be used as a reasonable proxy for the national average. Where I refer to these numbers prior to 1989, I am, in fact, using the North Central/Midwest figures. Further, the USDA keeps three sets of data for each year according to income variants. I refer to the middle variant for all years. Finally, all updating of costs to 2011 constant dollars are done using the Bureau of Labor Statistics Consumer Price Index Inflation Calendar. www.bls.gov/data/inflation_calculator.htm.)

3. Carolyn Summers, "USDA Estimates of the Cost of Raising a Child: Midwest," USDA Miscellaneous Publication No. 1411, 1985.

4. Mark Lino, "Expenditures by Families on Children, 2007," U.S. Department of Agriculture, Center for Nutrition Policy and Promotion, Miscellaneous Publication No. 1528–2007 (2008). http://www.cnpp.usda.gov/ExpendituresonChildrenbyFamilies.htm

5. Pamela Paul, *Parenting, Inc.: How we are Sold on $800 Strollers, Fetal Education, Baby Sign Language, Sleeping Coaches, Toddler Couture, and Diaper Wipe Warmers—and What It Means for Our Children* (New York: Times Books, 2008), 9.

6. *Ibid.*, 10.

7. National Association of Child Care Resource and Referral Agencies, "The High Price of Child Care, 2008 Update," 2008.

8. Sandy Baum and Jennifer Ma, "Trends in College Pricing: 2011," The College Board, 2011. http://trends.collegeboard.org/college_pricing/report_findings/indicator/Enrollment_Patterns_by_Selected_Characteristics

9. *Ibid.*

10. *Ibid.*

11. *Vital Statistics of the United States, 1965, Volume 1–Natality*, U.S. Department of Health, Education, and Welfare (1967), Table 1–6: Total

Fertility Rates and Birth Rates by Age of Mother, by Color: United States, 1940–65. http://www.nber.org/vital-stats-books/nat65_1.CV.pdf

12. Suzanne M. Bianchi, Melissa A. Milkie, and John P. Robinson, *Changing Rhythms of American Family Life*, American Sociological Association (2006), 59–125.

13. *Ibid.*

14. *Ibid.*

15. Bryan Caplan, *Selfish Reasons to Have More Kids: Why Being a Great Parent Is Less Work and More Fun Than You Think* (New York: Basic Books, 2011), 20.

16. Bianchi *et al.*, *Changing Rhythms*, Table 5A.1.

17. *Ibid.*, Table 5A.6. This figure of 12.6 hours of childcare per week encompasses all mothers; the figure for working mothers is still a whopping 10.6 hours per week.

18. *Ibid.*

19. Phillip Longman, *The Empty Cradle: How Falling Birthrates Threaten World Prosperity, and What To Do About It* (New York: Basic Books, 2004), 72.

20. "Current Population Survey, 2008: Annual Social and Economic Supplement," U.S. Census Bureau, 2008. http://pubdb3.census.gov/macro/032008/perinc/new03_001.htm

21. "Current Population Survey, 2008: Annual Social and Economic Supplement," U.S. Census Bureau, 2008. http://pubdb3.census.gov/macro/032008/perinc/new03_037.htm

22. National Association of Realtors, "4th Quarter Metro Area Home Prices Down as Buyers Purchase Distressed Property," February 12, 2009. http://www.realtor.org/press_room/news_releases/2009/02/4th_quarter_metro_area_home_prices_down

23. Longman, *The Empty Cradle*, 80.

24. Social Security Administration, "2013 Social Security Changes," 2013. http://www.ssa.gov/pressoffice/factsheets/colafacts2013.htm

25. Claire Hintz, "The Tax Burden of the Median American Family," Special Report 96, Tax Foundation, March 1, 2000. http://www.taxfoundation.org/article/tax-burden-median-american-family

26. Diane Macunovich, *Birth Quake: The Baby Boom and Its Aftershocks*, Online Appendix to Chapter 4: Alternative Measures of Male Relative Income. http://newton.uor.edu/Departments&Programs/EconomicDept/macunovich/birthquake/chp04app.pdf

27. Longman, *The Empty Cradle*, 77.

28. Robert Stein, "Taxes and the Family," *National Affairs*, 2 (Winter 2010): 35–48. http://www.nationalaffairs.com/publications/detail/taxes-and-the-family

29. Claudia Goldin *et al.*, "The Homecoming of American College Women," *Journal of Economic Perspectives*, volume 20, number 4 (Fall 2006): 133–156. http://www.princeton.edu/~kuziemko/gkk_jep.pdf

30. Claudia Goldin, "Career and Family: College Women Look to the Past," in *Gender & Family Issues in the Workplace*, edited by Francine D. Blau and Ronald G. Ehrenberg (New York: Russell Sage Foundation, 1997), 23 (http://tinyurl.com/9r35382). See also: U.S. Census Bureau, "Educational Attainment in the United States: March 1995," Population Characteristics P-20 Series (March 1995), 87 (http://www.census.gov/prod/www/abs/p20.html#eduattn).

31. Organisation for Economic Co-Operation and Development, ALFS Summary Tables, Labour Force Statistics by sex and age–indicators. http://stats.oecd.org/

32. Karin L. Brewster and Ronald R. Rindfuss, "Fertility and Women's Employment in Industrialized Nations," *Annual Review of Sociology* 26 (2000): 271–296. http://tinyurl.com/9skhm3m

33. David R. Francis, "Why Do Women Outnumber Men in College?" *NBER Digest*, January 2007. http://www.nber.org/digest/jan07/w12139.html

34. U.S. Census Bureau, "Median Age at First Marriage, 1890–2010." http://www.infoplease.com/ipa/A0005061.html

35. T.J. Matthews and Brady Hamilton, "Mean Age of Mother, 1970–2000," *National Vital Statistics Report* 51, no. 1 (December 11, 2002). http://www.cdc.gov/nchs/pressroom/02news/ameriwomen.htm

36. Sandy Baum and Marie O'Malley, "College on Credit: Results of the 2002 National Student Loan Survey," Nellie Mae Corporation, 2003. http://www.nelliemae.com/library/research_10.html

37. BabyCenter.com, "The Effect of Age on Fertility." http://www.babycenter.com/0_chart-the-effect-of-age-on-fertility_6155.bc

38. Vanessa Grigoriadis, "Waking Up From the Pill," *New York Magazine*, November 8, 2010. http://nymag.com/news/features/69789/

39. "Women's Fertility Drops 'Almost to Zero' After Age 43," Baylor College of Medicine Public Affairs Office (January 2, 2004). http://web.archive.org/web/20060907234231/http://www.bcm.edu/news/item.cfm?newsID=66

40. Mara Hvistendahl, *Unnatural Selection: Choosing Boys Over Girls, and the Consequences of a World Full of Men* (New York: Public Affairs, 2011), 254.

Chapter Three: SEX! (and maybe marriage)

1. Jean H. Baker, *Margaret Sanger: A Life of Passion* (New York: Farrar, Straus and Giroux, 2011), 10.

2. Lara V. Marks, *Sexual Chemistry: A History of the Contraceptive Pill* (New Haven: Yale University Press, 2001), 51–52.

3. Elaine Tyler May, *America and the Pill: A History of Promise, Peril, and Liberation* (New York: Basic Books, 2010), 17–34.

4. Margaret Sanger, "The Eugenic Value of Birth Control Propaganda," *Birth Control Review*, October 1921. http://www.nyu.edu/projects/sanger/webedition/app/documents/show.php?sangerDoc=238946.xml

5. Margaret Sanger, *Margaret Sanger: An Autobiography* (New York: W.W. Norton, 1938), 374–375. http://archive.org/stream/margaretsangerau1938sang#page/374/mode/2up

6. Margaret Sanger, "Apostle of Birth Control Sees Cause Gaining Here," *New York Times*, April 8, 1923, XII. http://select.nytimes.com/gst/abstract.html?res=F30B10FE345416738DDDA10894DC405B838EF1D3

7. Margaret Sanger, "National Security and Birth Control," *Forum and Century*, March 1935, 139–141. http://www.nyu.edu/projects/sanger/webedition/app/documents/show.php?sangerDoc=236613.xml

8. Margaret Sanger to Katharine McCormick, October 27, 1950 (Sanger Papers, Smith College). http://www.pbs.org/wgbh/amex/pill/filmmore/ps_letters.html

9. "Intelligent or Unintelligent Birth Control" (editorial), *The Birth Control Review* (Margaret Sanger, ed.), Vol. III, No. 5, May 1919, 12. http://library.lifedynamics.com/Birth%20Control%20Review/1919-05%20May.pdf

10. Miriam Kleiman, "Rich, Famous, and Questionably Sane: When a Wealthy Heir's Family Sought Help from a Hospital for the Insane," *Prologue Magazine* 39, no 2 (Summer 2007). http://www.archives.gov/publications/prologue/2007/summer/mccormick.html

11. May, *America and the Pill*, 2.

12. W. D. Mosher and J. Jones, "Use of Contraception in the United States: 1982–2008," *Vital Health Statistics*, Series 23, no. 29 (2010). http://www.cdc.gov/nchs/data/series/sr_23/sr23_029.pdf

13. *Ibid.*

14. *Ibid.*

15. *Ibid.* This number is constructed using the data in Table I, p. 34.

16. Pearce, *The Coming Population Crash*, 27.

17. The Alan Guttmacher Institute, "In Their Own Right: Addressing the Sexual and Reproductive Health Needs of American Men," 2002. http://www.guttmacher.org/pubs/fb_10-02.html

18. If you care, for men in 2002, average age for first sexual intercourse was 16.9 years; average age of first marriage was 26.7 years; average age of first birth was 28.5 years; and by 33.2 years, the average man intended to have no more children.

19. Christine A. Bachrach and Marjorie C. Horn, "Marriage and First Intercourse, Marital Dissolution, and Remarriage: United States, 1982," *NCHS Advanced Data*, no. 107, April 12, 1985. http://www.cdc.gov/nchs/data/ad/ad107acc.pdf

20. U.S. Census Bureau, "Annual Social and Economic Supplement: 2003 Current Population Survey, Current Population Reports, Series P20–

553"; "America's Families and Living Arrangements: 2003" and earlier reports. "Table MS-2. Estimated Median Age at First Marriage, by Sex: 1890 to Present," 2004. http://www.census.gov/population/socdemo/hh-fam/tabMS-2.pdf

21. U.S. Census Bureau, Current Population Survey, and Annual Social and Economic Supplements, March 2010 and earlier (census.gov).

22. Brady E. Hamilton and Stephanie J. Ventura, "Fertility and Abortion Rates in the United States, 1960–2002," *International Journal of Andrology* 29 (2006): 34–45.

23. U.S. Department of Health, Education, and Welfare, *Vital Statistics of the United States: 1960, Volume 1: Natality*, 1–11. http://www.cdc.gov/nchs/data/vsus/nat60_1.pdf

For 1960, there were 4,257,850 live births; 224,330 of which were out of wedlock.

24. U.S. Department of Health, Education, and Welfare, *Vital Statistics of the United States: 1980, Volume 1: Natality*, 4–11. http://www.cdc.gov/nchs/data/vsus/nat80_1acc.pdf

For 1980 there were 3,612,258 live births, 665,747 of which were reported or inferred to be out of wedlock.

25. Brady E. Hamilton, Joyce A. Martin, T.J. Matthews, Michelle J.K. Osterman, Paul D. Sutton, and Stephanie J. Ventura, "Births: Final Data for 2008," *National Vital Statistics Reports* 59, no. 1 (December 2010): 2. http://www.cdc.gov/nchs/data/nvsr/nvsr59/nvsr59_01.pdf

26. Christine A. Bachrach and Stephanie J. Ventura, "Nonmarital Childbearing in the United States, 1940–99," *National Vital Statistics Reports* 48, no. 16 (October 18, 2000): 8. http://www.cdc.gov/nchs/data/nvsr/nvsr48/nvs48_16.pdf

27. Brady E. Hamilton, Sharon Kirmeyer, Joyce A Martin, Fray Menacker, Martha L. Munson, Paul D. Sutton and Stephanie J. Ventura, "Births: Final Data for 2005," *National Vital Statistics Reports* 56, no. 6 (December 5, 2007): 8. http://wonder.cdc.gov/wonder/sci_data/natal/detail/type_txt/natal05/Births05.pdf

28. Brady E. Hamilton, Joyce A. Martin and Stephanie J. Ventura, "Births: Preliminary Data for 2009," *National Vital Statistics Reports* 59,

no. 3 (December 21, 2010): Table 2. http://www.cdc.gov/nchs/data/nvsr/nvsr59/nvsr59_03.pdf

For 2009, there were 4,131,019 total births, 1,543,190 of which were to mothers over 30.

29. Stephanie J. Ventura, "Changing Patterns of Nonmarital Childbearing in the United States," *NCHS Data Brief*, no. 18 (May 2009): 4. http://www.cdc.gov/nchs/data/databriefs/db18.pdf

30. U.S. Department of Health and Human Services, "Marriage and Cohabitation in the United States: A Statistical Portrait Based on Cycle 6 (2002) of the National Survey of Family Growth," *Vital and Health Statistics*, Series 23, no. 28 (February 2010): 1. http://www.cdc.gov/nchs/data/series/sr_23/sr23_028.pdf

31. Russell Hittinger, "Abortion Before *Roe*," *First Things*, October 1994. www.firstthings.com/article.php3?id_article=4494

32. Ramesh Ponnuru, *Party of Death: The Democrats, the Media, the Courts, and the Disregard for Human Life* (Washington, D.C.: Regnery, 2006), 13.

33. "Abortion Surveillance—United States, 2003," Centers for Disease Control and Prevention, Mortality and Morbidity Weekly Report 55, no. SS-11 (November 24, 2006): 18. http://www.cdc.gov/mmwr/PDF/ss/ss5511.pdf

34. Alan Guttmacher Institute. http://www.nrlc.org/abortion/facts/abortionstats.html

34. National Right to Life Committee, "Abortion Statistics." http://www.nrlc.org/uploads/factsheets/FS01AbortionintheUS.pdf

35. *Ibid.* See also Guttmacher Institute, "Characteristics of U.S. Abortion Patients, 2008," May 2010. http://www.guttmacher.org/pubs/US-Abortion-Patients.pdf

37. Steve Sailer, "The Baby Gap," *American Conservative*, December 20, 2004. http://www.isteve.com/babygap.htm

38. Jacob Alex Klerman, "U.S. Abortion Policy and Fertility," *American Economic Review* 89, no. 2 (1999): 261–264. http://www.rand.org/pubs/research_briefs/RB5031/index1.html

39. James Q. Wilson, *The Marriage Problem: How Our Culture Has Weakened Families* (New York: HarperCollins, 2002), 11.

40. Linda J. Waite and Maggie Gallagher, *The Case for Marriage* (New York: Doubleday, 2000).

41. Vladimir Canudas-Romo and Robert Schoen, "Timing Effects on First Marriage: Twentieth Century Experience in England and Wales and the U.S.A.," *Population Studies* 59, no. 2 (July 2005): 135–146. http://www.jstor.org/stable/30040452

42. W. Bradford Wilcox, *The State of Our Unions: Marriage in 2010: When Marriage Disappears*, University of Virginia National Marriage Project and the Institute for American Values, December 2010. http://www.virginia.edu/marriageproject/pdfs/Union_11_12_10.pdf

43. *Ibid.*, 19.

44. David Popenoe and Barbara Defoe Whitehead, *The State of Our Unions: The Social Health of Marriage in America 1999*, University of Virginia National Marriage Project (June 1999): Figure 2. http://www.virginia.edu/marriageproject/pdfs/SOOU1999.pdf

45. U.S. Department of Health and Human Services, "Marriage and Cohabitation in the United States, Cycle 6."

46. Larry L. Bumpass, Andrew Cherlin, and James A. Sweet, "The Role of Cohabitation in Declining Rates of Marriage," *Journal of Marriage and Family* 53, no. 4 (November 1991): 913–927. http://www.jstor.org/stable/352997

47. U.S. Department of Health and Human Services, "Marriage and Cohabitation in the United States, Cycle 6," 27–28.

48. Bumpass, Cherlin, and Sweet, "The Role of Cohabitation in Declining Rates of Marriage." The effects of cohabitation on the marriage rate vary by group, obviously, with the 60 percent figure standing in for the most general cohorts.

49. U.S. Department of Health and Human Services, "Marriage and Cohabitation in the United States, Cycle 6," 17.

50. Bumpass, Cherlin, and Sweet, "The Role of Cohabitation in Declining Rates of Marriage," 917–918.

51. J. McDonald and S.H. Preston, "The Incidence of Divorce Within Cohorts of American Marriages Contracted Since the Civil War," *Demography* 16 (February 1979): 1–25. http://www.ncbi.nlm.nih.gov/pubmed/428602

52. W. Bradford Wilcox, "The Evolution of Divorce," *National Affairs*, 1 (Fall 2009): 81. http://www.nationalaffairs.com/publications/detail/the-evolution-of-divorce

53. Vladimir Canudas-Romo and Robert Schoen, "Timing Effects on Divorce: 20th Century Experience in the United States," *Journal of Marriage and the Family*, 68 (August 2006): 749–758.

54. Larry Bumpass and R. Kelly Raley, "The Topography of the Divorce Plateau: Levels and Trends in Union Stability in the United States After 1980," *Demographic Research* 8 (April 2003): 245–260. http://www.demographic-research.org/Volumes/Vol8/8

55. Meg Jay, "The Downside of Cohabiting Before Marriage," *New York Times*, April 14, 2012. http://www.nytimes.com/2012/04/15/opinion/sunday/the-downside-of-cohabiting-before-marriage.html

56. Mary Ann Glendon, *The Transformation of Family Law* (Chicago: University of Chicago Press, 1989), 188.

57. James Q. Wilson, *The Marriage Problem*, 162.

58. Douglas W. Allen and Maggie Gallagher, "Does Divorce Law Affect the Divorce Rate?" *iMAPP Research Brief* 1, no. 1 (July 2007). http://www.marriagedebate.com/pdf/imapp.nofault.divrate.pdf

59. James Q. Wilson, *The Marriage Problem*, 65–105.

Chapter Four: What You Can, and Cannot, Measure

1. Tatiana Zerjal *et al*. "The Genetic Legacy of the Mongols," *American Journal of Human Genetics* 72, no. 3 (March 2003). http://www.pubmedcentral.nih.gov/articlerender.fcgi?artid=1180246

2. Yali Xue, at al., "Recent Spread of a Y-Chromosomal Lineage in North China and Mongolia," *American Journal of Human Genetics* 77, no. 6 (December 2005). http://www.pubmedcentral.nih.gov/articlerender.fcgi?artid=1285168

3. Laoise Moore *et al.*, "A Y-Chromosome Signature of Hegemony of Gaelic Ireland," *American Journal of Human Genetics* 78, no. 2 (February 2006). http://www.pubmedcentral.nih.gov/articlerender.fcgi?artid=1380239

4. Massimo Livi-Bacci, *A History of Italian Fertility During the Last Two Centuries* (Princeton: Princeton University Press, 1977).

5. *Ibid.*, 45.

6. Jean-Pierre Bardet, "Rouen in the XVIIth and XVIIIth Centuries: Change of a Social Environment," Societe D'Edition D/Ensieignement Superieur, 1983.

7. Vegard Skirbekk, "Fertility Trends by Social Status," *Demographic Research* 18 (March 28, 2008). http://www.demographic-research.org/volumes/vol18/5/18-5.pdf

8. *Ibid.*, 157.

9. *Ibid.*, 150.

10. *Ibid.*, 153, quoting Michael R. Haines, "Occupation and Social Class during Fertility Decline: Historical Perspectives," in *The European Experience of Declining Fertility, 1850–1970: The Quiet Revolution*, John R. Gillis, Louise A. Tilly, and David Levine, eds. (Cambridge, Mass.: Blackwell, 1992) 224.

11. Skirbekk, "Fertility Trends by Social Status," 150.

12. Jonathan V. Last, "Notes from the Nanny State," *Weekly Standard*, October 6, 2008. http://www.weeklystandard.com/Content/Public/Articles/000/000/015/616vsefb.asp

13. Nicholas Jackson, "Old, Weird Tech: Baby Cage Edition," *The Atlantic.com*, October 8, 2010. http://www.theatlantic.com/technology/archive/2010/10/old-weird-tech-baby-cage-edition/63819/

14. Robert S. Sanders, Jr., *Dr. Seat Belt: The Life of Robert S. Sanders, M.D. Pioneer in Child Passenger Safety* (Armstrong Valley Publishing, 2008).

15. U.S. Census Bureau, *Current Population Survey*, June 1976–2006, "Table H2. Distribution of Women 40 to 44 Years Old by Number of Children Ever Born and Marital Status: Selected Years, 1970 to 2006." http://www.census.gov/hhes/fertility/data/cps/historical.html

16. U.S. Census Bureau, *Current Population Survey*, June 2010, Table 1: Table 1. Women by Number of Children Ever Born by Race, Hispanic Origin, Nativity Status, Marital Status, and Age. http://www.census.gov/hhes/fertility/data/cps/2010.html

17. Steve Sailer, "The Dirt Gap," *American Conservative*, February 14, 2005. http://www.isteve.com/2005_Dirt_Gap.htm

18. Robert W. Burchell, William Dolphin, and David Listokin, "Residential Demographic Multipliers: Projections for the Occupants of New Housing," Fannie Mae Foundation (June 2006). Not available online, but a summary is available here: http://tinyurl.com/96eleeb

19. Clyde V. Kiser, "Differential Fertility in the United States," *Demographic and Economic Change in Developed Countries* (UMI, 1960), 87. http://www.nber.org/chapters/c2383.pdf

20. Willystine Goodsell, "Housing and Birth Rate in Sweden," *American Sociological Review* 2, no. 6 (December 1937): 1410–1427. http://www.jstor.org/stable/2084364

21. Warren S. Thompson, "The Effect of Housing Upon *Population* Growth," *Milbank Memorial Fund Quarterly* 16, no. 4 (October 1938): 359–368. http://www.jstor.org/pss/3347951

22. Marcus Felson and Mauricio Solaún, "The Fertility Inhibiting Effect of Crowded Apartment Living in a Tight Housing Market," *American Journal of Sociology* 80, no. 6 (May 1975). http://www.jstor.org/pss/2777301

23. Ali A. Paydarfar, "Effects of Multi-Family Housing on Marital Fertility in Iran," *Social Biology* 42, no. 3–4 (Fall/Winter 1995): 214–225. http://ncbi.nlm.nih.gov/pubmed/8738547

24. V. Krishnan, "Homeownership: Its Impact on Fertility," Research Discussion Paper 51 (Edmonton: University of Alberta, 1988).

25. Kenneth T. Jackson, *Crabgrass Frontier: The Suburbanization of the United States* (New York: Oxford University Press, 1985), 231–245. http://us.history.wisc.edu/hist102/readings/Jackson_BabyBoom.pdf

26. U.S. Census Bureau, Housing and Household Economic Statistics Division, "Historical Census of Housing Tables-Units in Structure," October 31, 2011. http://www.census.gov/hhes/www/housing/census/historic/units.html

27. William G. Axinn, Daniel H. Hill, and Arland Thornton, "Reciprocal Effects of Religiosity, Cohabitation, and Marriage," *American Journal of Sociology* 98, no. 3 (November 1992): 628–651. http://www.jstor.org/pss/2781460

28. W. Bradford Wilcox and Nicholas H. Wolfinger, "Happily Ever After? Religion, Marital Status, Gender, and Relationship Quality in Urban Families," *Social Forces* 86 (2008): 1,311–1,337. http://www.fcs.utah.edu/~wolfinger/SFfinal.pdf

29. Amy M. Burdette, Christopher G. Ellison, and W. Bradford Wilcox, "The Couple that Prays Together: Race and Ethnicity, and Relationship Quality among Working-Age Adults," *Journal of Marriage and Family* 72, no. 4 (Aug. 2010): 963–975. http://www.virginia.edu/marriageproject/pdfs/coupleprays.pdf

30. Norman B. Ryder and Charles F. Westoff, *Reproduction in the U.S., 1965* (Princeton: Princeton University Press, 1961), 66–77.

31. Charles F. Westoff, Elise F. Jones, "The End of 'Catholic' Fertility," *Demography* 6, no. 2 (May 1979): 209–217. http://www.jstor.org/pss/2061139

32. Joseph Carroll, "Americans: 2.5 Children Is 'Ideal' Family Size," Gallup News Service, June 26, 2007. http://www.gallup.com/poll/27973/Americans-25-Children-Ideal-Family-Size.aspx

33. Sarah R. Hayford and S. Philip Morgan, "Religiosity and Fertility in the United States: The Role of Fertility Intentions," *Social Forces*, 86, no. 3 (2008): 1,163–1,188. http://www.ncbi.nlm.nih.gov/pmc/articles/PMC2723861/pdf/nihms117862.pdf

34. Eric Kaufmann, "A Dying Creed? The Demographic Contradictions of Liberal Capitalism," Economic and Social Research Council, March 2007. http://www.sneps.net/RD/uploads/UPTAP%20Kaufmann%20-%20draft2.pdf

Chapter Five: Very Bad Things

1. Kate Appleton, "Death in Venice: Residents plan the city's funeral," *Newsweek*, November 11, 2009. http://current.newsweek.com/budgettravel/2009/11/a_funeral_for_the_death_of_ven.html

2. Nick Squires, "Venice Stages Its Own 'Funeral' to Mourn Its Population Decline—60,000 and Falling," *Telegraph* (London), November 14, 2009. http://www.telegraph.co.uk/news/worldnews/europe/italy/6568754/Venice-stages-its-own-funeral-to-mourn-its-population-decline-60000-and-falling.html

3. Laura Allsop, "Battling to keep the 'real' Venice afloat," CNN.com, June 9, 2011. http://www.cnn.com/2011/WORLD/europe/06/09/venice.under.threat/index.html

4. Kingsley Davis, "Reproductive Institutions and the Pressure for Population," *Sociological Review*, Vol. 29 (July, 1937), pp. 289–306. http://www.jstor.org/pss/2137577

5. W.S. Thompson, "Population," *American Journal of Sociology* 34 (1929), pp. 959–975.

6. Ron Lesthaeghe and D. Van de Kaa, "Twee demografische transities?" *Groei of Krimp*, Deventer (Netherlands), (1986); 9–24.

7. Wilhelm Flieger and Nathan Keyfitz, *World Population: An Analysis of Vital Data* (Chicago: University of Chicago Press, 1968), viii.

8. Ted C. Fishman, *Shock of Gray: The Aging of the World's Population and How it Pits Young Against Old, Child Against Parent, Worker Against Boss, Company Against Rival, and Nation Against Nation* (New York: Scribner, 2010), 13.

9. Richard Smith, "A Brief History of Ageing," *Research Horizons*, Issue 4 (September 2007). http://www.research-horizons.cam.ac.uk/spotlight/a-brief-history-of-ageing.aspx

10. Flieger and Keyfitz, *World Population*, ix.

11. Ron Lesthaeghe, "Second Demographic Transition," *Blackwell Encyclopedia of Sociology*, University of Maryland (2007). http://www.blackwellreference.com/public/tocnode?id=g9781405124331_yr2011_chunk_g978140512433125_ss1-59

12. S. Philip Morgan and Miles G. Taylor, "Low Fertility at the Turn of the Twenty-First Century," *Annual Review of Sociology* 32 (2006): 378. http://www.ncbi.nlm.nih.gov/pmc/articles/PMC2849172/pdf/nihms185225.pdf

13. Philippe Ariés, "Two Successive Motivations for the Declining Birth Rate in the West," *Population and Development Review*, Vol. 6, No. 4 (1980), pp. 645–650.

14. D. Van de Kaa, "The Idea of a Second Demographic Transition in Industrialized Countries," Paper presented at the Sixth Welfare Policy Seminar of the National Institute of Population and Social Security (Tokyo, Japan, January 29, 2002), 4.

15. Ron J. Lesthaeghe and Lisa Neidert, "The Second Demographic Transition in the United States: Exception or Textbook Example?" *Population and Development Review* 32, no. 4 (December 2006): 669–698.

16. Van de Kaa, "The Idea of a Second Demographic Transition," 6.

17. *Ibid.*, 18.

18. Tomas Frejka and John Ross, "Paths to Subreplacement Fertility: The Empirical Evidence," *Population and Development Review* 27 (2001): 213–254.

19. Van de Kaa, "The Idea of a Second Demographic Transition," 26.

20. Ron Lesthaeghe and Lisa Neidert, "The Political Significance of the 'Second Demographic Transition' in the U.S.: A Spatial Analysis," Annual Meetings of the Population Association of America, New York City, March 28–30, 2007.

21. S. Philip Morgan, "Is Low Fertility a Twenty-First Century Demographic Crisis?" *Demography* 40, no. 4 (November 2003): 589–603. http://www.ncbi.nlm.nih.gov/pmc/articles/PMC2849155/pdf/nihms185195.pdf

22. United Nations, Department of Economic and Social Affairs, Population Division, *World Population Prospects: The 2010 Revision*, 2011. http://esa.un.org/unpd/wpp/index.htm

23. Morgan, "Is Low Fertility a Twenty-First Century Demographic Crisis?" 2.

24. United Nations, Department of Economic and Social Affairs, Population Division, *World Population Prospects: The 2010 Revision*, 2011. http://esa.un.org/unpd/wpp/Sorting-Tables/tab-sorting_fertility.htm

25. Nicholas Kulish, "In East Germany, a Decline as Stark as a Wall," *New York Times*, June 18, 2009. http://www.nytimes.com/2009/06/19/world/europe/19germany.html

26. United Nations, Department of Economic and Social Affairs, Population Division, *World Population Prospects: The 2010 Revision*, 2011. http://esa.un.org/unpd/wpp/index.htm

27. *Ibid.*

If fertility remains constant, then by 2100, there will be 4.5 million Germans under the age of 15 and 16.6 million over the age of 65.

28. Fred Pearce, *The Coming Population Crash: And Our Planet's Surprising Future* (Boston: Beacon Press, 2010), 90.

29. Kulish, "In East Germany, a Decline as Stark as a Wall."

30. Annegret Haase, Dagmar Haase, and Sigrun Kabisch, "Beyond Growth—Urban Development in Shrinking Cities as a Challenge for Modeling Approaches," UFZ Centre for Environmental Research, Department of Urban Environmental Sociology, 2006. http://shrinking.ums-riate.fr/Ressources/Conclu/KAB_06.pdf

31. Nicholas Eberstadt, "Japan Shrinks," *Wilson Quarterly*, Spring 2012. http://www.wilsonquarterly.com/article.cfm?AID=2143

32. Josef Nipper, Kristina Schulz, and Eva Wiratanaya, "Germany's demographic changes and its implications for shrinking cities: disaster or development opportunities," Viessmann European Research Center Fall 2009 Conference (University of Cologne), 11. http://www.wlu.ca/viessmann/Integration/Nipper_Schulz_Wiratanaya.pdf

33. Kulish, "In East Germany, a Decline as Stark as a Wall."

34. Nipper, Schulz, and Wiratanaya, "Germany's Demographic Changes," 10.

35. Charles Hawley, "Wolves Solidify Paw-Hold in Germany," *Der Spiegel*, October 26, 2007. http://www.spiegel.de/international/europe/0,1518,509181,00.html

36. Fishman, *Shock of Gray*, 7.

37. Pearce, *The Coming Population Crash*, 233.

38. Norimitsu Onishi, "Village Writes Its Epitaph: Victim of a Graying Japan," *New York Times*, April 30, 2006. http://www.nytimes.com/2006/04/30/world/asia/30japan.html?pagewanted=all

39. Kieran McMorrow and Werner Roeger, *The Economic and Financial Consequences of Global Aging*, European Commission, 2004. Paul S. Hewitt, *Meeting the Challenge of Global Aging*, Center for Strategic and International Studies (2002). http://csis.org/publication/meeting-challenge-global-aging

40. Ben J. Wattenberg, *Fewer: How the New Demography of Depopulation Will Shape Our Future* (Chicago: Ivan R. Dee, 2004), 117.

41. U.S. Census Bureau, Population Estimates Program, GCT-T2-R, Median Age of the Total Population (geographies ranked by estimate), Data Set 2009.

42. Mara Hvistendahl, *Unnatural Selection: Choosing Boys Over Girls, and the Consequences of a World Full of Men* (New York: Public Affairs, 2011), 245.

43. David S. Reher, "Towards Long Term Population Decline: Views at a Critical Juncture of World Population History," *European Journal of Population* 23 (2007): 189–207. http://demoblography.blogspot.com/2008/04/towards-long-term-population-decline.html

44. Nicholas Eberstadt, "Global Demographic Outlook to 2025: Risks and Opportunities for the World Economy," Lecture for the Economic Conference on Demography, Growth and Wellbeing, The Progress Foundation, Zurich, Switzerland, November 30, 2006. http://www.progress-foundation.ch/PDF/referate/93_Lecture%20Nicholas%20Eberstadt%20inkl.PPT_30.11.2006_E.pdf

45. Gilbert Cette, Yusu Kocoglu, and Jacques Mairesse, "Productivity Growth and Levels in France, Japan, the United Kingdom and the United States in the Twentieth Century," National Bureau of Economic Research, Working Paper 15577 (December 2009): 31, Table 2. http://www.nber.org/papers/w15577

46. *Ibid.*, 32.

47. José Ernesto Amorós, Niels Bosma, and Donna Kelley, *Global Entrepreneurship Monitor: 2010 Global Report*, Global Entrepreneurship Monitor (2011), 22–23.

48. *Ibid.*, 33.

49. Kieran McMorrow and Werner Roeger, *The Economic and Financial Market Consequences of Global Ageing* (Berlin, Germany: Springer-Verlag, 2004), 9.

50. Pearce, *The Coming Population Crash*, 237.

51. *Ibid.*, 100.

52. *Ibid.*, 101.

53. Wattenberg, *Fewer*, 136.

54. *Ibid.*, 137.

55. World Bank Data Catalog. http://data.worldbank.org/data-catalog

56. Cette, Kocoglu, and Mairesse, "Productivity Growth," 33.

57. World Bank Data Catalog. http://data.worldbank.org/data-catalog

58. Ambrose Evans-Pritchard, "It's Japan we should be worrying about, not America," *Telegraph* (London), November 1, 2009. http://www.telegraph.co.uk/finance/comment/ambroseevans_pritchard/6480289/It-is-Japan-we-should-be-worrying-about-not-America.html

59. Daniel Gros, "The Japan Myth," Project Syndicate, January 6, 2011. http://www.project-syndicate.org/commentary/gros18/English

60. "Historical Background and Development of Social Security," Social Security Administration, 2003. http://www.ssa.gov/history/briefhistory3.html

61. "Ratio of Social Security Covered Workers to Beneficiaries, 1940–2000," *Social Security Administration 2000 Trustees Report*. http://www.ssa.gov/history/ratios.html

62. *Ibid.*

63. *The Future of Social Security*, Social Security Administration, Publication No. 05–10055, ICN 462560, April 2008. http://www.adap.net/socialsecurity/The%20Future%20of%20Social%20Security.pdf

Alternative study from ECS: http://www.adap.net/socialsecurity/The%20Future%20of%20Social%20Security.pdf

64. "Social Security and Medicare Tax Rates, 1937–2009," The Tax Foundation. http://www.taxfoundation.org/taxdata/show/24682.html#soc_security_rates_1937-2009-20090504

65. Veronique de Rugy, "Medicare Costs Over Time," Mercatus Center, George Mason University, June 20, 2011. http://mercatus.org/publication/medicare-costs-over-time

66. The Boards of Trustees, Federal Hospital Insurance and Federal Supplementary Medical Insurance Trust Funds, *2011 Annual Report*, Cen-

ters for Medicare and Medicaid Services (2011), 4–7. https://www.cms.gov/ReportsTrustFunds/downloads/tr2011.pdf

67. *Ibid.*, 51.

68. *Ibid.*, 80.

69. *Ibid.*, 12.

Chapter Six: The Bright Side

1. Warren G. Harris, "Teatro Puerto Rico," CinemaTreasures.org. http://cinematreasures.org/theaters/7786

2. "History Matters: Pioneros," US-PuertoRicans.org. http://www.us-puertoricans.org/index.php?option=com_wrapper&Itemid=79

3. Clara E. Rodríguez, "Puerto Ricans: Immigrants and Migrants" module for the Americans All curriculum project conducted by The Coordinating Committee for Ellis Island, Inc. (Washington, D.C.: 1989), 1–60. http://www.americansall.com/PDFs/02-americans-all/9.9.pdf

4. National Puerto Rican Day Parade, Inc. http://www.nationalpuertoricandayparade.org/history.html

5. Box Office Mojo, All Time Adjusted Gross. http://www.boxofficemojo.com/alltime/adjusted.htm

6. Rodríguez, "Puerto Ricans," 3. Office of Immigration Statistics, *Yearbook of Immigration Statistics: 2010*, U.S. Department of Homeland Security (August 2011), 16. http://www.dhs.gov/xlibrary/assets/statistics/yearbook/2010/ois_yb_2010.pdf

7. United Nations, Department of Economic and Social Affairs, Population Division, *World Population Prospects: The 2010 Revision*, 2011. http://esa.un.org/unpd/wpp/index.htm

8. CIA, *World Factbook*, Puerto Rico. https://www.cia.gov/library/publications/the-world-factbook/geos/rq.html

9. Jonathan V. Last, "U.S. and Immigration," *Philadelphia Inquirer*, February 26, 2006.

10. Steven A. Camarota, *Immigrants in the United States, 2007: A Profile of America's Foreign-Born Population*, Center for Immigration Studies, November 2007. http://www.cis.org/immigrants_profile_2007

11. "Abortion Statistics: United States Data and Trends," National Right to Life Committee Educational Trust Fund, January 2012. http://www.nrlc.org/Factsheets/FS03_AbortionInTheUS.pdf

12. United Nations, Department of Economic and Social Affairs, Population Division, *Replacement Migration: Is it a Solution to Declining and Ageing Populations?* (New York: United Nations, 2001). http://www.un.org/esa/population/publications/migration/migration.htm

13. Phillip Longman, *The Empty Cradle: How Falling Birthrates Threaten World Prosperity, and What To Do About It* (New York: Basic Books, 2004), 23.

14. George J. Borjas, "The Analytics of the Wage Effect of Immigration," Harvard University, August 2009. http://www.hks.harvard.edu/fs/gborjas/publications/working%20papers/AnalyticsAugust2009.pdf

15. Paul Krugman, "Notes on Immigration," *New York Times*, March 27, 2006. http://krugman.blogs.nytimes.com/2006/03/27/notes-on-immigration/

16. Congressional Budget Office, *A Description of the Immigrant Population: An Update* (June 2011), 2. http://www.cbo.gov/ftpdocs/121xx/doc12168/06-02-Foreign-BornPopulation.pdf

17. United Nations, Department of Economic and Social Affairs, Population Division, *World Population Prospects: The 2010 Revision*, 2011. http://esa.un.org/unpd/wpp/index.htm

18. World Bank Data Catalog (http://data.worldbank.org/data-catalog). See also Robert M. Dunn Jr., "Mexican Immigration Will Solve Itself," *American*, June 29, 2007. http://www.american.com/archive/2007/june-0607/mexican-immigration-will-solve-itself/

19. Nicholas Eberstadt, "The Changing Demographics of the U.S. Southern Security Perimeter," *Comparative Strategy* 25 (2006): 81–108. http://www.aei.org/article/24726

20. Carl P. Schmertmann, "Immigrants' Ages and the Structure of Stationary Populations with Below-Replacement Fertility," *Demography*, November 1992, 595-612. Quoted in Steven A. Camarota, "Projecting Immigration's Impact on the Size and Age Structure of the 21st Century American Population," Center for Immigration Studies,

December 2012. http://cis.org/sites/default/files/camarota-projecting-age-structure.pdf

21. Steven A. Camarota, "Birth Rates Among Immigrants in America," Center for Immigration Studies, October 2005. http://www.cis.org/articles/2005/back1105.html

22. S. Philip Morgan and Emilio A. Parrado, "Intergenerational Fertility Among Hispanic Women: New Evidence of Immigrant Assimilation," *Demography* 45, no. 3 (August 2008): 651–671. http://www.ncbi.nlm.nih.gov/pmc/articles/PMC2782440/pdf/dem-45-0651.pdf

23. Paul D. Sutton, Brady E. Hamilton, T.J. Mathews, "Recent Decline in Births in the United States, 2007–2009," NCHS Data Brief, No. 60 (March 2011). http://www.cdc.gov/nchs/data/databriefs/db60.pdf

24. Gretchen Livingston and D'Vera Cohn, "U.S. Birth Rate Falls to a Record Low; Decline Is Greatest Among Immigrants," Pew Research Center, November 29, 2012. http://www.pewsocialtrends.org/files/2012/11/Birth_Rate_Final.pdf

25. U.S. Census Bureau, "U.S. Population Projections," 2008. http://www.census.gov/population/www/projections/methodstatement.html

26. D'Vera Cohn and Jeffrey S. Passel, "U.S. Population Projections: 2005–2050," Pew Research Center, February 2008. http://pewhispanic.org/files/reports/85.pdf

27. Emilio A. Parrado, "How High Is Hispanic/Mexican Fertility in the U.S.? Immigration and Tempo Considerations," Population Studies Center, PSC Working Paper Series, June 22, 2010.

28. S. Philip Morgan and Heather Rackin, "The Correspondence Between Fertility Intentions and Behavior in the United States," *Population and Development Review*, 36 no. 1 (March 2010): 91–118.

29. Joshua Goldstein, Wolfgang Lutz, and Maria Rita Testa, "The Emergence of Sub-Replacement Family Size Ideals in Europe," *Population Research and Policy Review* 22 (2003): 479–496. http://user.demogr.mpg.de/goldstein/publications/goldstein_lutz_testa.pdf

30. Lydia Saad, "Americans' Preference for Smaller Families Edges Higher," Gallup, June 30, 2011. http://www.gallup.com/poll/148355/Americans-Preference-Smaller-Families-Edges-Higher.aspx

31. General Social Survey SDA. Row "CHLDIDEL," Column "YEAR," Weight "COMPWT," Filter "SEX(2) AGE (18–45)." http://sda.berkeley.edu/cgi-bin/hsda?harcsda+gss08

32. Kellie J. Hagewen and S. Philip Morgan, "Intended and Ideal Family Size in the United States, 1970–2002," *Population and Development Review* 31, no. 3 (September 2005): 507–527. http://www.ncbi.nlm.nih.gov/pmc/articles/PMC2849141/

33. General Social Survey SDA, *op. cit.*

34. Hagewen and Morgan, "Intended and Ideal Family Size," 509.

35. Goldstein, Lutz, and Testa, "Emergence of Sub-Replacement Family Size," 484.

36. *Ibid.*, 490.

37. Maria Rita Testa, "Childbearing Preferences and Family Issues in Europe," *Special Eurobarometer 253*, Wave 65.1, Vienna Institute of Demography, Austrian Academy of Sciences (October 2006), 30. http://ec.europa.eu/public_opinion/archives/ebs/ebs_253_en.pdf

38. Ingrid Hamm, "The Demographic Future of Europe—Facts, Figures, Policies: Results of the Population Policy Acceptance Study (PPAS)," Robert Bosch Stiftung, Federal Institute for Population Research (2006), 10. http://www.bosch-stiftung.de/content/language1/downloads/PPAS_en.pdf

Chapter Seven: Domestic Politics, Foreign Policy

1. Virginia State Board of Elections. http://www.sbe.virginia.gov/ElectionResults/2004/Nov2004/l_01.htm

2. Bill Bishop, *The Big Sort: Why the Clustering of Like-Minded America Is Tearing Us Apart* (New York: Houghton Mifflin, 2008).

3. *Ibid.*, 10.

4. U.S. Census Bureau, "Current Population Survey Historical Geographical Mobility/Migration Tables," Table A-1, "Annual Geographical Mobility Rates, By Type of Movement: 1947–2011." http://www.census.gov/hhes/migration/data/cps/historical.html

5. Joel Kotkin, "There's No Place Like Home," *Newsweek*, October 8, 2009. http://www.thedailybeast.com/newsweek/2009/10/08/there-s-no-place-like-home.html

6. Bishop, *The Big Sort*, 44.

7. Peggy Fletcher Stack, "More Mormons Exiting Salt Lake City and Moving to the Suburbs," *Salt Lake Tribune*, July 17, 2008. http://www.sltrib.com/ci_9913722?source=rv?source=sb-reddit

8. Utah Lieutenant Governor's Office, Division of Elections. http://elections.utah.gov/election-resources/election-results

9. Ron Lesthaeghe, Lisa Neidert, "U.S. Presidential Elections and the Spatial Pattern of the American Second Demographic Transition," *Population and Development Review*, 35:2 (June 2009): 391–400.

10. Steve Sailer, "The Baby Gap," *American Conservative*, December 20, 2004. http://www.isteve.com/babygap.htm

11. Keith T. Poole, "The Decline and Rise of Party Polarization in Congress: Debunking the Myth," *Extensions: A Journal of the Carl Albert Congressional Research and Studies Center* (Fall 2005): 6–9. http://www.ou.edu/special/albertctr/extensions/fall2005/Poole.pdf

12. Bishop, *The Big Sort*, 24.

13. William Voegeli, "Days of Rage, Years of Lies," *Claremont Review of Books*, Vol. 11, No. 3 (Summer 2011) pp. 14–20. http://www.claremont.org/publications/crb/id.1830/article_detail.asp

14. CIA, *World Factbook*. https://www.cia.gov/library/publications/the-world-factbook/geos/ir.html

15. Gunnar Heinsohn, "Ending the West's Proxy War Against Israel," *Wall Street Journal*, January 12, 2009. http://online.wsj.com/article/SB123171179743471961.html Lionel Beehner, "The Effects of 'Youth Bulge' on Civil Conflicts," Council on Foreign Relations, April 27, 2007. http://www.cfr.org/publication/13093/ Christopher Caldwell, "Youth and War: A Deadly Duo," *Financial Times*, January 6, 2007. http://www.ft.com/cms/s/0/652fa2f6-9d2a-11db-8ec6-0000779e2340.html

16. Daniele Anastasion, Richard P. Cincotta, and Robert Engelman, *The Security Demographic*, Population Action International, 2003. http://

www.populationaction.org/Publications/Reports/The_Security_Demo-graphic/Stress_Factor_1_-_the_Youth_Bulge.shtml#fisanchor0

17. Jack A. Goldstone, "Population and Security: How Demographic Change Can Lead to Violent Conflict," *Journal of International Affairs* 56, no. 1 (Fall 2002).

18. United Nations, Department of Economic and Social Affairs, Population Division, *World Population Prospects: The 2010 Revision*, 2011. http://esa.un.org/unpd/wpp/index.htm

19. Jeffrey J. Brown and Samuel Foucher, "A Quantitative Assessment of Future Net Oil Exports by the Top Five Net Oil Exporters," *Energy Bulletin*, Post Carbon Institute, January 7, 2008. http://www.energybul-letin.net/node/38948

20. Mark Steyn, *America Alone: The End of the World as We Know It* (Washington, D.C.: Regnery, 2006), xvi. Anastasion, Cincotta, and Engel-man, *Security Demographic*, 42. United Nations, Department of Economic and Social Affairs, Population Division, *World Population Prospects: The 2010 Revision*, 2011. http://esa.un.org/unpd/wpp/index.htm

21. CIA, *World Factbook*. https://www.cia.gov/library/publications/the-world-factbook/geos/ym.html

22. CIA, *World Factbook*. https://www.cia.gov/library/publications/the-world-factbook/geos/SY.html

23. CIA, *World Factbook*. https://www.cia.gov/library/publications/the-world-factbook/geos/ae.html

24. Stephen Trimble, "Benchmark contest: F-35 cost vs F-22 cost," *Flight Global*, May 19, 2010. http://www.flightglobal.com/blogs/the-dew-line/2010/05/benchmark-contest-f-35-cost-vs.html

25. "China Aircraft Carrier Confirmed by General," BBC News, June 8, 2011. http://www.bbc.co.uk/news/world-asia-pacific-13692558

26. "China's Achilles Heel," *The Economist*, April 21, 2012. http://www.economist.com/node/21553056

27. Nicholas Eberstadt, "The Global War Against Baby Girls," *The New Atlantis* 33 (Fall 2011): 3–18. http://www.thenewatlantis.com/publications/the-global-war-against-baby-girls

28. Mara Hvistendahl, *Unnatural Selection: Choosing Boys Over Girls, and the Consequences of a World Full of Men* (New York: Public Affairs, 2011), 203–206.

29. Mara Hvistendahl, "Has China Outgrown The One-Child Policy?" *Science* 329, no. 5998 (September 2010): 1458–1461. http://www.sciencemag.org/content/329/5998/1458.short

30. Nicholas Eberstadt, "Drunken Nation: Russia's Depopulation Bomb," *World Affairs* 171, no. 4 (Spring 2009). http://www.worldaffairsjournal.org/article/drunken-nation-russia%E2%80%99s-depopulation-bomb

31. Nicholas Eberstadt and Apoorva Shah, "Russia's Demographic Disaster," *Russian Outlook*, American Enterprise Institute, May 2009. http://www.aei.org/outlook/100037

32. Eberstadt, "Drunken Nation."

33. *Ibid.*

34. United Nations Statistics Division, *Demographic Yearbook 2009–2010*, Table 24 "Divorces and Crude Divorce Rates." http://unstats.un.org/unsd/demographic/products/dyb/dyb2009-2010.htm

35. William Robert Johnston, "Historical Abortion Statistics, Russia." http://www.johnstonsarchive.net/policy/abortion/ab-russia.html

36. World Bank Data Catalog. http://data.worldbank.org/data-catalog

37. Sergei N. Bobylev and Anatoldy G. Vishnevsky, "Russia Facing Demographic Challenges," *National Human Development Report: Russian Federation*, United Nations Development Programme (Moscow), 2009. http://hdr.undp.org/en/reports/nationalreports/europethecis/russia/NHDR_Russia_2008_Eng.pdf

Chapter Eight: Losing Battles (What Not to Do)

1. Judith G. Bryden and David M. Heer, "Family Allowances and Population Policy in the U.S.S.R." *Journal of Marriage and the Family* 28, no. 4 (November 1966): 514.

2. *Ibid.*

3. Leonid Brezhnev, *Population and Development Review* 7, no. 2 (June 1981): 372–4. http://www.jstor.org/pss/1972650

4. Ben J. Wattenberg, *The Birth Dearth: What Happens When People in Free Countries Don't Have Enough Babies?* (New York: Pharos Books, 1987), 41.

5. World Bank Data Catalog. http://data.worldbank.org/data-catalog

6. Nicholas Eberstadt and Apoorva Shah, "Russia's Demographic Disaster," *Russian Outlook*, American Enterprise Institute, May 2009. http://www.aei.org/outlook/100037

7. Fred Weir, "A Second Baby? Russia's Mothers Aren't Persuaded," *Christian Science Monitor*, May 19, 2006. http://www.csmonitor.com/2006/0519/p01s04-woeu.html

8. Daniel Gross, "Russia's campaign to increase its birthrate," *Slate*, May 25, 2006. http://www.slate.com/id/2142366/

9. Yasha Levine, "How Russia's baby-boosting policies are hurting the population," *Slate*, July 10, 2008. http://www.slate.com/articles/news_and_politics/dispatches/2008/07/incentivized_birth.html

10. Sara Rhodin, "A Holiday from Russia with Love," *New York Times*, July 9, 2008. http://www.nytimes.com/2008/07/09/world/europe/09russia.html

11. James R. Holmes, "Strategic Effects of Demographic Shocks," in *Population Decline and the Remaking of Great Power Politics*, edited by Susan Yoshihara and Douglas A. Sylva (Washington, D.C.: Potomac Books, 2012), 43.

12. Carl Ipsen, *Dictating Demography: The Problem of Population in Fascist Italy* (Cambridge: Cambridge University Press, 2002), 73.

13. Robo Daily, "Japanese baby-bot with runny nose teaches parenting skills," SpaceDaily.com, March 10, 2010. http://www.spacedaily.com/reports/Japanese_baby-bot_with_runny_nose_teaches_parenting_skills_999.html

14. United Nations, Department of Economic and Social Affairs, Population Division, *World Population Prospects: The 2010 Revision*, 2011. http://esa.un.org/unpd/wpp/index.htm

As a point of explanation, that's 108 million using the 2010 median variant or 99 million using the constant-fertility variant.

15. Daniel Gross, "Why Japan Isn't Rising," *Newsweek*, July 16, 2009. http://www.newsweek.com/id/207063

16. Yuki Yamaguchi, "Elderly at Record Spurs Japan Stores Chase [to] $1.4 Trillion," Bloomberg.com, May 9, 2012. http://www.bloomberg.com/news/2012-05-09/elderly-at-record-spurs-japan-stores-chase-1-4-trillion.html

17. Nicholas Eberstadt, "Japan Shrinks," *Wilson Quarterly*, Spring 2012. http://www.wilsonquarterly.com/article.cfm?AID=2143

18. Naohiro Ogawa and Robert D. Retherford, "Japan's Baby Bust: Causes, Implications, and Policy Responses," Population and Health Series, No. 118, East-West Center, April 2005. http://www.eastwestcenter.org/fileadmin/stored/pdfs/POPwp118.pdf

19. Michael Hassett, "Where did all the babies go?" *Japan Times Online*, June 10, 2008. http://search.japantimes.co.jp/cgi-bin/fl20080610zg.html

20. Joel Kotkin, "The Kid Issue," *Forbes*, September 7, 2009. http://www.joelkotkin.com/content/0055-kid-issue

21. CIA, *World Factbook*. https://www.cia.gov/library/publications/the-world-factbook/geos/ja.html

22. Mara Hvistendahl, *Unnatural Selection: Choosing Boys Over Girls, and the Consequences of a World Full of Men* (New York: Public Affairs, 2011), 125.

23. Statistics Bureau Japan, "Statistical Handbook of Japan 2011," Chapter 2, Section 4 (2011). http://www.stat.go.jp/english/data/handbook/co2cont.htm#cha2_4

24. Phillip Longman, *The Empty Cradle: How Falling Birthrates Threaten World Prosperity, and What To Do About It* (New York: Basic Books, 2004), 51.

25. Peggy Orenstein, "Parasites in Prêt-à-Porter," *New York Times*, July 1, 2001. http://www.nytimes.com/2001/07/01/magazine/parasites-in-pret-a-porter.html

26. *Ibid.*

27. Harold Fuess, *Divorce in Japan: Family, Gender, and the State, 1600–2000,* Stanford University Press (2004), p. 102. http://www.bsos.umd.edu/gvpt/lpbr/subpages/reviews/fuess1004.htm

28. *Ibid.*, 145.

29. Danielle Demetriou, "Tokyo Sees Rise in 'Divorce Ceremonies,'" *Telegraph* (London), June 13, 2010. http://www.telegraph.co.uk/news/worldnews/asia/japan/7822356/Tokyo-sees-rise-in-divorce-ceremonies.html. (The full statistic is actually "number of divorces per 1,000 people aged 15–64.")

30. U.S. Census Bureau, *Statistical Abstract of the United States: 2011*, "Table 1335. Marriage and Divorce Rates by Country: 1980 to 2008," 840. (This figure, too, is for divorces per 1,000 people aged 15–64.) http://www.census.gov/compendia/statab/2011/tables/11s1335.pdf

31. Eberstadt, "Japan Shrinks."

32. Ogawa and Retherford, "Japan's Baby Bust," 16.

33. Nico Keilman, "Concern in the European Union about Low Birth Rates," *European View* 7 (2008): 333–340. http://folk.uio.no/keilman/EV.pdf

34. Johann Hari, "Are There Just Too Many People in the World?" *Independent* (London), May 15, 2008. http://www.huffingtonpost.com/johann-hari/are-there-just-too-many-p_b_144065.html

35. Commission on the European Communities, *Promoting Solidarity Between the Generations*, Green Paper, 2007. http://eur-lex.europa.eu/Notice.do?checktexts=checkbox&val=448793

36. European Commission, *Europe's Demographic Future: Facts and Figures on Challenges and Opportunities* (Luxembourg: Office for Official Publications of the European Communities, 2007). http://ec.europa.eu/social/main.jsp?catId=502&langId=en&pubId=78&type=2&furtherPubs=yes

37. "The Demographic Future of Europe," European Parliament Resolution: 2007/2156(INI), February 21, 2008. http://www.europarl.europa.eu/sides/getDoc.do?pubRef=-//EP//TEXT+TA+P6-TA-2008-0066+0+DOC+XML+V0//EN

38. Keilman, "Low Birth Rates," 335.

39. CIA, *World Factbook* (accessed December 11, 2012). https://www.cia.gov/library/publications/the-world-factbook/fields/2127.html

40. Jan M. Hoem, "Why does Sweden have such high fertility?" Working Paper, Max Planck Institute for Demographic Research, April 2005. http://www.demogr.mpg.de/Papers/Working/wp-2005-009.pdf

41. Marie-Thérèse Letablier, "Fertility and Family Policies in France," *Journal of Population and Social Security*, Supplement to Vol. 1 (2003): 245–261.

42. CIA, *World Factbook*. https://www.cia.gov/library/publications/the-world-factbook/geos/fr.html

43. Christopher Caldwell, *Reflections on the Revolution in Europe: Immigration, Islam, and the West* (New York: Doubleday, 2009), 18. Douglas A. Sylva, "Europe's Strategic Future and the Need for Pronatalism," *Population Decline and the Remaking of Great Power Politics*, edited by Susan Yoshihara, Douglas A. Sylva (Washington, D.C.: Potomac Books, 2012), 107.

44. Jan M. Hoem, "The Impact of Public Policies on European Fertility," *Demographic Research* 19 (July 2008): 249–260. http://www.demographic-research.org/Volumes/Vol19/10/19-10.pdf

45. Therea Wong and Brenda S.A. Yeoh, "Fertility and the Family: An Overview of Pro-natalist Population Policies in Singapore," Asian MetaCentre Research Paper Series, No. 12, June 2003. http://www.populationasia.org/Publications/RP/AMCRP12.pdf

46. World Development Indicators Database. http://www.nationmaster.com/time.php?stat=hea_fer_rat_tot_bir_per_wom-rate-total-births-per-woman&country=sn-singapore

47. Family Population and Planning Board, Singapore. http://www.a2o.com.sg/a2o/public/html/etc/07_family.htm

48. Lee Kuan Yew, "Talent for the Future" (speech), August 14, 1983, quoted in Theresa Wong and Brenda S. A. Yeoh, "Fertility and the Family: An Overview of Pro-Natalist Population Policies in Singapore," Asian MetaCentre Research Paper Series (no. 12), 8. http://www.populationasia.org/Publications/RP/AMCRP12.pdf

49. *Ibid*.

50. Goh Chok Tong, "National Rally Day Speech," August 4, 1986, quoted in Wong and Yeoh, "Fertility and the Family," 11.

51. "Singapore Family Planning and Population Board Repeal Act, Chapter 300, 1970 Ed. Cap. 168," Government of Singapore, 1986. http://policy.mofcom.gov.cn/english/flaw!fetch.action?id=34dba3a5-deb1-431f-8c82-b4f20a3bbb7c

52. Mui Teng Yap, "Singapore's 'Three or More' Policy: The First Five Years," *Asia-Pacific Population Journal* 10, no. 4 (1995): 39–52. http://www.un.org/Depts/escap/pop/journal/v10n4a3.htm

53. Government of Singapore, "Enhanced Government-Paid Maternity Leave (GPML) Scheme," 2004. http://fcd.ecitizen.gov.sg/ProFamilyLeaveScheme/GovernmentPaidMaternityLeave.html

54. Wang Hui Ling, "Concern over 'anti-women' policies in PM Goh's speech," *Straits Times* (Singapore), August 28, 1994.

Chapter Nine: How to Make Babies

1. G. Tsuladze, N. Maglaperidze, A. Vadachkoria, *Demographic Yearbook of Georgia, 2008* (via Georgian Centre of Population Research). http://gcpr.ge/statistics/en

2. Ministry of Labour, Health and Social Affaires of Georgia (via Georgian Centre of Population Research). http://gcpr.ge/statistics/en

3. Department for Statistics of Georgia (via Georgian Centre of Population Research). http://gcpr.ge/statistics/en

4. *Ibid.*

5. *Ibid.*

6. CIA, *World FactBook.* https://www.cia.gov/library/publications/the-world-factbook/geos/gg.html

7. Irina Badurashvili, Revaz Cheishvili, Ekaterine Kapanadze, Mariam Sirbiladze, and Shorena Tsiklauri, "Gender Relations in Modern Georgian Society," Georgian Centre of Population Research (2008), 74.

8. Tom Esslemont, "Church Leader Sparks Georgian Baby Boom," BBC News, March 26, 2009. http://news.bbc.co.uk/2/hi/europe/7964302.stm

9. Badurashvili *et al.*, "Gender Relations," 75.

10. Bryan Caplan, *Selfish Reasons to Have More Kids: Why Being a Great Parent Is Less Work and More Fun Than You Think* (New York: Basic Books, 2011), 15.

11. Chris M. Herbst and John Ifcher, "A Bundle of Joy: Does Parenting Really Make Us Miserable?" (working paper) May 16, 2012. http://dx.doi.org/10.2139/ssrn.1883839

12. Kevin Milligan, "Subsidizing the Stork," *The Review of Economics and Statistics* 87, no. 3 (August 2005): 539–555. http://faculty.arts.ubc.ca/kmilligan/research/babies2004.pdf

13. Marcus Walker, "In Estonia, paying women to have babies pays off," *Wall Street Journal*, October 20, 2006. http://www.post-gazette.com/pg/06293/731744-82.stm

14. World Bank Data Catalog. http://data.worldbank.org/datacatalog

15. A.H. Gauthier and J. Hatzius, "Family Benefits and Fertility: An econometric analysis," *Population Studies* 51 (1997): 295–306.

16. Karin L. Brewster and Ronald R. Rindfuss, "Fertility and Women's Employment in Industrialized Nations," *Annual Review of Sociology* 26 (2000): 286. http://tinyurl.com/9skhm3m

17. Jan M. Hoem, "The impact of public policies on European fertility," *Demographic Research* 19 (July 2008): 249–260. http://www.demographic-research.org/Volumes/Vol19/10/

18. Robert Stein, "Taxes and the Family," *National Affairs*, 2 (Winter 2010): 35–48. http://www.nationalaffairs.com/publications/detail/taxes-and-the-family

19. Longman, *The Empty Cradle*, 173.

20. Cesar Conda and Robert Stein, "Tax Cuts for Kids," *Weekly Standard*, July 9, 2007. http://www.weeklystandard.com/Content/Public/Articles/000/000/013/826odihu.asp

21. Ramesh Ponnuru, "A Tax Reform to Run With," *National Review*, April 24, 2006. Subscriber only. http://www.nationalreview.com/nrd/?q=MjAwNjAoMjQ=

22. David Leonhardt, "Even for Cashiers, College Pays Off," *New York Times*, June 25, 2011. http://www.nytimes.com/2011/06/26/sunday-review/26leonhardt.html

23. Jacques Steinberg, "Plan B: Skip College," *New York Times*, May 15, 2010. http://www.nytimes.com/2010/05/16/weekinreview/16steinberg.html

24. Associated Press, "Universities Racking Up the Endowments," May 22, 2005. http://www.msnbc.msn.com/id/7887394/ns/business-personal_finance/t/universities-racking-endowments/

25. Walter Russell Mead, "The Ice Cream Party and the Spinach Party," *Weekly Standard*, February 6, 2006. http://weeklystandard.com/Content/Public/Articles/000/000/006/650qaifa.asp?pg=2

26. Haifang Huang and Yao Tang, "Residential Land Use Regulation and the U.S. Housing Price Cycle Between 2000 and 2009," Department of Economics, University of Alberta, Working Paper No. 2010–11 (November 2010). http://www.uofaweb.ualberta.ca/economics2/pdfs/WP2010-11-Huang.pdf

27. Nicholas Kulish, "Things Fall Apart: Fixing America's Crumbling Infrastructure," *New York Times*, August 23, 2006. http://www.nytimes.com/2006/08/23/opinion/23talking-points.html?pagewanted=all

28. To take just one comparison year, in 2005 the general fertility rate (that's births per 1,000 women aged 15 to 44) in Los Angeles County was 69.5. In Dallas County it was 76.5—that's 10 percent higher than Los Angeles. California Department of Public Health, "General Fertility Rate and Birth Rates by Age of Mother, California Counties, 2005" (http://www.cdph.ca.gov/data/statistics/Documents/VSC-2005-0230.pdf). Texas Department of State Health Services, "2005 Natality" (http://www.dshs.state.tx.us/CHS/VSTAT/vs05/nnatal.shtm).

29. Christopher Caldwell, *Reflections on the Revolution in Europe: Immigration, Islam, and the West* (New York: Doubleday, 2009).

30. Daily Mail Reporter, "Nicolas Sarkozy Joins David Cameron and Angela Merkel View that Multiculturalism has Failed," *Daily Mail* (London), February 11, 2011. http://www.dailymail.co.uk/news/article-1355961/Nicolas-Sarkozy-joins-David-Cameron-Angela-Merkel-view-multiculturalism-failed.html

31. Phillip Longman, "Missing Children: How Falling Birthrates Turn Everything Upside Down," *The Family in America* 25, no. 1 (Winter 2011): 1–20.

32. Leigh Phillips, "Hungarian mothers may get extra votes for their children in elections," *Guardian* (London), April 17, 2011. http://www.guardian.co.uk/world/2011/apr/17/hungary-mothers-get-extra-votes

33. Jonathan V. Last, "Demeny Voting," *Weekly Standard*, July 7, 2011. http://www.weeklystandard.com/blogs/demeny-voting_576394.html

34. Eric Kaufmann and Vegard Skirbekk, "'Go Forth and Multiply': the Politics of Religious Demography," in *Political Demography: Identity, Conflict and Institutions*, edited by J. A. Goldstone, Eric Kaufmann and Monica Duffy Toft (Boulder, Col.: Paradigm Publishers, 2011). http://www.sneps.net/RD/uploads/1-Kaufmann&Skirbekk-draft1.pdf

35. *Ibid.*

36. *Ibid.*

37. Eric Kaufmann, Anne Goujon, and Vegard Skirbekk, "Secularism, Fundamentalism, or Catholicism? The Religious Composition of the United States to 2043," *Journal for the Scientific Study of Religion*, 49 (2010): 302.

38. Jennifer Senior, "All Joy and No Fun," *New York Magazine*, July 4, 2010. http://nymag.com/print/?/news/features/67024/

39. Theodore Roosevelt, "Address Before the National Congress of Mothers," March 13, 1905, *Presidential Addresses and State Papers*, volume III (New York: Reviews, 1910), 288. http://archive.org/stream/president ialaddi5roosrich#page/288/mode/2up

40. Joseph Ratzinger, "The Universalization of European Culture and the Ensuing Crisis," in *Without Roots: The West, Relativism, Christianity, Islam* (New York: Basic Books, 2006), 64–74. http://www.catholic-culture.org/culture/library/view.cfm?recnum=7089

Index

9 781594 037313